Driving Miss Smith

Also by Warren Lakin (with Ian Parsons)

I Think the Nurses are Stealing My Clothes:
the Very Best of Linda Smith (ed.)

Driving Miss Smith

Warren Lakin

HODDER &
STOUGHTON

First published in Great Britain in 2007 by
Hodder & Stoughton

An Hachette Livre UK company

I

Copyright © Warren Lakin 2007

A CIP catalogue record for this title is available from the British Library

ISBN 978 0 340 93278 0

Typeset in MT Sabon by Hewer Text UK Ltd, Edinburgh

Printed and bound by Mackays of Chatham plc, Chatham, Kent

Hodder & Stoughton policy is to use papers that are natural, renewable
and recyclable products and made from wood grown in sustainable forests.
The logging and manufacturing processes are expected to conform
to the environmental regulations of the country of origin.

Hodder & Stoughton Ltd
338 Euston Road
London NW1 3BH
www.hodder.co.uk

This book is dedicated to my mum, Sheila Lakin, to Margaret Barraclough of Sheffield, and to Denise Fitzpatrick of Brampton Bierlow (Cortonwood).

And is in memory of my late dad, Leslie Lakin; Linda's late mum, Bessie Smith; Linda's late aunt, Helen Locke; the late Dave 'Deep Soul' Godin; and the late great Ian Dury.

It's what we did and who we knew
And that's what makes this story true

Ian Dury

I think it comes back to stories. People carry stories about them on, I think people live on in the memories of their family and friends, not just memories, I don't mean that in a passive way. The stories, the kind of vibrations of everything they did, carry on through the narratives that they've left behind.

Linda Smith

Contents

PROLOGUE
Taking Stock in Tavistock

'Hello Tavistock – that's a nice friendly welcome . . . This is a lovely town, very impressive, very dinky. A town devoted to the production of potpourri. Could it be any more twee? Nothing happens here that's louder than a scone being buttered . . .'

It was 21 September 2002 and Linda was greeting her expectant Saturday-night audience just before the autumn tour of one-night stands entitled 'Linda Smith Live'. The early part of Linda's act was always fuelled by great observational material about the town she was visiting, mercilessly plundering its history, its appearance, its inhabitants and above all its quirkiness – that's if it had any. Her fans enjoyed indulging her in this. Whatever she said about their home town, she was most probably going to be equally scathing about the next-door neighbours.

Linda had quirks of her own, of course. For one thing, she achieved status as an acclaimed comedian and writer without possessing a mobile phone, a computer (or typewriter), or a driving licence. Linda did own a mobile phone once, but after using it a couple of times, she put it in a drawer and left it there for evermore. She loved to chat on the landline for hours on end, but resented the intrusiveness of the 'field telephone'. Although I bought her a personal computer, to try and wean her off me as her script typist, she preferred to write longhand and was a relentless scribbler of notes.

As for the car, why learn to drive when you've got a driver? Linda would regularly suffer public transport, but her preferred mode of travel to work was the motor car – with me at the wheel, a tape cassette or CD of upbeat music in the machine or a Radio Four programme of choice. As kids we both loved *Thunderbirds* so I suppose I could describe us as comedy's answer to Lady Penelope and her faithful chauffeur Parker. The analogy falters a bit after that because rather than driving a pink Rolls-Royce, we were cruising the motorways in a hired economy car.

Throughout most of our relationship, we were constantly on the road, especially after Linda began packing them in at theatres and arts centres across the UK from early 2001. After a long apprenticeship as a live performer, working more often than not on a shared bill, she was finally touring in her solo show. It gave her a real buzz to be performing in venues that had sold out months in advance, to audiences that had paid serious money to come and spend an evening with her. It had been her dream for a very long time.

We used to try and concentrate the touring work on Fridays, Saturdays and Sundays, because Linda liked to be available, where possible, for recording *The News Quiz* on Radio Four on Thursdays. Working weekends also meant that I could get away from my job – as a fundraiser for arts and culture – to moonlight as 'Parker'. In my spare time I was Linda's booker, negotiator, troubleshooter, driver and general right-hand person.

If I got my touring compass right, we could go to an area of the country and do Friday, Saturday and Sunday gigs, and then drive home late on Sunday night, arriving back in time for me to get a few hours' sleep before going into work on the Monday morning. Some tours were made up of one-nighters, in which case we'd always do our utmost to get home at the end of each gig. Linda hated being away from her garden, particularly in spring and summer.

In September 2002, Linda and I were living in a modest former railway worker's cottage in Stratford, east London. Small house, huge garden. Linda spent a lot of her off-duty time outdoors tending to her various families of plants and entertaining friends on the patio. Tea was served all day and often into the night. She was extremely sociable and particularly loved seeing friends at home, because she spent so much time on the road.

Show days would usually begin with a trip to the garage to fill up the car and buy newspapers. I'd scan the tabloid front pages and if I saw something funny, I'd point it out to Linda and she might weave it into her act. But generally she'd read the *Guardian* or the *Independent* on the way to a gig. It always amazed me how she managed to read in the car without feeling sick. We'd also have the radio news on from time to time. Almost everyone in the audience would have seen or heard the six o'clock news before coming to the show and it would be embarrassing to be unaware of a big story when it came to doing topical material.

The onus was on me as the driver with regard to time-keeping, because Linda only had the very vaguest idea of how long it would take to get anywhere. I was the only one with a watch, though Linda would occasionally borrow mine if she needed to time a speech or was doing a short set and needed to judge when her twenty minutes were up. We found perfect harmony in our haphazard timekeeping, but to give Linda her due, she would often be genuinely upset about keeping people waiting, whereas I tend to be very laid back and blame it all on living in London and the unpredictability of travel. Problem is, this doesn't sound very convincing when you're miles away from the capital.

But when a show time has been advertised as 7.45 p.m. and people are coming along expecting it to start then, you've got to do your level best to honour that. Linda would want to be at the venue an hour and a half beforehand, which gave her ample time to relax, have a cup of tea (she never ate anything before going on stage) and a sound check, get everything done on the technical front, get a feel for the place, meet the staff, think about her material and put her show head on.

Meanwhile, I'd go on a reconnaissance mission to find out a bit of local information from the venue staff, about rival towns and posh areas and where to find this or that locally. Linda would then get to work on incorporating local references into her material. The staff always enjoyed getting involved.

If we were delayed because I'd misjudged the times, or the traffic was appalling for whatever reason – a meteor crashing into the A127 – sometimes Linda would have to do final preparation in the car, including looking at her notes and jotting stuff down. That would mean feeling hurried and rushed, which wasn't part of the deal. It was tantamount to asking her to make her face up in the car – unthinkable, really. There was no worse sound than that of *The Archers'* theme tune at 7 p.m. – the witching hour, as I came to think of it. It meant a court appearance for me, even if it wasn't my fault. Sometimes we cut it very fine indeed and Linda had to draw on years of experience not to get flustered.

But on this particular occasion, our journey to Tavistock, the cream tea capital of the West Country, had been trouble-free. This gig had been planned as a one-off, giving Linda

the chance to get into her stride and try out some new material before her autumn tour started in earnest the following
weekend, with three consecutive gigs from Friday to Sunday.

Tavistock is a long way to go for a single gig, so we decided
to make a weekend of it. We left London and stopped
overnight at a hotel in the wilds of Wiltshire, having failed
to secure anything more nourishing en route than a giant-
size teacake and a hot drink at a Little Chef service stop
somewhere on the outskirts of dismal Andover. We drove
around the town seeing T-shirted squaddies and their bare-
legged lasses staggering along the streets from pub to pub,
leaving a leery slug-like trail through this Friday-night open-
air pleasure dome. It's probably not fair to single out
Andover. There are hundreds of similar scenes acted out in
small-town Britain every weekend and we witnessed a good
number of them during years of touring.

We took the scenic route across Dartmoor and arrived in
the pleasant market town of Tavistock on the western edge
of the moor, a relatively short distance from the prison. We
arrived at the Bedford Hotel in mid-afternoon, just a hop
from that evening's venue, The Wharf, about half a mile
down the Plymouth Road.

Linda had a lie-down; she hadn't been feeling well and
wanted to relax before we headed out for a light tea. It had
been a very busy year and she'd been working hard on several
fronts: touring live; writing the second series of her radio
sitcom; and making regular appearances on TV and radio.
Health, as well as work, had dominated the year so far. We
were both reeling from my father's death in February, which
had left me stunned, sickened and saddened beyond belief.
After many months of chemotherapy treatment he had
become desperately ill and died in peace at home, nursed

by my wonderful mum. Suddenly, the person who was my primary influence, my best mate for most of my life, was no longer there.

Linda was deeply affected by Dad's death. She and Dad had a sweet, easy-going relationship that was both very funny and affectionate. Mum and I still enjoy replaying a series of hilarious episodes featuring my dad at his most outrageous, Larry David-style. One incident, based on our refusal to associate with him outside the house while he was wearing a ridiculous pair of divers' protective goggle glasses to fend off the wind, left Linda and me convulsed with laughter for about ten minutes, rolling around the hallway floor.

After Dad died, I took a week off work to comfort Mum and help her sort out his affairs, which were in typically impeccable order. Linda soldiered on with her work engagements, which were shaping up well – plenty of variety and a decent financial return. Within two weeks she was gigging again and I was driving her to Leicester for the first show of her spring tour.

Because of Linda's writing and recording commitments, we decided to go easy on live bookings for a short while after the tour. There was another reason, too.

Linda loved playing in venues with a bit of atmosphere – anything from a traditional proscenium arch theatre with plush seats to an imaginative conversion of an old building. Among her favourites were the Hackney Empire, the wonderful Georgian Theatre Royal in Richmond, Yorkshire, and Huntingdon Hall in Worcester, which was once a Methodist chapel. I'm not saying she disliked modern arts centres, but she definitely found some of them a bit soulless.

You often remember venues according to how good they were to you backstage – how efficient they were at providing everything you asked for, whether the staff were welcoming and the stage crew co-operative. Sometimes the attitude to performers was appalling. I've never understood why. Surely it stands to reason that you'll get a better show out of the person you are paying to perform if you provide them with a clean, well-ventilated dressing room. The more traditional theatres tend to be better because actors need proper lights and mirrors to get into costume and make-up, but if the accent of a venue was more on music, you could sometimes find yourself in a dressing room littered with overflowing ashtrays and half-empty beer bottles left over from the night before. It could really get you off on the wrong foot.

No such problems at The Wharf in Tavistock, I'm glad to report. The Wharf described itself in its comprehensive seasonal programme as 'West Devon's Premier Arts and Entertainment Centre'. It's hard to argue with that. Nevertheless, it always augurs well when the booker, in this case a lovely warm woman called Margaret Hurdwell, greets you and makes you feel immediately at home, like a long-lost friend.

The opposite could often be true, as Linda joked in her live show: 'It makes a difference – a welcome when you arrive somewhere . . . you know, you get somewhere like (softly) – Telford . . . there you are, travelling all day . . . and there to meet you is this woman, standing at the door like this – you know those people, semi-filleted . . . weakened by thirty years of veganism . . . consequently, hardly got the strength to support her own skeleton . . . standing there in a dress made of Quorn . . . previous job: administrator in a vegetarian circus – where the most exciting thing that happened was a man placing his head into the mouth of a live yoghurt . . . standing there . . . "Oh, hello, you're here, are you? I'm afraid nobody's coming – I don't know why – Marjorie's put a leaflet in the library." How could it fail?'

Tonight's show had been booked almost a year earlier, which is quite unprecedented for a smaller arts centre seating 210. This lot were very good at their business; they had sold out with minimal publicity. Like a lot of small venues, The Wharf was self-financing and run by a voluntary committee, meaning no one was paid. They were doing it for love, believe it or not.

The brochure made clear what it took for a place like The Wharf to survive, let alone flourish. A section under the heading, 'Help! Help! Help!' read as follows: 'Our steward secretary has had to resign because of family commitments. Are there any Friends who would like to be co-opted onto the committee? We are also in need of box-office volunteers – sessions are no longer than three hours – could you offer either a regular slot or as a fill-in? The car boot sale raised £38. The committee would like to hear from any Friends who have ideas for ways of raising funds . . .' It was a genuine hand-to-mouth arts organisation, somehow managing to keep its doors open to provide a real service to its locality.

It had to offer an incredibly varied arts programme to survive, from opera to poetry and musical theatre. That season you could see Maria Gibbs with 'The Best of Joyce Grenfell' (although surely the great Maureen Lipman is the best Joyce Grenfell), or you could have gone mad and treated yourself to the magic of Geoffrey Durham, the Great Soprendo (formerly Mr Victoria Wood). We never got to meet Geoffrey, but Linda must have appeared at dozens of theatres and arts centres where he had recently been or was due to make a disappearance.

Now The Wharf also unwittingly contributed to Linda's

'I Spy' book of absurdly named rock tribute bands. We began collecting them in earnest in 2001 when the trend for 'not the real thing' acts really seemed to have taken hold. Established combos like Bjorn Again (Abba) and The Bootleg Beatles (The Beatles or, at a stretch, The Rutles) had been doing the rounds for years. The Wharf's line-up included: T-Rextasy (T-Rex); Floydian Slip (Pink Floyd); Limehouse Lizzie (Thin Lizzy); Into the Bleach (Blondie) and – wait for it – Whole Lotta Led (Led Zeppelin, of course). Linda often cited the imaginary The Dours (a Yorkshire equivalent of The Doors) as one of her favourite trib outfits. But her personal top of the pops was the real Bon Jovi tribute band, 'By Jovi'.

That night, as Linda was preparing in the dressing room, I was out front of house in my customary role of surveillance officer, clocking the punters and studying their social profile. 'What are they like?' she asked when I popped back.

'A mixture – maybe as many as forty per cent greys, quite a few Radio Four types,' I replied. There were always a good smattering of men of a certain age – 'Harold Shipman look-a-likeys' is how Linda described them. You know: beard, specs, tweed jacket and slacks (sort of country casuals).

In the last thirty to forty minutes before she went on, Linda would consolidate new bits from her last performances and incorporate all the local references. A lot of consideration went into how to start the show. Had something happened to us on the journey? Genuinely – or would she make it up? Had something big happened in the town that week? She couldn't miss any obvious targets; they would provide her with the perfect way into the show.

The key was to come on and fuse it all together so that she'd have a nice warm presence immediately, but also to get a first laugh pretty damn quickly. Then she could judge what the crowd was like. Were they listening? Were they smart? Were they a bit slow? Were they up for it?

The emphasis, after starting on the right foot, was on keeping the energy going. Even in a stand-up set of nearly two hours you can't dip; you can't afford peaks and troughs. If you sink a bit, the audience will drop down with you and then you've got your work cut out to bring them back up. It takes some doing: to take them up, keep them up, and bring them back up there again after the interval. It requires real stamina, as well as clever footwork. What's more, you've got to get it right first time, because you can't go back and explain something a second time. During quiet passages and when you're going into new areas, you've got to know that they're with you.

Where possible, I tried to sit in the audience once the show had started. It's a very different view from being backstage or listening on a monitor in the green room or dressing room, or with a technician. Linda preferred me to be out front as well. During the interval she'd say, 'How do you think it's going?' I'd give my perspective on the audience's responses, and she'd make tactical decisions accordingly. It could get quite analytical. Some nights it seemed best to cut the sports section right down, because we sensed that the punters just wouldn't be interested. Other nights you knew they were going to love hearing Linda's take on rugby, cricket and golf. It was rare for a woman even to go near such traditionally male subjects.

Linda was great on her feet, always improvising. If, once the show had begun, she thought something would work better later rather than earlier, she would switch the material around. She would always know what her route was from beginning to end, but during that route she was able to swing off into a lay-by or down a B road and come back onto the A route a different way. It was an amazing process to witness, night after night. I was always struck by her recall. I'd be sitting there thinking, 'Oh no, she's going to forget to do that bit about Nazis on TV.' But then twenty minutes later, up it popped. It was as if she were shuffling a pack of cards in her head. No two shows were ever the same.

Once, during an interval, I was flicking through a local magazine while Linda was having a cup of tea and thinking about the second half. An advertisement caught my eye and I pointed it out. Five minutes later, Linda used it in her act: 'I was having a little look through the *Villager* magazine and I'd never thought – before the Cats Protection League alerted my attention to it – that cat-neutering vouchers make a good gift. It's a little tip, isn't it – probably best for cat owners . . .'

After the show Linda would want to write the new stuff down immediately, but inevitably she'd lose the scrap of paper, or forget where she'd put it. Luckily she had an excellent memory, and so just before the next show she'd suddenly remember that new bit about Bush or Blair – or cats – and rework it, so that it was freshly minted just in time. Equally, she might never use it again.

Back in the dressing room immediately after the curtain came down, we'd do a quick post-show analysis before anyone got the chance to disturb us. We'd stop talking the moment someone knocked at the door, preferring to wait to chat things through, perhaps until we were in the car again. Once we were alone, Linda would always be concerned about how any new material had gone down with the audience. 'Do you think it worked?' It was important to her. She wanted truthful feedback. 'Did people really find that funny or was it just the odd person?' Even if at the end of the show people were on their feet clapping and cheering, it wasn't necessarily the whole story. 'Do you think it's worth keeping that in again, or just leaving it? Should I be doing less on that subject? What do you think?'

She could get annoyed with me if I wasn't very clear about what I was saying. 'What do you mean? Oh, you don't think that went well. No, you're just saying that. You don't really mean it went well.'

'Yes, of course it went well.'

I had to think hard about what I said and how I said it. I had to be honest. I was her sounding board. There was no one else she could ask. Was I being unnecessarily kind? Was I not being truthful? Was I doing it just to calm her fevered brow? She expected me to be dead straight with her, not just placate her. Looking back, I think I had more responsibility than I realised at the time. Often I'd have to be justifying my remarks while negotiating my way out of town on the road, and it might be some time before we could relax into the journey home. It was like a set piece and we played it through for years and years. It was all part of the comedown from the show. I miss it badly.

Taking leave of Tavistock was a very different experience, however, as was the pre-show warm-up that September night. During the late summer, Linda had begun to sense that something wasn't right with her health. Sometimes it was a nagging backache, more often than not a very uncomfortable pain and bloating, which she seemed to be experiencing in the lower abdominal region. She definitely wasn't feeling herself. Still, she was the kind of person who took pain relief and got on with things. 'We'll carry on as long as I feel up to it,' she assured me. She began relying on that old showbiz fallback, 'Dr Theatre', to get her through. And so he did – up to a point.

By this evening, though, we both knew something was not right. A few days before the show, our GP had sent her for an ultrasound scan and arranged an appointment near to home with a specialist at Newham General Hospital. So now we were getting a bit frayed waiting for the results.

Possibly as a side-effect of all this, Linda was finding it increasingly difficult to slip into her favourite performing suit; the trousers were tight and needed adjusting. As show-time approached she was desperate to change into a more comfortable pair. There was only one thing for it – I had to make a mercy dash back to the hotel, find a spare pair of black trousers with a more generous waistband and plead with a chambermaid to find an iron and board so that I could make them presentable to a paying audience. This mission restored my sagging faith in human nature; the young woman not only found the equipment for me, she insisted on pressing the trousers.

By the time I had rushed back to The Wharf, the clock was showing less than fifteen minutes to start time. But Linda, like the supremely unflappable trouper that she was, pored over her notes for a couple of precious moments, then strode out to backstage, pacing back and forth in time with the music we normally supplied for pre-show warm-up (The Skatalites' 'Lucky Seven' – Linda loved ska.) She waited behind the black curtain for the introduction. As I often did, I made the off-stage announcement. 'And now will you give a big warm Tavistock welcome to . . . Linda Smith!'

Linda coped marvellously that evening, as she always did. The show went very well, but she was far from well. We both knew that it was time to take stock of the situation and that, if necessary, the tour would have to be put on hold while she underwent further medical investigations. The journey back to London the next day seemed interminable.

I

Bubble Car to Birmingham

Erith to Smethwick

Linda's first experience of drawing a crowd came early, although the audience was not strictly hers, but belonged to a small motorised vehicle. Back in the early 1960s, her elder sister Barbara and Barbara's boyfriend Terry were the proud owners of an eye-catching three-wheeler grey bubble car.

Barbara and Terry were the first in the family to own a car. Terry got the bubble car because, not having a reverse gear, it could be driven on a scooter licence, and this came in handy while Terry was under seventeen. When he was seventeen he put the reverse on it and passed his driving test straight away. The bubble car had a bench seat, and the steering wheel was in the door, so as the door opened the steering wheel went with it.

Legend has it that the bubble car, an Isetta, turned heads on its arrival outside the family maisonette in Erith, south-east London. The whole family and several neighbours would flock onto the street for a closer inspection of this mobile curiosity. The whole family except for Linda, of course, who sat proudly in the middle of the front bench seat, not a seatbelt in sight, no doubt enjoying her first taste of the limelight.

In those days, Christmas was spent with Linda's father's family in the Smethwick district of Birmingham. Her dad, Ray Smith, would lead the annual expedition to the Midlands to spend time with his mother Lily, aka Granny Smith, and his sister Linda.

Three years in a row Terry and Barbara took Linda to Birmingham at Christmas, to her Granny Smith's, while Linda's parents took the train. Apparently, the journey from south-east London to Birmingham took at least five hours, with the bubble car excelling at speeds up to 40 mph but most of the time cruising along the all-so-quiet motorway at a comfortable 30 mph.

Linda often talked about her mum and she incorporated various autobiographical elements into her live act, but she rarely spoke to me or to anyone else about her feelings towards her dad. I must admit, the more I've heard about Linda's dad, the more I feel that he and Linda's mum were not exactly a perfect match. From the sound of it, Linda's mum's first marriage – to Barbara's dad, Thomas Boyce – was a lot happier than her second marriage to Ray.

Linda's mum was called Bessie, more by accident than design. The story goes that when her father went to register her birth, her mother had said they would call her Elizabeth Evelyn, but Bessie for short. Ostensibly, her father got it wrong and called her Bessie Elizabeth Evelyn. Bessie was born in North Heath, Erith, on 4 July 1918 to Maria and John Locke, just four months before the end of The First World War.

Maria had been raised in Great Yarmouth, but had lived most of her life in the Erith area, whereas John was a coal miner from Ebbw Vale. He had come to London for work when a lot of the pits in South Wales closed. Bessie had two sisters and two brothers. Of the three sisters, Bessie was in the middle, Margaret was the eldest and Helen the youngest. John was the first son and Roy was the baby of the family.

He was the last of the siblings to die, about three or four years ago.

Bessie met her future husband, Thomas Boyce, when she was 21. They were married during the Second World War and had their only child, Barbara, in 1944. Thomas was only 38 when he died in 1952, of tuberculosis, like his father before him. An electrical engineer, he wasn't called up during the war because he was needed at home; his job was categorised as a reserved occupation. But he was badly injured when a bomb dropped through the ceiling of a local factory and, in an act of true bravery, he threw himself on a pregnant woman, saving her life by taking the full force of the blast himself.

Barbara has strong memories of the years of her father's illness. Bessie wouldn't let Thomas go into hospital and looked after him at home. Then, at the age of three, Barbara developed tuberculosis and was sent to Norfolk to a sanatorium for a year. 'Dad was bedridden for years, but there were happy times,' Barbara told me. 'My parents were marvellous. They were very happy together. We had good times with my grandparents, aunts and uncles, and I had several cousins who visited a lot. I can remember the day Dad died. My cousin Jean took me and my other cousin to the cinema and when we got back she said, "Come into the bedroom. I want to tell you something." And she sat me down and told me my dad had died. My mum was very, very sad. She was just 34. After that, we never spoke about my dad – never, ever – at least, not until I had my son Scott.'

After Thomas died, Bessie went out to work on an assembly line, making televisions at a factory called Burndetts, where she made a couple of good friends, Mirrie and Barbara. Shy and chubby, she was very much a stay-at-home type. At weekends there were family outings to Southend, where she would often seek out the services of a fortune teller. She was highly superstitious, according to Barbara. 'If a gypsy wanted her to buy a bit of heather she would. I used to say, "Don't buy it." Mum would say, "They put a curse on you if you don't."'

When Barbara was nine or ten, a gypsy woman told Bessie that she could see her holding the hand of a child, a little girl. 'That child is going to grow up to be exceptionally clever. And you are going to be so proud of her. Her IQ is going to be so high. She is going to be loved by everyone,' the gypsy pronounced. Bessie believed every word of it.

Three years after Thomas died, Bessie's life changed again when her friends Barbara and Mirrie talked her into going on a factory beano to Southend-on-Sea. There she met Ray Smith, at the time a steel erector, who was on a pub outing from Camberwell, where he was lodging.

Ray was tall, handsome, funny and 'charming to the outside world', says Barbara. 'Mum was very vulnerable. I think she was flattered. He walked into a ready-made home; that's what attracted him. He was quite outgoing, but he had lots of issues with people. He didn't have many friends. When I met him I thought he was wonderful, but I was also a bit embarrassed. My friends would say, "He's a bit of all right, your stepdad."' He was also demonstrative. 'We hadn't seen that kind of affection before. I was happy that my mum was happy. He treated me fine and his family was very good to me.'

Ray and Bessie courted for about a year before they got married. Ray was ten years her junior, but apparently the age gap wasn't very noticeable. What was impossible to ignore, as time went on, was Ray's volatile temperament.

Just a few hours after the wedding ceremony, he accused his best man of trying to get off with his new bride. A huge row ensued and Ray's best friend stormed off into the night, mortally offended, shaking his fist in rage. The family never saw the friend again.

From the evidence presented to me over the years, it would be fair to surmise that life was hardly domestic bliss at the Smiths' matrimonial home in downtown Erith, but Ray could be very generous. In the pub he'd treat everyone to a drink. He'd buy his wife presents and would later become a beloved granddad to Barbara's young sons. When she was younger, Linda adored him for his sense of humour and his quirkiness. They were the best of pals – until Dr Jekyll became Mr Hyde. Then the spirit of generosity could evaporate in moments to reveal a very ugly side to this man. Insecurity would give way to irrational jealousy and his behaviour could very quickly become abusive.

I met Ray only once and then hardly spoke to him other than to make a formal greeting. But I picked up from Linda during our early years together, and from Barbara, the impression of someone who wasn't especially contented with his lot. He was a railway track maintenance worker. Barbara remembers him as 'a real worker, a grafter' and, like Linda, she felt that he was frustrated. 'He was a highly intelligent man, a big reader, who never fulfilled himself. He was very radical, a trade union official, a shop steward – very, very political, very left wing. We used to wake up on Sunday mornings to IRA revolutionary songs on the record player. Though I don't think there was any Irish connection.

'When he was okay, he was a very funny man. Linda definitely got her love of reading from him and used to go to the library with him. When she was quite young, between five and ten, they were very close, because they had the same interests. Sometimes she'd go to the tracks with him. But as she grew more aware, she began to pull away from him. She was very protective of her mum.'

Linda's protectiveness was due to the fact that, sadly, there was a violent element to Bessie and Ray's relationship. 'Linda slept in the same bed as me,' Barbara remembers. 'When the awful business was going on – shouting and screaming in the middle of the night – I'd put my hands up to her ears so that she didn't hear, but she obviously did. He never, ever hurt me, never touched me, but I grew to hate him, because I saw what he did to my mum. When I was 13 he said to me, "Why don't you call me Dad?" I said I could never call him Dad unless he acted like a dad and a husband.

'I used to have a go at him and he would say, "You keep out of this. It's nothing to do with you; it's between your mother and me."' He always kept my mum short. He wouldn't allow her to have any money and he wouldn't allow her to work. He would go to the shops with her. Mum became very withdrawn, but she was still a wonderful mother.

'We tried to protect Mum's mum from it. As I grew older I used to go down there a lot because we lived in the same road and I was very close to them. I'd often go in and I'd be crying all night. "Whatever's wrong?" she'd ask. "Oh, nothing."

'Mum's brothers lived just up the road and round the corner, so on a few occasions I ran up to get them to come down to stop him. They came down, so they knew, and as the years went on they all knew. That didn't stop him. It's like an illness. I believe it stems from something in his early years.

'He was a big, big drinker. That was half his problem. He was a gambler too. It was worse when he had been drinking.

Just something stupid would set him off. Mum would serve up dinner. "It's rubbish," he'd say, and it would start.

'His mother knew what he was like, but she wouldn't accept it. When Linda was a baby it was getting quite bad and my mum told her; she had to bring her into it. But Granny Smith would say, "You must do something to provoke him. You must ask for it. You know he likes to do this and likes to do that and you as a wife should do what he says." It was never his fault.'

Bessie had Linda about three years after she married Ray, when she was 40. Linda Helen Smith was born in the Hainault Maternity Hospital, Erith, at 5.45 on the morning of 29 January 1958. Her baby book, which was lovingly maintained in the early years by members of her immediate family, reveals that Linda weighed in at 6lb 9oz. She was described as having dark-blue eyes, corn-coloured hair and a peaches-and-cream complexion. There are various remarks about the infant Linda being energetic, vigorous and very mischievous; nothing changed there then. Her early health record mentions she had a bad cold at thirteen months, stating that it was 'caused by talking'.

For Barbara, the day Linda was born was 'the best day of my life'. She doted on her little sister, even though her arrival meant that the focus of the family shifted away from her onto the baby.

Up until then, Ray's mother Granny Smith had always treated Barbara to lots of presents, taking her on shopping trips to Selfridges to buy new coats and shoes. 'When they said Mum was pregnant, I was absolutely over the moon, but I'll never forget when Granny Smith came in and said, "Your nose will be pushed out now, my dear." Her whole attitude changed.

'She went on holiday when Linda was two and brought back a solid gold watch, a big gold cross and a bracelet of little sea pearls and rubies. They were for Linda, so Mum put them away for when she was old enough. I didn't get anything after that, but I can say with my hand on my heart that it did not bother me because that little girl was like my own child. The whole family spoilt her rotten.'

Soon afterwards, Barbara, 15, met Terry Giles, 16, at Allhallows-on-Sea in Kent. Terry's parents had a caravan there and Barbara's boss at the hairdresser's salon where she worked had a caravanette and speedboat. Barbara was on the beach with a friend when Terry and a mate strolled past. There was a battery-powered record player perched on Terry's shoulder – a Dansette – which was pounding out 'Shakin' All Over' by Johnny Kidd and The Pirates.

Terry soon found out that his fifteen-year-old girlfriend came as a package with her two-year-old little sister. 'We took her everywhere and people used to think that she was ours. In the sixties it was quite frowned upon, no wedding ring. We used to get funny looks. I liked having her with me, but Terry didn't. He used to moan at me. Linda was extremely loving to me at that age, so I coveted her from day one, because we weren't a demonstrative family.

'She used to tell Terry "I don't like you". We'd be sitting on the settee in the front room at Mum's, playing music, and she'd come in and plump herself in the middle. She was terrible.'

Linda later said that she hated the idea of Barbara getting married, 'because I didn't want her to go away'. This was particularly understandable in the circumstances. Without Barbara, there would no longer be anyone to act as a buffer between Linda and her warring parents, to block her ears in the night during a row. Linda admitted that she didn't like the prospect of losing a member of her captive audience, either: 'I was always doing little shows for the family. Not entirely with their consent, I suppose. Trapped in the front room and I would do little songs and things. I was quite good at pushing other kids off the sofa if I thought they were getting a little bit too much attention.'

After Barbara and Terry got engaged, Linda made a last attempt to scupper their marriage plans. 'The vicar came round to check where we lived,' Barbara says. 'He knocked at the door and said, "Are Barbara and Terry here?" Linda said, "No. Nobody of that name here." She was six or seven at the time. "Oh," he said. "Barbara and Terry? Terry Giles and Barbara Boyce." "No, nobody here," Linda insisted, and slammed the door.'

Recalling the same incident, Linda said: 'I slammed the door and thought, "That's it, wedding's off." I thought that would be the end of it. Mortified when he worked out that actually it was the right address. I really hated the idea of them getting married.'

Still, she got used to the idea in time for the big day, and dressed up in 'a nice blue satin affair'. Barbara drew on her hairdressing skills to do the bridesmaids' hair like Dusty Springfield's, with piled-up curls and a blue satin band.

Submitting to this early makeover went against the grain for Linda, who had a reputation for being a tomboy. 'She always had a gang. They were mostly boys. She was not a girly girl,' Barbara says. 'I tried to make her girly. When she was little I used to buy her all these frilly dresses.' There is a photo of Linda, aged one, dressed up in Barbara's big china doll's dress and doll's hat. 'When we were sharing, my bedroom was all pink. Mum was a great one for making beautiful curtains and bed covers and doilies for the dressing table, all to match. The satin stuff went when I moved out, and Linda went on to plaster the walls with Alice Cooper posters.'

As the years passed, Linda and Terry became very fond of each other, but the initial years were difficult. When Barbara and Terry had a bust-up early on in their relation-ship, the family took Barbara's side and told her that she was well rid of him. It took a while for them to reconcile; they took it a step at a time. Terry would go over to Sunday lunch, but was prohibited from staying the night.

One Sunday lunch, young Linda piped up, 'You're allowed to have lunch with us but you're not staying. You're never staying in our house again.' You could have cut the atmos-phere with a knife, apparently.

Ray was very possessive of Bessie, and his jealousy also extended towards Linda and Barbara, particularly when Barbara started going out with Terry. When Barbara went on holiday with some friends, he said, "Why would you need to go away with friends when you've got your family?" Ray Smith and Terry got on on the surface, but Terry disliked him for how he treated Bessie.

In their early married years, Barbara was worried about leaving home, because of the situation with Ray. Terry wanted to emigrate to Canada, but Barbara could never have left Linda and her mum. She and Terry had their own place nearby and Linda would often stay with them, and visit on Sundays. Although Linda had lots of little pals, she must have been lonely within the family set-up. The age difference between her and Barbara meant that she was very much an only child. Barbara, especially after she left home, was more of an aunt to her than a sister.

When Linda was eight, Bessie was badly injured in a road accident and spent several months in hospital. Barbara remembers getting a phone call on Christmas Eve, the year after she married Terry. Bessie was in a coma and very close to death after being run over by a motorbike on her way to take Linda to Brownies. Her legs and arms were broken, and she had a fractured skull. The prognosis was bad: she was not expected to survive the night, but if she did, by some miracle, she would be completely disabled, perhaps even paralysed.

Bessie's absence from home brought family tensions to the surface. Barbara and aunt Helen organised for Linda to be taken care of by Bessie's sister, Margaret, but Granny Smith was having none of it. She put her foot down. In her opinion it was up to the Smiths to look after their own; no one else could or should fulfil that role. She drafted her daughter Linda down from Birmingham to cook and clean for Ray and Linda, while she supervised.

Fortunately, Bessie was either made of stronger stuff than the doctors gave her credit for, or she was extremely lucky. She made a complete recovery and came home after four months, at Easter. That day is still vivid in Barbara's memory. 'Mum came out of hospital on two sticks. Old Granny Smith was there and she said to me – and I'll never forget it – "Right, I've looked after mine. Now it's your turn. You can look after yours." And she left, just like that, taking Aunt Linda with her.'

Fortunately, Linda and Barbara had other close relatives with somewhat sunnier personalities than Granny Smith's. Linda's favourite aunt, Bessie's sister Helen, was a constant presence; she had a big influence on the sisters. Indeed, Barbara has a strong sense that, although Linda did have a dad, they grew up without a father as such, and had two mums, Bessie and Helen.

Helen Locke, who never married, was six foot tall, slim, elegant and very graceful. She worked for many years as a lady's maid for Lord and Lady Inverforth at the family's grand home and garden in Hampstead, north London. Every day she commuted from a municipal tower block flat in Slade Green, near Erith, to a millionaires' row across London. She was a faithful and conscientious employee, doing most things for 'the lady' and indulging her eccentricities – Helen's duties included seeing to her ladyship's pet parrot, which had its own quarters.

In common with a lot of working-class people who devote their days to serving the upper classes, Helen brought home a low wage for her labours. But there were perks to supplement her income. She would often be given objects from the Inverforth household. When 'the lady' was getting rid of designer and hand-rolled silk scarves, costume jewellery, pots or vases, Helen would take them home on the train and often distribute them to her sister and nieces, once giving Linda a handsome Lalique vase.

Helen always dressed well. She would save up and buy a pair of shoes costing £100 – an outrageous sum in those days – and Lady Inverforth would buy her lovely handbags. So she had a lot of good stuff carefully boxed and hanging up in the wardrobe of her council flat, including beautiful cashmere coats. Bessie used to complain that Helen had given Linda and Barbara expensive tastes. 'It's your fault these two have grown up wanting these things,' she'd say.

Helen was a lovely, caring person with a smashing sense of humour. I'm sure Linda inherited a love of beautiful and stylish objects from her, possibly along with her dress sense.

I suppose Helen was also a bit quirky; she kept garden gnomes. During the summer they lived outdoors, but they would winter below her fireplace, protected from the cold weather. I'm the proud inheritor of two of them and they have pride of place in the shade of my garden. But no, I don't bring them in for the winter.

For me, a welcome by-product of knowing and loving Linda was an introduction to the good women of Erith who dominated her family, namely her mum Bessie, aunt Helen, and sister Barbara. It is a privilege to have known them.

2

Good Luck in the Future

Erith to Bexleyheath [By bus]

There are men in the village of Erith
Whom nobody see'eth or heareth
And there looms on the marge
Of the river, a barge
That nobody roweth or steereth.

Anon.

'I am from London, but not a particularly nice bit of London; a horrible little place, a grim little place on the outskirts, called Erith. A place so grim and miserable and meaningless and depressing, it's not actually twinned with anywhere but it does have a suicide pact with Dagenham. That's the kind of town it is.

'I thought I would move away from there because it's a horrible place. The sort of place where people don't just keep pit bull terriers, they have to have photos of them in the window. Big pit bull terrier's mush with "I Live Here – Break In, Make My Day", which is daft really, because when you meet the people who live there, a photo of them would be more effective.'

Commonly known by locals as 'the town that Hitler missed' (although its waterfront suffered heavy casualties in the war), Erith was an irresistible comic target for Linda. It is not a pretty place. Even the most partisan of the natives of this Thames-side settlement would have to admit that.

But what you said privately about the town was one thing. To go public was quite another, as Linda discovered when she stirred up a huge kerfuffle with an appearance as a guest stand-up comic on the Channel Four late-night comedy series *Packet of Three*, fronted by her old chum Henry Normal, in August 1991.

Unlike the Luftwaffe, Linda's scathing comments about Erith scored a direct hit that was reflected in the bulging postbags of the local newspapers for the next few weeks. We knew nothing of it until Linda's aunt Helen sent us some of the clippings. It is rare for comic material of this nature to fall into a comedian's lap, but on this occasion Linda was given a gift-wrapped present that lasted many years and became a regular segment in the home town section of her solo show. Little remains of old Erith, situated on the south side of the Thames. Historically, it is bound up with the river and its estuary. Once part of Henry VIII's naval dock-yard, it later became a popular resort for day-trippers arriving on pleasure boats in mid-Victorian times, and was developed for docks and industry by entrepreneurs in the late nineteenth century.

The Erith waterfront Linda knew was very run down, all wreckers' yards and factory chimneys belching out thick clouds of foul, discoloured smoke. Burnt-out cars were a common sight; illegal dumps of rubbish littered the docks and pavements. This was industrial Erith, once the site of armaments factories linked to the Royal Arsenal at nearby Woolwich. Heavily targeted during the Second World War, it never recovered, going into almost terminal decline for decades.

The river now hosts water sports: a yacht club and a rowing club. There has even been a degree of gentrification achieved through new-build riverside apartments. 'Who would have thought it?' Linda would have exclaimed in wide-eyed disbelief. She used to say that you'd know you were near the end of civilisation if they started building luxury apartments on the waterfront at Erith.

The town centre has been pretty much modernised out of existence and is barely identifiable now. Linda mourned the passing of the old town, which by 1980 had been bull-dozed and sacrificed to make way for anonymous modern shops, offices and car parking spaces. A further major rede-velopment took place in the late 1990s, when two plain-looking shopping centres made way for new social housing and better-quality shops.

Today its cultural hot spot is the Erith Playhouse, the largest public theatre space in the borough. It was presenting *Accidental Death of an Anarchist* – a Linda favourite – the last time I passed by. A helpful local museum is run on very limited opening hours.

Although at least one other person of artistic note was born within its precincts – the poet Wendy Cope – Erith was not a place you would necessarily associate with creative beginnings. Linda's early years were notably lacking in kindred companions. It wasn't until much later on that she met a group of like-minded friends, people who were inter-ested in art, theatre and books. But she was bright from the word go. Her sister Barbara remembers Linda, aged ten or eleven, solving an apparently insoluble problem on a BBC schools TV programme. 'The form teacher couldn't believe it. It was the talk of the class and the family.'

Lessness Heath Primary School on Erith Road, Belvedere, where Linda spent the years from 1962 to 1969, was predomi-nantly working class and white, reflecting its surroundings.

There were two entrances, one on the Upper Belvedere side, where most of the residents were owner-occupiers, and the other on the Erith side – where Linda came from – in the middle of a council estate.

Anyone remotely different stood out 'like a sore thumb', according to Sharyn Smith, who sat next to Linda during their final two years at the school. Her memories of Lessness Heath are still very vivid. 'One very posh boy in our class was given a lot of grief. He spoke in an accent that seemed very alien to most of us, the Queen's English as it might have been described then, and he did not play football with the rest of the lads.'

An Asian girl who arrived in the final year was even more of a curiosity. 'The class was fascinated by her. The level of interest was a reflection of how strange and exotic people from other cultures seemed in that part of the world at that time. I don't think there was much awareness of how this could be construed as lack of tolerance, but since moving away and returning as an adult, one notices a certain narrow-mindedness that is very unpleasant. I'm sure this is something that would not have been lost on Linda.'

Linda was tall and blonde, Sharyn says. 'Her appearance didn't change much as she grew up. She was instantly recognisable as the Linda I knew at the age of ten or eleven, even when she was in her forties. She was quiet and watchful. I didn't ever think that she was shy, but she was not particularly gregarious. I imagine that she was one of life's observers even at a young age.

'She did not have a particular close friend and was not part of a particular friendship group, but I enjoyed sitting next to her. I have a visual memory of her running in the school hall in her big baggy school knickers and white vest to the sound of "Lily the Pink", with her long hair streaming behind her.'

Her form teacher, Dennis Cunningham, had a cavalier attitude to lessons. No national curriculum for him; he taught what he fancied, according to his mood. As a result of his penchant for technical drawing, the pupils in his class became adept at using protractors and compasses, producing perfect pentagons and complex 3-D shapes. Sharyn remembers Mr Cunningham fogging up the classroom with his heavy smoking, and shouting 'SEX!' in order to get the class to shut up and listen.

In later years Linda recalled doing sketches at playtime, 'directing my friends in spoof game shows and adverts'. She was also developing a definite feisty side to her character that stood her in good stead in the playground. 'I remember making a sarcastic quip at her expense once in class, as boys do,' recalls Ian Williams, another classmate. 'After all, she was only a girl. I thought no more of it until playtime, when Linda got her revenge. She landed a right hook on me!'

She might sometimes have cut a somewhat eccentric figure at this time, as Bessie's passion for knitting meant that Linda was always decked out in colourful cardigans, a quirk that went on to inspire an hilarious segment of her show:

'The thing with my mum was, it wasn't recreational knitting . . . she wasn't in control of it. No – it was a kind of woolly Tourette's – it was a compulsion . . . She would be dragged around the house by the needles, with smoke coming out of them, and great tapeworms of this useless stuff – knit purl, knit purl, knit purl – consequently, every stitch I left the house in was knitted . . .

'Then, the twinsets – Fair Isle of course – with pleats cunningly knitted in a fashion so bizarre . . . even Vivienne

Westwood hasn't attempted it. Socks, shoes, satchel, sand-wiches, pencils – just everything . . . I looked like a time-travelling Ovalteenie on my way to school. Oh and Christ, if it rained . . . the weight of this stuff, I would be dragged to the ground like a driftnet . . . like a little pastel beached Grimsby trawler, trudging through the woods . . . seagulls going squawk, squawk, squawk, following me all the way. To be honest, we had the EC round a couple of times asking me mum to use bigger needles – we were catching stuff that should have been chucked back . . . the Erith silver fish population has yet to recover.'

On Sundays, Linda received religious instruction at the local church Sunday school. She later recollected feeling an early affinity with Christianity, at around the age of eight. In fact, on several occasions in later life she confessed to having been struck by the romance and drama of Easter and the idea of Jesus rising from the dead.

'As a kid I loved Sunday school,' she once said. 'We had a very good vicar called the Reverend Barnes who was quite a scruffy and eccentric character, and he smoked roll-ups and told really good stories. Looking back, these had quite a humanist core to them. He was a great bloke actually, and he made Sunday school really good fun.' Her parents weren't particularly religious. 'They'd put "C of E" on forms, because it fitted the slot, which is quite small,' she joked. 'The religious duties are not too onerous really – sweet sherry of a Christmas.'

Sunday school served a purpose for everyone. It got Linda out of her parents' way on a Sunday morning and was a pleasurable social activity. 'All my friends went. That's why I went.' Characteristically, it wasn't long before she began to question the stories and imagery. 'As you get older, the stories get more ambiguous and you start thinking things like, "Why did Jesus blight that fig tree then? It couldn't help it that it didn't have any fruit on it. I'm nine and I wouldn't do that. I'm beyond that sort of nonsense." It just seemed like a fit of pique, the sort of thing you'd get told off for if you did it. "How childish!"'

Meanwhile at Lessness Heath, Mr Cunningham's teaching methods, although sometimes unorthodox, obviously worked for certain sections of the class. Unusually for the school, Sharyn and Linda, along with the other two children on their table, all passed the Eleven-Plus exams. Linda chose not to make use of this qualification and go to grammar school, instead attending Bexleyheath School, a large comprehensive. There she did the regulation five years from 1969 to 1974, plus a short stint in the sixth form before she became disillusioned, refused a prefecture, and left.

The overriding feature of Linda's secondary-school career was very erratic attendance. Sometimes she missed between four and six weeks of a term, which must have been a severe handicap in the race for results. Her sister Barbara blames the domestic situation. Ray's abusive behaviour towards their mum meant that Linda felt compelled to stay at home and defend Bessie rather than go to school and leave her exposed to more torment.

Barbara says: 'When Linda was about twelve, I remember my mum saying, "Barb, come and speak to Linda. She won't go to school. I know she's not ill." So I told Linda, "You've got to go to school. You've got your exams." "How can I go to school?" she said. "I'm too worried. I don't know what he's going to do next."'

I suspect the school and teachers knew little or none of this. The following extract from an end-of-term report by her second-form teacher is a fairly typical Bexleyheath School assessment: 'Linda is capable of producing a high standard of work but she is disorganised and dreamy, particularly where written work is concerned. She must make a determined effort to discipline herself to give written work more careful attention, and to give it in when required.' Other comments from that time included criticism of her 'scatter-brained memory' and the way her 'attitude impedes her progress'.

At home, Linda retreated into books and was a constant visitor to the library. Subsequently, her affinity with religion enjoyed a brief surge. 'Catholicism crossed my mind a bit,' she said. 'I think I was just reading too much Oscar Wilde and Graham Greene and things like that. And thinking, Catholicism! for a brief fleeting moment. But then I thought, "Hold on a minute, this is terrible . . ."'

Music, as well as literature, was a great escape, and her favourite groups included Sparks, Roxy Music and Simon and Garfunkel. Never one to follow the crowd, she preferred David Bowie to David Cassidy and idolised Alice Cooper.

But her biggest heroes, by far, were Peter Cook and Dudley Moore. 'I loved them,' she said. 'I used to watch television with my parents, but *Not Only . . . But Also* baffled them. I got the book of *The Dagenham Dialogues* out of the library and would put on the record of Pete and Dud and follow and join in the dialogue. I memorised it. I knew every word of *The Dagenham Dialogues*. I'd take the Peter Cook role, because I was tall. I still am; I haven't let myself go in that respect.'

I shared Linda's passion for the work of Peter Cook and Dudley Moore – including *Derek and Clive*. Linda was always quoting lines from 'Pete and Dud at the Art Gallery' and 'Sex Fantasies'. In 'Sex Fantasies', the pair recount how they've been pestered for romance by various film stars (including 'bloody Greta Garbo' and 'bloody Anna Magnani'). They claim to have evicted the stars from their bedrooms by fairly brutal means, ordering them never to come back. The words 'tap, tap, tapping' at the windows just did it for us.

We loved the exchanges between the Dagenham flat caps. They were probably the highlights of each of the three series of *Not Only . . . But Also*, which ran between 1965 and 1970. I know Linda was precocious when it came to her comedy favourites, but this stuff must have taken root gradually. It requires a much longer digestion period than the sight gags of Tommy Cooper or Morecambe and Wise.

When I first met Linda she had a garment in her wardrobe that she lovingly referred to as her 'Wisty Mac', a raincoat dedicated to the one and only E. L. Wisty – perhaps Peter Cook's greatest character invention, who would appear decked out in such a raincoat. As a tribute to Linda and her raincoat, I will remind you of Wisty's finest hour. In 1964, Wisty and Spotty Muldoon formed the World Domination League, declaring, 'We shall move about in people's rooms and say, "Excuse me, we are the World Domination League. May we dominate you?" Then, if they say, "Get out," of course we give up.'

I have this image of her pacing the byways of the Erith badlands reciting Pete and Dud sketches as a teenager. Barbara reports that she also enjoyed mainstream comedy like *The Two Ronnies, Porridge, Rising Damp, On the Buses, Morecambe and Wise, Sykes* and *Last of the Summer Wine*.

Her own ability to make people laugh was already well developed, and proved useful at Bexleyheath School. 'As I got older it turned out to be a very handy thing from the bullying point of view, because it sort of made you a bit of a non-combatant if you were funny. It meant they didn't bother with you too much and you could stand on the sidelines and watch other people being bullied,' she said.

'There would be a bit of a fight, two little gangs, and one would start picking on me and someone else would say "Don't bother with her, silly as arse 'oles!" And that was it. It was like being a stretcher bearer in the First World War, in the line of fire. Actually, that's a bad analogy, it was like being a general in the First World War; you weren't actually in the line of fire.'

Linda wasn't the only one in her class to use humour as a distraction of one kind or another. 'There was a little group of us that were a bit funny . . . and weren't serious about school generally and were quite bright, but not necessarily applying themselves to school, applying it more to writing funny little sketches and things like that.'

Although no one appears to have diagnosed Linda's mild dyslexia, the drama and English teachers were very encouraging to her, and acting was mooted as a possible career. She took a bow in the school production of a Hans Christian Andersen story, 'The Tinderbox', though she was annoyed when she was chosen to play the part of the princess. She was keen to avoid blonde stereotypes and wanted the part of the witch. I hope she got herself a new agent after that debacle.

Linda's final report from Bexleyheath School in 1974 was inauspicious. 'Has not really given much to school life. I hope her attitude improves in the future,' wrote the headmaster, signing off with the obligatory, 'Good luck in the future.'

Looking back on her school years on BBC Radio Four's

The News Quiz, Linda finally got her own back: 'Yes, that's a great thing to go out into the world with, isn't it. I would have to say that, sadly, my attitude hasn't changed and it's provided me with a pretty good living. Rather better than the little typing job that I'm sure you had in mind for me. I don't know why they don't just scrap school altogether; it's a complete waste of time in my opinion. I don't know how many years of geography I did; I can't get from here to Euston . . . I spent twenty years colouring maps of the world. South America and its produce. Colouring in little tubs of palm oil and maize. Maize. It comes from everywhere, goes everywhere, then you never see it.'

Linda left Bexleyheath with four O-levels (English literature, English language, history, geography) and three CSEs (biology, German, mathematics). I found this A4 printed form – presumably from around this time – with the heading 'Personality Profile'. It required Linda to tick adjectives about herself. These are the ones she chose as 'Very' rather than 'Fairly':

Unorthodox
Intellectual
Generous
Dominant
Sensitive
Eccentric
Stupid (added at the bottom, inked in her own handwriting).

She blamed the school for putting her off God once and for all. 'I suddenly thought in assembly that this was all rubbish, all these stupid old gits like the headmaster and the deputy headmaster reading out this piffle and all these sulky kids moving their mouths to these hymns. I do remember enquiring whether or not you could be removed from assembly on the grounds of being an atheist, but I was told that it didn't count. You could only be excluded if you were Jewish, Catholic or Muslim. But not believing in God was not a valid reason.'

At home she also began standing up for her beliefs. When Granny Smith was nasty to Bessie, Linda told her where to get off. 'Granny was going out with this chap she worked for,' Barbara recalls. 'He had a fish and chip shop in Camberwell. (She later ran her own very successful fish and chip shop in Smethwick.) He had a disabled wife, but Granny used to go on holiday with him and they started coming down to my mum's on a Sunday.

'We all felt uncomfortable about it and Mum didn't like it. Then one day there was a bit of an argument about it and Granny Smith said to my mum something along the lines of, "To think of all the things I've bought in this house!"

'Mum said, "Well, take them with you when you go."

'Granny then turned round to Mum and said something really horrible, and that got Linda going. "Get out, piss off out of our house," Linda said. "None of us want to see you again."

'Gran said to Linda, "I shall cut you out of my will."

'And I'll never forget this – we often laughed about it afterwards. Linda said, "I don't want your . . . money and nor does Barbara. Nor does Mother want it. We don't want anything from you. Now go."'

3

No Swearing Please, We're English

Sheffield to Erith

In the late 1980s, I had the pleasure of driving Linda, her mum and her aunt Helen to several destinations for day trips and a couple of holidays. For the longer trips we were based in Scarborough to tour the coast and moors of North Yorkshire, and once Torquay was our base for a sunny week on the Devon Riviera. They were ideal companions and we had much fun as a quartet. At this time, Linda's mum's health was failing and she had limited mobility. Our walks had to be restricted, but we still managed to get out and about a lot. I think Bessie could have rivalled Nana, that's my mum's mother, for her malapropisms. Linda and I always laughed affectionately about the way she misread menus, for example, turning 'Chicken Cacciatore' into 'Chicken Caricature'. One incident sticks in my mind. It took place near the public car park overlooking picturesque Robin Hood Bay in North Yorkshire. Before we set off on any of these journeys, I had to make a pact with Linda not to swear in front of her mum and aunt. I usually managed to honour this non-swear agreement, but I let the side down badly on this occasion, provoked by a motorist who came close to involving us in a collision through sheer stupidity.

Without realising it, I unleashed the f-word expletive and reduced my three companions to an eerie silence. I tried to disperse this atmosphere by joking and making light of what had happened. But my momentary foul language was, it seems, more offensive than a stranger's reckless driving. It felt like I'd been catapulted into a scene from a family sitcom and incurred the disapproval of a group of characters all played by Patricia Routledge.

In Linda's late teens, the potential for such moments grew daily. On a simple level, there was the generation gap. From an early age she'd been conscious of having older parents, in particular a mum who said, 'Thank you, driver,' on the bus rather than the younger, trendier, 'Ciao!' used by her friends' parents. By the time she started studying for her A-levels at Erith College of Technology in 1976, the divergence was even more obvious. Years later, on stage at the Lescar Hotel in Sheffield in 1993, she joked about the chasm between young and old:

'No matter how old you get, your family never know you, do they? And I tell you what makes you realise this – the cards they send you on your birthday. Always, if you're a lad, it's a picture of a vintage car or fly fishing. If you're a girl, pony trekking or ballerinas . . . all very popular activities in south London, I can tell you. You open it with a sinking heart to read this mawkish verse, because you know your auntie or granddad has spent hours choosing a *nice verse*.

'And it'll be something like – "On your birthday / Be happy for ever / A chain of love / That time will not sever / Have a lovely time / My darling Trevor." And they've spent f . . . hours looking for that. And if they really knew you and they really understood your lifestyle, instead of the fly fishing and the Labradors and the rest of it, on the front of that card there'd be a few empty cans with some fags stubbed out in them . . . and the verse inside would be something like – "Dear grandchild / On your birthday enjoy a few jokes / Have shitloads to drink and a few lines of coke / My dear, on your vomit, please try not to choke." That would be more it, really, wouldn't it?'

Linda was known among her friends at Erith College for drinking real ale and smoking Dunhill cigarettes; she also started going out with boys. But these were not the only characteristics that marked the point at which she began to find a separate identity, distinct from the one she was brought up with. The more she read and absorbed culturally – the more plays she saw and opinions she exchanged – the less she had in common with the older members of her family. Of course, it didn't affect her love for them, but she would have been acutely aware of the shift. And for Bessie and aunt Helen, it must have been perplexing to see Linda with her head perpetually in books with names like *Nausea*, *Bleak House* and *Good and Bad Manners in Architecture*.

Literature was a great escape, but her real dream was to become a serious actress. After a false start in the sixth form at Bexleyheath School, she auditioned for RADA, where her boyfriend Saul was studying drama. Sharyn Smith, her primary-school friend, recalls seeing her just before the audition. 'Linda went to a different secondary school to me but we shared part of the same bus route home. My last memory of us together on the bus was when she told me that she was auditioning for RADA. I remember this clearly because it was a complete surprise. I would never have imagined that she would want to put herself on stage, as she seemed so quiet and unassuming. I asked her what she was going to do at the audition, and she replied, "A speech by Lady Macbeth!"'

The audition went ahead and RADA accepted Linda, who must have been over the moon. However, Bexley Council refused her a grant on the grounds that Britain's most prestigious drama school didn't offer a degree course. I wonder how different her life would have been had the funding been available. Would Linda have cut it as a top-class actress? She did a lot of theatre over the next few years, but I never saw her act, except in her own comic sketches, because by the time we met she was no longer appearing in university productions. So how would RADA have changed things? We shall never know, but I have a strong suspicion that she would have found her way into stand-up, one way or another.

Still, without a grant, RADA was an impossible dream and a disappointed Linda was forced to readjust her ambitions. Now she set her sights on Cambridge University, perhaps hoping to follow in the footsteps of her comic heroes Peter Cook and Dudley Moore, who had been undergraduates there more than a decade earlier. For university she needed qualifications, hence the move to Erith College, where she studied A-level English literature and economic history – along with general studies and elective studies – from 1976 to 1978. Here she really started to come into her own, intellectually and socially, on and off the stage.

Linda said later: 'Erith College was so, so much better than school. You could wear your own clothes, I was with a good bunch of bohemian misfits and the lecturers were often quite groovy. Brian Shade, the general studies teacher who did drama, was a proper actor and did professional productions.' Her admiration for Brian Shade was mutual. He maintained that she always had the potential to carve out a career as a comic actress. 'Linda had a dry sense of humour from the age of 18,' he told me. 'Her sense of timing was wonderful. She was brilliant.'

Finally she was getting the support and encouragement

that had eluded her at school – and she blossomed, appearing in two end-of-year productions at Erith College, both master-minded by Brian Shade. In April 1977 she played the part of Lady Cynthia Muldoon in *The Real Inspector Hound* by Tom Stoppard; in 1978 she played all but one of the five women characters in *The Golden Pathway Annual* by John Harding and John Burrows. 'She gathered real confidence from playing those women's parts,' Brian recalls. 'She'd go behind a screen, come up with another prop, and suddenly she was somebody else,' he continues. 'People believed her and they laughed because she was hilarious. I wanted her to go to drama school, but she decided to do the right thing, and went to university. By the way, there's a question I have to ask her: where is the essay I wrote on alternative theatre,* which she pinched nearly 30 years ago?'

One of Linda's haunts at the time was the Malt Shovel pub in Dartford, where she used to meet up with Erith's late-1970s answer to the Bloomsbury Group. 'One of the best lines I ever heard her say was in this pub,' says Peter Howard, a close friend from that time. 'It was a Sunday lunchtime and the Salvation Army came round collecting money. Linda said with beautiful RP, 'I'm terribly sorry, but most of my money seems to be tied up with Caesar at the moment!' The Salvation Army person just looked completely baffled.'

Linda's friends were in agreement that Erith College wasn't really geared up for A-levels. It was a technical college full of engineers and hairdressing students, and the A-level course alternated with a secretarial course. 'Our little cohort of A-level-only students numbered about nine and I was delighted

---

* Happily, I was able to reunite Brian and his essay in late 2006, when I found it as I was going through a collection of university papers that Linda had saved from that time.

to find that most had, in some shape or form, been rejected or themselves rejected more traditional schools,' says Philip Sanderson, a self-confessed grammar-school dropout from Strood in Kent.

Although the college had something of a laissez faire attitude, the A-level options were limited. A bizarre curricular quirk required the entire A-level group to study economic history, simply because it slotted in with what the secretarial students were doing at the same time. To complicate matters, the group's teacher was a Jethro Tull fan who modelled himself on lead singer Ian Anderson, endlessly filling his pipe while he taught this 'unimaginably dour' subject. 'I believe after two years we all failed this subject – or were awarded O-levels!'

Linda's closest friends were mainly boys who appeared with her in theatre productions, but the wider circle took in a mix of her drama course mates' girlfriends, boyfriends, brothers and sisters, soon developing into a massive and inclusive social group. Peter's younger brother Michael remembers an impromptu night at the Malt Shovel. 'Linda phoned out of the blue one Friday evening and asked where Peter was. I said he was out, so she asked if I fancied a drink. I suppose everyone else in the gang must have been busy – why else ask one of your mates' kid brothers out? We had a great time. She drank me under the table. I must have been only 16 because I remember cycling there and back after about six pints of Young's bitter.'

Linda always loved the Nina Simone song that goes, 'When I was a young girl I used to drink ale . . .' and by all accounts, she was a real ale fiend, only frequenting pubs that served the real thing, like the Malt Shovel and the Leather Bottle at Belvedere. Her book and pamphlet collection included specimens like, 'Brewing Beers Like Those You Buy'. She was a supporter of CAMRA, the Campaign for Real Ale. But trips to the Malt Shovel were usually driven by less esoteric concerns. According to Sean Hayden, perhaps her closest male friend at the time, 'We went to the Malt Shovel on Sundays mainly because Pete Howard's dad went there and would give us a lift and buy us pints. We were poor students, so we'd go along with any adult who was prepared to listen to us – particularly about politics – and buy us a pint.'

They were also in with a chance of picking up free or dirt-cheap theatre tickets for West End plays. 'Tickets to any play that was past its sell-by date, or was trying to pack the houses, used to filter through the amateur dramatic societies,' Sean told me. The Rotary Club, local fire service and taxi ranks all received a quota of tickets, which they sold off in the pub at twenty pence a pair. This was surely one of the only advantages of living in a town where, for much of the population, cultural activities ranked on a rough par with having your teeth pulled. During this time Linda saw a lot of Shakespeare and Restoration comedy, along with a smattering of Pinter and Galsworthy.

She already had a wide knowledge of plays and theatre. 'She was well ahead of the rest of us,' says Peter, recalling the time Brian Shade passed round handouts on Henrik Ibsen. 'Before the handout got to me, I'd written down "Henry Gibson"! But Linda knew all these people, from Ibsen to Chekhov.'

Saturday nights were spent at the Tramshed, Woolwich, enjoying a first experience of stand-up in the Fundation Show, featuring the as yet undiscovered comedy duo Hale and Pace. This was just before Tony Allen and the alternative cabaret scene exploded in London, and it drew audiences from far and wide. Linda appeared on the Tramshed stage herself when Off The Kerb Productions did 'South of Deptford', her first appearance being on 9 April, 1988. It must have felt quite strange to be performing at her first regular comedy haunt, the place where she had spent so many Saturday nights drinking beer and laughing at the acts.

For live music back then there was the Dartford Folk Club at the Railway Inn, next to Dartford Station. Linda would also have gone to listen to modern jazz at the Greenwich Jazz Club on a Sunday lunchtime at Greenwich Theatre. There wasn't a lot to do in Erith per se, especially on a student budget. Peter Howard remembered 'staring out of the window and there was the flat expanse of Essex on the other side of the water, which seemed to go on for ever . . . and then just nothing . . . it was just flat and boring. There was nothing on the cultural landscape – we did it all ourselves.'

Sean Hayden described 'hours and hours together in classrooms, canteens and going to the pub', where the group shared their love of plays, politics, books and comedy in endless conversations. When there wasn't enough money to go to the pub, Linda spent long evenings at Sean's or Peter's in Barnehurst.

'There was a lot of discussion of the arts. Linda was knowledgeable about everything. She was very clever, very witty, especially when it came to the one-line retort. She had a good command of facts – and an encyclopaedic knowledge of classical music – so she could intellectually crucify you if she chose to.'

Nearly everyone on the course was left wing, according to Philip Sanderson. These were turbulent times politically, punctuated by strikes, industrial action, cuts, inflation and the lead-up to the 1978 Winter of Discontent. Many of the lecturers were also left of centre. 'People didn't discuss politics all the time, but it informed the general student banter.' Linda and her friends went to Rock Against Racism gigs in London and marched in support of the Anti-Nazi League. Sean was president of the student union, running the committee for the benefit of entertainment (lots of discos) and sending delegates to the Labour Party Young Socialists' conference.

Punk was revolutionising music and the Erith College common room turntable began to favour the Sex Pistols over Santana and Camel. It was around this time that Linda developed an enduring admiration for the music of Ian Dury and the Blockheads. She also loved Elvis Costello. Fashion, too, was changing, yet many students ignored the trend for ripped clothes and safety pins. Linda is remembered for her long hair, gold-rimmed glasses, big baggy jumpers and black trench coat. Her brother-in-law Terry teasingly nicknamed her 'John Lennon'.

In her second year at Erith College, once she turned 18, Linda was required to pay £150 towards college fees, so money was desperately short. 'We jumble-saled ferociously and would wear mixtures of old and new with panache,' Alison Dark (then Alison Travers) told me.

Stewart Wentworth, who met Linda through friends at Erith College, was an inveterate party-giver, and the gang was always trooping along to his house of a Saturday night. There was a certain amount of drug taking at college, Philip Sanderson recounted. 'Probably pretty modest by today's standard – usually it was dope and speed. One time, most of the group took mescaline and spent a lot of time wandering

round the college gardens admiring how green the grass was.
But most of the time it was a half of lager at lunchtime
down the road at the pub.'

Most of Linda's college friends came from better-off
families. Sean and Pete lived in the posh area of Barnehurst;
her great friend Pauline Daniels (formerly known as
Pauline/Lucy Trask) came from Bexleyheath, which Linda
once referred to as 'a sneak preview of limbo – bugger all
to do and lots of time to do it in.' Pauline has many vivid
memories of Linda. 'Looking back, it's difficult to over-
estimate how much it meant meeting someone who was also
interested in books, ideas, films and the theatre. Linda was
like an oasis in the desert and I've never met anyone since
remotely as intelligent or fun loving.

'I remember Linda's mum as very homely in fluffy slippers,
quite shy and often knitting. She was very tolerant of Linda
bringing back her friends after the pub and only got slightly
annoyed one night when, after making coffee, Linda left the
new plastic kettle on a hotplate where it promptly melted.
Everyone else was oblivious to the acrid fumes emanating
from the kitchen.'

Bessie used to fret about making a good impression on
Linda's friends. 'Mum used to say, "She brings them boys
here and they all come from posh homes. What must they
think?" I'd say, "For goodness sake, Mum, they've come for
your apple pie!"'

Some of her friends were aware of the tension that existed
at home. 'We occasionally went back to Linda's parents,'
Sean Hayden told me. 'Her mum and dad would be bickering
all the time; that was probably one good reason not to be
there. It just wasn't the happiest of homes in my recollection.'
Pauline added, 'I only saw her dad on a couple of occasions

when he came in late in his working clothes, a donkey jacket with orange reflective shoulders. He was physically a powerful man and treated us with a sort of bemused tolerance (or maybe he was drunk, now I come to think of it), just occasionally putting his head around the door to see who was there.' Linda rarely brought friends home if Ray was likely to be there. Fortunately he did a lot of night work at the time.

Pauline, whose sister Barb was at college in Weymouth, remembers Linda staying over with Barb for a party and phoning her dad to ask him to send some money. A fiver arrived promptly the next day. 'A couple of days later, Linda was again short of cash and phoned her dad again. The cash duly arrived with a note that said, "Linda, I'm sending you the shirt off my back." They all thought that was highly amusing.'

Linda spent a fair amount of time at Pauline's house, usually after visits to the pub. 'It occurs to me that her fascination with northern camp began quite early on,' Pauline says. 'My mum was from Bradford and although she had lived in south-east London since just after the war, she still retained her accent and a no-nonsense approach to life, often expressed in quirky northern turns of phrase.' Linda delighted in these and would often quote them in conversation, adding a twist of her own. 'Now think on!' was a favourite admonishment, along with, 'Nay lass, 'ave a bit of decorum!'

'She always enjoyed coming around to our house and was endlessly amused by my mum's quaint Yorkshire take on life and her malapropisms ("How about a nice drop of Asti Sputum?"). In turn my dad enjoyed the company of our motley crew of friends and particularly liked to engage Sean in political debate. The banter was always good-natured.

Dad was genuinely intrigued by Linda, whom he saw as an intelligent and forthright girl with what he termed "far left views".'

One evening at Pauline's house, during the Winter of Discontent, she and her sister cooked a special meal and the usual crowd attended. Linda was resplendent in a satiny gentleman's evening suit, no doubt purchased at a charity shop. As the drink flowed, the inevitable ideological debates began. The fire station in Bexleyheath had a picket line and the subject of trade unions came up. 'It was then that Linda uttered the immortal line about profit being nothing but "unpaid wages",' Pauline says. 'The old man nearly fell off his chair. His incredulous reaction was really comical; he savoured that particular episode for years afterwards.'

Pauline admired her friend for what she described as her high-mindedness. 'In all our conversations I never heard her make a remark that was in any way crude or coarse. We didn't have that way of discussing very intimate or sexual things that girls seem to do now. There was just this real cerebral quality about her and the sorts of preoccupations she had, and this dignified stance on things seemed to come over in everything she said.'

She also remembers Linda for her 'very English Romantic streak'. 'At one time we used to have a thing about the artist Samuel Palmer, who had lived and worked at Shoreham, a village a few miles out into Kent. We were talking this over in the pub one Saturday night and were somehow seized with the idea of driving down there to locate the artist's house and experience his "valley of vision" by moonlight. Linda had a holiday job working in the parks department at Dartford and I was working twelve-hour weekend shifts at a children's home, which both called for early starts, so it wasn't the brightest thing to do. But we were hell bent on the idea and went anyway.

'During the course of a pretty raucous night spent trudging through fields and waiting for the sun to come up, Sean, a bit of a twitcher, said, "Shut up and let's just savour the owl." Linda immediately launched into an extravagant monologue about wildlife crisp flavours: "new crunchy bat" etc. It was the most brilliant piece of improvisation ever. We never actually found Samuel Palmer's house, but Linda's reverie stayed with me. It seems so extraordinary now. That was a fairly typical evening.

'We sometimes went to late-night films after an evening at the Tramshed, many of which I have forgotten, but I do recall seeing *The Producers* and *The Adventures of Barrie McKenzie* with Barry Humphries playing both Barrie and his Aunt Edna. Linda loved all the literary references and I remember particularly her delighted response when Edna innocently went into a house of ill repute, pausing briefly to note the name Radclyffe Hall on the gatepost.

'Linda also had a thing about crap records and could trot out a string of unlikely titles that she recalled hearing. We had a collection of particularly gruesome specimens, my best effort being a vinyl horror called "Bette Davis Sings", which she trumped with a collection of ballads sung by Eamonn Andrews.'

Linda was obviously enjoying the life of the mind. Then, in her second year at Erith College, she fell in love. Brian Pereira, who was studying for an HNC in business in the year below her, shared many of her interests and tastes. Pretty soon they became inseparable. Brian lived with his widowed mother and sister in nearby Slade Green. Pauline remembers him as being 'of a boyish type that Linda was attracted to then. He was a sensitive boy, slight with longish black curly hair and very fine, delicate hands. Mostly, he was easy to be with, but sometimes he seemed nervous and smoked a lot.'

Brian's family came from Goa, India. Linda's sister Barbara says that Linda's dad, who was 'an out and out racist', disliked Brian because of his colour. 'When Brian called, it was, "Wog at the door." Ray never asked him in. He just left him standing there.' But Linda's mum loved him. To her, he was a 'smashing bloke'. Mum would say, "Wouldn't they have lovely children?" Linda christened Brian the "curly-haired rascal".'

Pauline described Brian and Linda as a devoted couple, always hand-in-hand and deep in conversation. 'I think their relationship was a real meeting of minds and when I think of them together, I think of them like brother and sister. It seemed like a very chaste relationship.'

Chaste or not, it was an enduring relationship and lasted for some years, despite the charged climate of the late 1970s, when the National Front was very active and there was a real tension surrounding interracial romance. John Hogan, a close college friend of Linda's, recalled Brian being barred entrance to a club in Margate, and Linda told Pauline that he had been given a hard time in an Irish bar in London. Closer to home, when his best friend Justin Lorentzen met him at his local pub, Brian was told to leave the bar for his own safety. Later on, his mother suffered racial harassment in Slade Green and felt compelled to move house.

Fortunately, these outside pressures appeared to have little impact on Linda and Brian as a couple. Linda was a great letter writer, and in a letter to Pauline she recounts an outing to London with Brian.

'Last week we spent the day in the National Gallery, and quelle jour it was too! The highlight of the visit was when we walked into one of the rooms and were immediately rooted to the spot (metaphorically speaking) by Seurat's vast and stunning canvas, *Les Baigneurs Sur L'Herbe*. It was quite literally breathtaking. I've never seen such colour and light!'

Her appreciation of the arts did not translate into the academic results she needed to get into university, however, and she found herself retaking her A-levels in November 1978. In a letter to Pauline, she describes days with Brian after Sean and John went off to further education at Lanchester Poly. 'Brian and I spend a great deal of time together, reading, watching films, walking, wandering around bookshops and record shops. In a way it is idyllic, but it doesn't have the calming effect on me that you might expect. Under the surface, I feel very anxious about my examinations in November and my future in general . . .'

Her anxiety was understandable. It was imperative to get away from Erith. But for the moment Linda was stuck, and the future was very uncertain. One thing she knew for sure, however: her experience of holiday employment, which included stints at the Homepride bakery, a local petrol station and a summer at the Bexley Parks Department, had put her off the idea of a conventional job for ever. 'I always knew I didn't want a job,' she told Dawn French. 'That was the thing. Work never attracted me in any way. I had a few jobs when I was a student and it was horrible. It's so, so horrible, work.

'I had this job in a petrol station and the manager would always make you ask people if they wanted to buy oil. People know if they want oil. So every time they came in, he would stand over me while I went, "Do you want oil?" "Eh?" "Do you want oil?" "No!" Because oil is not an impulse buy. You don't think, I'll treat myself to a couple of gallons of two-stroke. Keep them by the till – they'll have them with a Mars bar.

'So I turned against work at an early age. And I thought, "I have got to find some way of not working yet staying alive." So I went to university. I thought it was a good way of putting off the dread day.'

By now her family were getting used to the idea of Linda, the bohemian intellectual, and they were very proud. For her twenty-first birthday, just before she left home for good, they gave her the complete works of George Bernard Shaw.

4

Pericles to Picket Lines

Erith/Bexley to Sheffield

Once upon a time, Sheffield was ranked the dirtiest city in the country. The central and west sections of the city weren't too bad, but a bus taking you east through the industrial heart of the steelworks area would be covered in a film of red iron oxide dust by the time it had been through Attercliffe. The people who lived near the steelworks had to wash their curtains every day.

After the Clean Air Acts of 1956 and 1968 were passed, Sheffield became one of the cleanest cities in the country. When I arrived there in 1983, I thought it was a very pleasant place, full of green spaces. But my digs were in the west end; as soon as I went east I saw a different city. By then many of the steelworks had closed or were closing down and the landscape was characterised by derelict houses, forges and furnaces. Linda called it 'Star Wars Valley'. The streets looked bombed out.

Still, Sheffield was a world away from London, where there was a distinct hostility on the streets. The pace of life here was slower and people talked to you at bus stops. The city centre felt old-fashioned in a nice way, full of local shops and businesses. Best of all, almost everywhere was within walking distance.

Linda arrived at Sheffield University to study English and philosophy in the autumn of 1979, when the city was on fire politically. Already a centre of political activism, it was about to ignite a nationwide controversy under its dynamic new Labour council leader, David Blunkett, who at 32 was one of the youngest council leaders in the country.

Declaring the city a nuclear-free zone and twinning it with Donetsk in the Ukraine, which was then part of the Soviet Union, the council introduced peace studies into schools and slashed bus fares to five pence a ride. On May Day, the red flag was hoisted to celebrate the workers' struggle. Dubbed 'The People's Republic of South Yorkshire', allegedly by the Conservative MP for Sheffield Hallam, Irvine Patnick, it was a notorious bastion against Thatcherism and definitely Linda's kind of place. She later satirised the council's zealous liberal tendencies in part of an early routine that centred on the great comic creation Clive Caring-Person, her imaginary right-on boyfriend.

'Clive . . . works for Sheffield City Council . . . it's a very liberal revisionist type of council and they have an equal opportunities scheme in their employment policy, which means they will even employ dickheads like Clive. He works in the alternative videos unit, a very worthwhile job. I expect you've heard of video nasties – Clive makes video nicies. He's employed to take disturbing material like Disney films that have very heavy bits in them, cut all the nasty bits out and make them suitable for the viewing of small children and nervous people – and Neil Kinnock and people like that. "More violence! I can't stand it when Bambi's dad dies."

'In Clive's film, Bambi's dad doesn't die; this is the thing, you see. He moves to a higher plane, a higher plane of existence, where they have a wonderful party with incense and candles and flowers to celebrate the fullness of life cycles, and Bambi and his mum trot happily off to live in a women's house. So it's an ill wind that blows nobody any good.'

It was a relief to escape Erith, although it wasn't easy leaving behind her real boyfriend, Brian. She was also anxious about the situation with Bessie and Ray. 'In one respect I'm worried because I'm leaving, but perhaps they might get on better if I'm not there,' she confided in Barbara.

'It was the same when I got married,' Barbara reflects. 'I was worried about leaving, but I thought things might get better if Ray had Linda to himself. Instead it just got worse. He was a big drinker and often used to disappear for a couple of days after getting paid on a Friday. Yet my mum would still cook his dinner and leave it ready. Linda would say, "Why are you still doing that, Mum?" Mum felt it was her duty.'

Despite her concerns, Linda went north and, true to form, arrived late, during the final half-hour of university registration. With nowhere to stay, she ended up in a depressingly grim little room in a hotel full of middle-aged salesmen who talked about sales units over breakfast. She told Helen Fox of *Northern Star* magazine in 1991: 'I got terrible flu, was ill for about four days and felt really miserable. I didn't go to any fresher events because I didn't know anyone and I didn't think I'd like them anyway. Sheffield was totally different to what I'd expected. My only image of the north was *Coronation Street*, like it is for most people.'

But she soon settled in and found a place to stay: a flat on the Ecclesall Road. Kate Collier was her flatmate in the first and second years. Like many of the friends Linda met between 1979 and 1982, Kate stayed put in Sheffield after graduation. She remembers lots of sitting around the flat, or the local pub, the Pomona, having the kind of conversations about art and literature that Linda's Erith College mates described. They also met up at the Beehive, the Hallamshire and the Washington, where Pulp frontman Jarvis Cocker and Richie Kirk of Cabaret Voltaire were regulars.

'I was very young and naive,' Kate said. 'I thought university was going to be full of really interesting people, life and politics. Linda skewed the picture for me for a while because she was into politics. She was into discussing things like books and music. So she represented what I thought university would be about, and I think I became disappointed when I realised that there weren't a lot of people like Linda.'

Three years older than Kate, Linda was like a big sister to her. 'She was fantastic and always made sure I was all right. At the end of my first year, I hadn't got any accommodation and didn't know what to do. Linda phoned me at my parents' and asked if I wanted a room in a shared house in Wiseton Road. She was doing me a big favour. I wasn't always as decent back as I could have been – I was very into being seen with the right people and all that crap – but she never held it against me. She wasn't a malicious person in any way. Of course, we hated Maggie Thatcher, things like that . . . but on a personal one-to-one level she wasn't malicious at all.'

That first year was marred by the climate of fear that had been created by Peter Sutcliffe, the Yorkshire Ripper, who killed three women and attacked two more between September 1979 and November 1980. The house in Wiseton Road was less than half a mile from Melbourne Avenue, where he was finally arrested. Kate remembers being stopped and warned by the police. 'They'd say, "You shouldn't be out. You're a woman alone." And Linda and I would say, "Why the f . . . hell should women not walk about freely, just because there's a psychotic on the loose?" I know it was about our safety, but we resented it all the same.'

Vibrant Sheffield was a world away from culturally dead Erith. Linda had eclectic tastes in music and slipped easily between the live concerts of Sun Ra and his Arkestra and Cabaret Voltaire supported by Throbbing Gristle. Tickets were a snip at £1.35 in advance and £1.60 on the door. One particularly memorable gig was The Smiths, who played in the tiny student's union bar just before they charted; Morrissey handed out gladioli to the packed audience.

On Wednesdays, there was a reggae night at the Limit Club and Kate remembers meeting Linda at a triple-bill gig featuring Madness, The Selecter and The Beat. 'Imagine seeing them for two pounds fifty! In those days you could literally go out for the night with a five-pound note.'

Linda made many enduring friendships at Sheffield. Julie Pearn, who along with her partner Araya Reddah remained among her best pals for the next twenty-five years, met her at a senior English lecturer's house in Linda's first year. 'My first impressions were that she obviously considered it a huge laugh. The "Prof" saw himself as a bit of a culture vulture. He would have social gatherings of university worthies to appreciate or execute music, art or literature. Linda and her student friend Celia [Woolfrey] were like a couple of gleeful naughty kids.'

Julie was studying first African, then Caribbean literature, an unusual choice at the time. 'All my colleagues were black African students – a situation I revelled in. My studies were a source of blank incomprehension for most of my white peers, but for Linda I am certain they were a positive reason for wanting to get to know me. Linda had a warm and welcoming attitude towards all reasonably humble human beings, so it was natural to her that any endeavour to open up cultural understanding and challenge racism was bound to be a good thing and should be supported with enthusiasm.'

Linda chose Sheffield because she liked the English department. But she didn't always stick to the required reading list. 'Although I was meant to read *Beowulf*, I must have faked reading it; I think I bought it. Sometimes in tutorials I would be quite lively, even though I hadn't read the book. I used to like practical criticism because you didn't have to prepare for it.'

She wasn't being lazy; it was a case of priorities, and many of the writers she was interested in were extra-curricular. For instance, she and Julie shared an enthusiasm for the poetry and performance of Louise Bennett, the Jamaican folklorist, writer and singer. 'We admired Miss Lou's earthy rooted humour and her stance as an artist – articulating grassroots perspectives through the grassroots voice of Creole,' Julie says.

It was a time for exploring, anything from music and literature to food and nature. One of Julie's earliest memories of Linda is being invited for a meal in 1980, and she credits Linda with introducing her to 'a whole new eating experience'. 'This time it was chicken satay. I had never tried a satay sauce before and the memory of its difference and deliciousness has remained with me. It seemed that Linda was bringing the eclectic cultural delights of London to spice up our more limited Yorkshire fare.' Another friend, Janet Bray, has never forgotten a particular Thai meal that Linda cooked.

Araya recalls long walks along the canal and occasionally in the Pennines. 'Linda had no room for small walks. Her stride was always bigger than most of us attempt in two. She was very striking and moved like a gazelle.'

Around this time, Linda was developing a strong interest in modern theatre, avidly following the work of ground-breaking companies like Belt and Braces and 7:84. So when the drama department at Sheffield created a new curriculum that allowed students to do a chunk of their degree in drama, she jumped at the chance. But first she had to sit an English language exam at the beginning of her second year, in order to get into the drama department as a full-time English student. This meant being stretched between exam prepa-ration and the department's first production of the year, Shakespeare's *Pericles*.

Because of the constraints on her time, her principal lecturer in drama, Frances Gray, suggested a cameo role as the goddess Diana, at the end of the play, which was self-contained and easier to rehearse.

'It was a real showstopper. She looked very striking,' says Frances. 'She'd let her hair right down to her waist and was wearing a blue and silver kaftan that made her look Wagner-ian. There was heavenly music coming from up above when she came on and she did her bit looking wonderful. Every-body said they remembered that part of the play. She must have been a good four inches taller than any of the guys in the show – it was a bit of a short year.'

During *Pericles*, Linda became friendly with Stephen Daldry, who got his dates wrong and turned up a week after the play had been cast. 'He ended up being general factotum and sat on the stage as prompter in a deckchair, because it was set on a beach,' Frances recalls. It was a humble start for the student who went on to become a major artistic force at Sheffield's Crucible Theatre, the Gate Theatre and the Royal Court Theatre in London, before becoming the Academy Award-nominated director of movies such as *Billy Elliot* and *The Hours*.

'We were a very resolutely poor theatre,' Frances recalls. 'It was a case of let the audience in free and do it! We never got any money anyway – thirty quid for a show – so that was our thing, doing bare boards stuff. We'd work out ways to get people to look good in their own clothes and in *Pericles* everyone was dressed in cheesecloth. It was cheap from Bradford Market.'

Perhaps not surprisingly, the drama course was becoming very political, especially after Sheffield became the much-televised hub of the first national steelworkers' strike in 1980. This was during the heightened tensions of Mrs Thatcher's first term, with the city and its flying wedge pickets on the political frontline.

'There were all sorts of big lefties like Howard Brenton coming up to do plays with us,' says Frances. 'We didn't do anything but Shakespeare and plays that had been written just this minute – about the strikes or whatever. There were four of us teaching drama at that time and we were all politically busy.'

Linda's next role was Baptista Minola, father of Katherine and Bianca in Frances's all-woman production of *The Taming of the Shrew*. 'At first she wasn't very happy to be cast as the father, because it looked like a small part, but then she realised how significant it was to be standing there betraying all the women on the stage. At the end, they all came down to the footlights with their fists up. It was really quite a big role compared to the number of lines she spoke. Her performance moved closer every day towards a nicely barbed impression of Prince Philip.'

In their second and third years at Sheffield, Stephen Daldry and Linda forged a terrific working partnership that had a significant impact on their peers. In 1981 they collaborated on a practical assessment course piece called '20 Lears – The First Three' – which considered the dramatic concept of madness, using a speech from the text of Act IV, Scene 6 of *King Lear*. Frances says, 'It started with Linda facing Steve. There was a long conversation and then she turned him round and he had a skull painted on him. It was a lovely moment. Linda and Stephen talked the same kind of language.'

Mea Webb was a fellow student in the drama group. 'Between them Stephen Daldry and Linda were head and shoulders above the rest of us and they probably taught us as much, informally, as our tutors,' she says. 'They had superior intellects and were just passionate and more focused towards their drama. They were better read, more informed and better able to focus. We were privileged to have spent that time with them.'

After Linda's death, Stephen made the following tribute: 'I know a lot of people carry on talking about Linda and her wit and her humour; my abiding memory of Linda is her piercing intelligence, overflowing creativity and indeed, passionate politics. For all of us growing up in the People's Republic of South Yorkshire at the time, the city was probably more of an education than the university, which was just as well because both Linda and I suffered a certain amount of dyslexia, Linda slightly more than myself.'

Stephen has not forgotten his role as Linda's fool in the Lear project. 'We couldn't really bear the arduous task of reading Shakespeare's original, so it was much more Linda's imaginings on what the play might be about. Given the fact that our professors never guessed this, maybe they had not read it either. We actually ended up with a first for our practical work, which is just as well because they could never possibly have read the essays we came up with.'

Through Stephen, Linda met Ann Lavelle, with whom she went on to form an important collaborative partnership after university, in comedy. 'Stephen always talked about Linda as fabulous. He really liked her,' says Ann. 'His house was a fun artistic little place and Linda used to come round there quite a lot. So we'd have basically late nights drinking and smoking and discussing into the night.

'Stephen was very imposing, clever and dynamic. He had that dynamism that has obviously propelled him to great things. And he's a very enthusiastic, fun person. I think he had a nickname for her, "Leapy Linda" or something like that. You knew he could see that little spark of madness or cleverness or genius. Linda was intense and very clever. She was a very special person.' It's interesting to note from a BBC News website that Stephen credits the Socialist Workers' Party students' Sheffield branch for giving him a 'political education' that became evident in both his stage and screen offerings.

Apart from the on-course association with left-wing playwright Howard Brenton, Linda became interested in the leading proponents of experimental theatre at the time, including Ken Campbell, Pip Simmons and the *People Show*. She also admired writers like Caryl Churchill. She went on to co-direct *Measure for Measure* with Frances. 'I set her up doing the brothel bit, which we made violently feminist.'

Mea Webb remembers Linda arriving at the drama department with 'a complete set of political views and values', which immediately gave her a presence and a voice. 'I thought at the time that this was what going to sixth-form college did for you,' says Mea. 'I was also aware she had grown up in an environment where politics were discussed. To me, who had a whole lot of growing up to do, this was very attractive, if a little intimidating.

'She wasn't at all intimidating as a person, though. My memory of Linda from those days was as someone who listened to you. She would stand slightly stooped over, almost looking up at you, with one hand holding back her long hair, slightly shy and usually serious. There was nothing frivolous or silly about her and I don't think she had much time for anyone who was. She wasn't always serious and often had a shine of laughter in her eyes. Mostly she was incredulous about something.

'We did a lot of work together, including *The Taming of the Shrew* and Brecht's *The Good Woman of Szechuan*. Linda brought an integrity to the roles she played. She often played the "older" parts with great gravitas – perhaps this was because of her height. The most remarkable thing I remember is the day we nearly threw our lecturer, Frances Gray, off the lighting tower. It sounds odd, but we had been doing a number of quite intense sessions that involved relaxation and meditation-cum-hypnosis, where we whipped ourselves up into a frenzy, much like a voodoo trance. Linda was very dominant in the group and I think she may have led us. Together we came seriously close to maiming Frances for life. I think this was because she was seen as the authority figure and the outsider. It was an altered state. I hadn't then – and have never since – been involved in anything like it.'

At the start of their second year, Linda and her friend Celia moved to a rented house in Attercliffe, in the heart of the steelworks area of Sheffield's east end. It was a rare and unlikely dwelling place for students, who mostly lived on the west side of town, near their regular facilities and watering holes. Linda developed a real affection for Sheffield's east end on the 'other' side of town.

She and Celia shared the house with Mark 'The Miner' Chamberlain, a coal miner at Dinnington pit near Sheffield, and his friend Roadie. Originally from Hull, Mark was incredibly generous, an enormous drinker and a *Guardian* reader. He had no trouble downing a dozen pints or more a night at the nearby Staniforth Arms. Celia says, 'Whenever I hear Van Morrison's "Moondance" I think of sunny Sunday mornings, everyone surfacing from the night before, in that house painted in pink, purple and lime green (by the landlord) with autumn leaf carpets and a hoover that belched garam masala – feeling happy.'

It seemed to be a good time for Linda too, though Celia remembers her saying how hard it was to get down to writing essays. Linda would run through it all in her mind, visualise writing it, handing it in and even the tutorial afterwards. Then she would snap out of her reverie and realise that three hours had gone by and she hadn't written a thing.

'She lived a lot in her head and gave the impression of being in a bit of a daydream,' Celia says. She recounts a time when Linda came home upset that she hadn't noticed an open drain in the road. She'd fallen down it and had to climb an iron ladder fixed to the side. 'There was a lot of thinking going on in Linda's life then – thoughts whirling around. Too many sometimes. But we had some exceptional times – a lot of laughs.'

Janet Bray recalls nights at the Station pub on the Wicker, where she and Linda enjoyed friendly sing-alongs with the locals. 'We shared a fascination with the wealth and depth of humanity found there. This was in the middle of the closure of the steelworks and there was a really apocalyptic feeling in the Don Valley. I think we both realised something historic was going on and wanted to understand it from the roots up, to be able to analyse what we saw at leisure.'

Their friendship began with artistic collaboration, when Linda was given a main role in Janet's play *Ladies of the Cross* in January 1982. Janet describes the play being very much in the vein of *The League of Gentlemen*. 'Linda was the only other student who understood the grotesque style I was after. The production hit many obstacles and she became my great ally and stuck by me throughout. It was the start of a friendship based on the same view of the world as a weird, grotesque and hilarious place, and a shared, pleasurable curiosity for the amazing weirdness of "ordinary" people.

'I have never enjoyed a night out so much with anyone. We could talk for hours analysing people and politics. We never talked about family, just politics, art and weird people. It was strange that we didn't talk about relationships, but I think we were just much better at sparking off about funnier and more analytical things.'

Perhaps this was also because Linda didn't particularly want to talk about Brian, who remained her boyfriend even though they spent so much time apart. By now Brian had developed a frustratingly elusive tendency, and Linda often found herself waiting in for his calls. He visited Sheffield occasionally, and she met up with him in London, but it was proving a struggle to keep the relationship on an even keel.

She stayed in touch with many of her friends from Erith, keeping up a regular correspondence with pals like Pauline Daniels (then Lucy Trask). 'Linda was a most loyal and generous friend and we exchanged letters regularly,' Pauline says. 'She really helped me through an emotionally sticky phase when I left my student nursing and was feeling very low; she encouraged me with her humour and good sense. Her letters, long missives, usually penned after a night at the pub, were terrific. It was all there – the quirky turns of phrase, the love of word-play and the surrealist flights of fancy which were her hallmark.'

Pauline and her partner Paul visited Linda in Sheffield when she was living in a house in Wincobank, the next square in the never-ending game of rented accommodation. Linda's landlords were going to Australia, so it seemed the ideal time to visit. 'After quite a bit of trouble locating the house, we arrived just in time to see the somewhat startled owners leaving for the airport. Brian was already there and the four of us had the best time. I remember the meal Linda cooked – mackerel with lime and soy sauce – which impressed me no end. She had just bought the Tom Waits' album *Heart Attack and Vine*, and was playing it non-stop.

'The next day we went into town and Linda took us to the Frog and Parrot pub and to several great second-hand bookshops, where she found a signed copy of Eric Fenby's biography of Delius and gave it to me. We had seen Ken Russell's film based on the book and she must have remembered how much I loved the music. It was just the kindest gesture.

'She adored the vintage clothes shops and we were delighted to find some great 1940s frocks, which we promptly bought and wore to the pub later in the evening. Mine had a trademark label in the collar – 'It's a Symphony!' – which afterwards became something of a catchphrase between us when we really rated something.'

Linda's time at university was nearing an end and all was

going well in the pressured lead-up to her final exams during the spring of 1982. But her preparations were suddenly and severely disrupted when news reached her from home that her dad had disappeared. Ray had done his usual vanishing act on Friday, but when he still had not returned by the Monday, Bessie and Barbara started to wonder if an accident had befallen him. Linda took the next train home.

'Linda phoned the railway depot and the depot said he was on a week's holiday,' Barbara says. 'But she eventually tracked him down through his workmates and discovered that he'd got another woman. She found him with this woman, shacked up really comfortably. And yet all these years he had been accusing my mum of having affairs. Linda asked him when he was going to collect his clothes and stuff from home. She said she didn't want him seeing Mum. She also said that the kindest thing he had ever done for Mum was to leave her after twenty-five years of marriage.

'After about a week or so, he wanted to come back. Linda said, "Mum, you're not to." Mum was sixty and she had been having it all those years. We used to beg her to come and live with us – we had a big house – but she would say it was Linda's dad and it was her duty. In later years Linda would say, "Why didn't you leave him, Mum?" "Because of you," she said.'

Bessie had become sadly downtrodden over the past few years, which had become increasingly horrendous. One of the worst things was that everybody knew what was going on. Despite it all, though, Bessie kept her dignity and this time, Ray was going for good.

'He begged her to take him back,' says Barbara. 'He was crying at the door. I took Mum to a solicitor and dealt with the divorce. She successfully filed for divorce on the grounds of mental cruelty. Linda and I both said Mum had eight good years after that before she died.

'He kept writing to Linda and Linda wouldn't have anything to do with him. And he wrote to me and asked if he could carry on seeing the boys every week, if he could take them out. He was a wonderful granddad, but I felt so bitter towards him. I said, "You can't ever see my children for as long as I live. You'll never see them and if that hurts you then that's good." And that's how I felt and I never regret it. I spoke to Linda about it and we both agreed. She refused to see him. He kept writing and sending her money for birthdays, and she'd send it back. Then, around ten years ago, his sister got in touch with Linda to say that Ray was ill in hospital after a bad accident on the railway. She said, "Why would you think I care? Why are you telling me?"

'When Mum died, Linda said to me, "Barbara, I blame him for Mum having breast cancer. It's all his fault. I never want to see him again for as long as I live." And she never did.'

In late August 1982, Linda went up to Edinburgh with a group of students under the banner of Sheffield University Theatre Group. They were set to perform at the Edinburgh Fringe Festival venue St Columba's by the Castle, presenting *The Diggers*, about a seventeenth-century peasants' land occupation. According to Ann Lavelle, Stephen Daldry and his then girlfriend Jo Henderson were the driving force behind the show.

'Stephen and Jo oversaw the whole creative concept. They went up to Edinburgh, found the venue and sorted everything out. We just tagged along – we didn't do any of the hard work. Stephen and Jo did all the organisation and the flyers and getting the play in the programme. It was great fun and a bit of a mad thing. It was the first time Linda and I worked together.'

Commercial station Radio Forth 194 described *The Diggers* as 'an enormously powerful performance'. The reviewer from the *Scotsman* newspaper wasn't anywhere near as indulgent. '*The Diggers* starts with a racket, gets noisier and ends in bitter dissent and disorder, having battered across a stark sense of frustrated rage, not much else.'

Among the cast was Dave Rees. 'The reviewer seemed to be under the impression we were an army of unemployed from the streets of Sheffield,' he says. 'I remember he met us in the pub afterwards and ranted on about something deep and profound he had somehow seen in the production. I think we all thought he was just a bit loony.'

Stephen Daldry still has fond memories of the production. 'We decided we would take a show to the Edinburgh Festival, much against the advice of the student union because they had lost so much money taking student shows up there in the past. But Linda prevailed and we spent many months trying desperately to get a show together . . . I can't say it was a particularly successful investigation into the English Revolution.

'Linda really put her finger on the pulse when we got to Edinburgh by saying, "The important thing about this show, Stephen, is that it is crap." She decided that the point of the show was to give the audience their money back. Word of this got back to Sheffield and the finance director was dispatched to stop it happening. He turned up at the end of our press performance, when Linda was already amongst the audience with wads of cash saying, "It's a crap show. Here, have your money back." The finance director began yelling at Linda to take the money back. "You have to give Linda the money back!" he told the audience.

'There was a little bit of banter and then Linda delivered a speech to the finance director in front of everybody about the nature of crap art and crap unions and moral responsibility. I suppose, looking back on it, you could say it was Linda's first ever stand-up. And of course, as far as the audience were concerned, it was all part of the show and we got rather good notices.'

Coincidentally, this was the first year I had gone to the Edinburgh Fringe, with a show featuring the 'Ranting Poets' of the moment – Little Brother, Seething Wells, Benjamin Zephaniah and Attila the Stockbroker – all acts we had promoted heavily at New Variety cabaret in London. So it's quite possible that our paths may have crossed that summer. However, Linda and I were not to meet for another year.

5
Linda's in Love Again

Broomhill to Sheffield Trades and Labour Club

'Misery loves company. I find married people, they're always encouraging you to get married if you're not. And the next thing that they do is assume that you, as a child-free person, are inevitably going to have kids. So they'll be changing some stinking nappy and they look at you and say, "Ooh, you've got all this to come." I always say, "No, when my boyfriend's incontinent he's going straight in a home."

'I rather question the phrase "Happy Hour" when you look at the people availing themselves of this facility. It's more, "I'm trapped in a loveless marriage which is why I'm drinking tequila at thruppence a flagon instead of getting the 8.33 back to Chislehurst, bloody hell I never wanted to live there anyway" Hour.'

Linda and I met in the summer of 1983, after I'd been in Sheffield for a few months. I was there to begin life as a mature student reading politics and sociology at the university, aged 29. She was there because she had stayed on after graduation, unable to see herself joining what she called 'the working world'. In later years, neither of us liked the idea of having 'a career'. We just did what we did.

Still, there's no denying that my work path ultimately led me to Linda. When I left school, I started out as a trainee accountant, but that only lasted a few dismal months. My dream was to be a sports reporter, yet the general consensus seemed to be that this was an unlikely ambition for the son of a bookkeeper – totally pie in the sky. Undeterred, I wrote to two or three newspaper groups in the Essex area asking whether any of them would take on a trainee. Bingo! The Essex and East London Newspaper Group, based in Dagenham, were about to open a new plant in the Southend area and I was offered a three-year indentured traineeship.

All in, I spent five years working as a reporter in south-east Essex. At 20, I became shop steward or Father of the Chapel of the National Union of Journalists and took part in various strikes and disputes. I'd picked up my politics from my dad and was quite a bit left of the Labour Party, later joining the International Socialists. I quit the paper because I was tired of its provincial nature. The editor and the editorial director weren't keen on me writing political exposés, and a story I was compiling about police corruption in south-east Essex was spiked. It was very frustrating; I had been working on the story for weeks and a similar version later came out in the *News of the World*.

While still working as a reporter, I became involved in promoting arts events in Southend – anything from theatre groups to jazz and rock bands. One day I got chatting to the director of a mobile theatre company about the groups that I'd been booking. He seemed impressed and said, 'If you ever come to London, look us up.' I thought, 'Wow, people actually get paid to do this!'

So when I finished at the newspaper, I decided to find out more about this life where you get paid to do stuff you enjoy doing. Before long, a guy in a van arrived to pick me and my possessions up from my mum's house and move me to a shared house in Forest Gate, east London. My first job was as an administrator of a children's and community theatre group called Soap Box Theatre. It was 1978 and I was 24.

A year earlier I'd seen a play called *Joe of England* by John McGrath, at a youth club in Basildon. A proponent of 'popular theatre', McGrath also wrote *A Good Night Out*, which became a bit of a bible to Linda and me. In the book he explains how theatre can work very well away from the traditional proscenium-arched space, employing a much less formal structure and a looser relationship between performers and audience. *Joe of England* was a turning point for me. It was theatre with a message that didn't hit you over the head – fun and credible, with great language, acting and original live music. I thought, 'Bloody hell, this is fantastic!' I definitely wanted a piece of it.

I'd been at Soap Box Theatre for six months when I bumped into Roland Muldoon, the director who had told me to look him up if I ever came to London. He was the co-founder of CAST, a well-known left-wing theatre group on an Arts Council grant. That afternoon, after meeting his partner and wife, Claire Muldoon, at their flat in Paddington, I gave in my notice at Soap Box and went to work for CAST.

CAST had a history and a half. Founded by Claire and Roland in 1965, it had been a vehicle for campaigns against the Vietnam War and apartheid, among other causes. But after Thatcher became prime minister, the government started cutting back grants for groups with left leanings. Roland rightly judged that the writing was on the wall for CAST unless we diversified, and that's how New Variety came into being in January 1982.

It was a huge success: a cabaret of lots of different acts, including stand-up, physical comedy, live music, ranting poets, magic and juggling. In fact, anything that was entertaining and had some politics to it could be found on the New Variety stage. It caught on like wildfire and after a GLC grant was awarded we spread to five new venues. But by 1983 I needed some headspace. Having honed my skills as a national tour organiser, booker and cabaret programmer in London, I left CAST feeling the need for a change. University seemed a good idea. And that's how I landed in Sheffield.

I had a mate there who was talking about forming a theatre company and developing a new kind of political theatre. I'd worked with him in London and liked what he was saying. Since I was starting my degree in Sheffield in October, it seemed sensible to go up early and start collaborating. I arrived in May and we set to work immediately. Within a few months we were looking for people to join us. And that's where Linda came in.

Linda had been having a bad time. The drama with her father had taken its toll emotionally and there was worse to come. Still reeling some months later, she received a letter from Brian, her boyfriend, ending their relationship. She turned to her friend Celia Woolfrey for support. 'She called round to see me and showed me the letter,' Celia says. 'She was in a state of shock; she couldn't believe it.' Brian vanished from her life completely after that. Linda took it badly.

'Brian was studying journalism,' says Barbara, Linda's sister. 'He used to visit her in Sheffield and Linda would go to see him. They were together for about four years. But when the relationship became very serious and it seemed that they were going to settle down together after university, Brian's family objected. Suddenly he disappeared off the scene. It was like those *Without a Trace* programmes.

'Linda was absolutely devastated. She came to stay at my house and tried to find him. I went down to his mum's, but she said she didn't know where he was. I kept going down, but nothing came of it; he wasn't around. We all thought at the time that maybe his family had taken him away somewhere.

'Linda and I used to phone each other nearly every day, especially when she was having all these problems. She suffered terribly after Brian – more than you can imagine. I often went up on the InterCity train for the day and met her for lunch. It was a really tough time for her, especially after what had happened with her dad.'

We can only speculate about the circumstances surrounding Brian Pereira's disappearance. We don't know if Linda ever saw him again. They may have spoken on the telephone. But the love affair was over. In the winter of 1982/3 Linda fell into a dark depression. Then, in spring, she moved house again, this time to live with Ben Lowe and his partner Alex Manning in the Hunters Bar area of Sheffield.

Alex remembers Linda arriving at their house in a very low state. 'I was working in London during the week, so I only saw Linda at weekends. I just couldn't understand why Ben chose Linda to share the house with him. She just didn't want to talk or engage at all. But Ben said she had a spark and as time went on I realised she did want to engage.

'She said that her father had left home. She attributed her lowness of mood to the break-up of a relationship with a man she had been going out with, who had seemingly been able to move on and cast her aside as having belonged to his past. She was caustic about this man. So it was really a double whammy of being left by men.

'We lived next door to a policeman who no doubt had a

name but was always known to us as "Plod". He had no personality to speak of and his conversational style was that of someone reading evidence from a notebook to a court. It became Linda's hobby to engage "Plod" in conversation at every possible opportunity and then to recount the results to Ben and me. I began to feel her humour.

'She managed to worm out of him that he had been selling insurance before he joined the police, but had found the work too boring. Linda thought that surely it must be that he was too boring for insurance sales rather than it was too boring for him! I used to save up South Yorkshire-isms that I heard at work, knowing that she'd appreciate them. "Lower than lino" – how damning of someone is that? "Spitting coloured lights" – about as angry as it is possible to be. Even now when I hear odd quirks of speech I think of how Linda would have liked them.'

It was at Ben and Alex's house that I first met Linda in the summer of 1983. Ben is now a solicitor living and working in Bradford, but back then he was a journalist-researcher who spent much of his free time as a DJ for a progressive disco that gave its services to a host of benefit causes.

Ben recommended Linda to my mate and me as someone who might be interested in the new theatre company we were trying to set up. Our aim was to place political theatre – theatre with a message – in a community setting, but we also needed to make money with commercial shows. At this point we were about to take the name Commonstage and had just one event under our belts – a hastily arranged but ultimately successful cabaret night called 'Solidarity for Nicaragua', which attracted a big crowd to the Sheffield University lower refectory hall. I think Linda was there in the audience to witness me on stage.

I don't think Sheffield had seen a night quite like it before. Influenced by the New Variety format, it offered a dose of quick-fire comedy and political sketches, along with a multi-cultural fusion of music. Another night had already been planned for October, this time to benefit the fight for freedom and justice in El Salvador. As you might have gathered by now, Sheffield was home to a lot of keen and committed supporters of liberation struggles in Latin America. A size-able group of Chileans had been granted exile/refugee status by the city council.

I remember the day I met Linda at Ben and Alex's house. She had a lovely presence and I was immediately taken by her. What's more, she seemed to be on our wavelength imme-diately and was very interested in the ideas we were putting forward. We talked for hours and it became abundantly clear that she was very eligible for membership of our group. We were looking for a commitment from someone who genuinely understood what we were about. It didn't matter if they weren't practised in the ways of putting together political theatre in a community setting.

Linda could see that there was no shortage of material for a political theatre company in Sheffield, and she instantly seemed to grasp the potential for using issue-based material derived from people's experiences – from local industrial disputes to domestic violence. With thousands of jobs lost in the steel industry since the 1980 steelworkers' strike, Sheffield had begun to feel like a city going downhill fast. So this would be Sheffield fighting back, defending services against Tory cuts, rate capping and the rest. We were looking to do our own sketches about the political issues of the day, which would earn money, but over time we hoped to drop the commercial side and put together a group that would get the community involved, and get local people onto a stage.

Linda was perfect for the group in many ways: she shared our ideas; she had seen New Variety in London and was familiar with some of the political theatre work we'd been involved in; and she'd done plenty of performing, even though we hadn't actually seen her on stage. So she was in.

That first time we met, four of us talked tactics about what we wanted to do and how. But when the meeting broke up and the others left, I stayed on for more tea and chat with Linda. We found we had lots in common. We really hit it off. Linda's friend Ann Lavelle remembers it well. 'Linda and Warren went together so perfectly,' she says. 'I remember them first meeting each other and they actually spent the entire night talking about political theatre, which I think says a lot about them and the couple they became.'

Lots of meetings followed, with conversations continuing into the night, and it soon became obvious that Linda and I had taken a shine to each other. We discussed and debated the big issues affecting the world; we laughed a lot; we sparked. I think we were both knocked out by our almost instant compatibility. I thought Linda was divine. She was passionate about all the things that I held dear. She was strikingly good looking and fresh faced in a very English, pre-Raphaelite way.

We both loved comedy and the new 'alternative' comedians like Alexei Sayle; we loved movies, particularly gangster films; we loved music, particularly modern jazz. That, I declare, made Linda the only *young* woman I had ever met who wasn't bullshitting me about liking jazz. She could trade on equal terms about Charles Mingus, Dexter Gordon and Miles Davis. What a wheeze.

We were both Londoners 'up north'. Linda had done her time at Sheffield University and I was soon to start a degree course at the very same establishment. There was a difference there, however. I couldn't settle to it, didn't like it and flunked it within a term. So I quit and returned to life in the fast lane. I wasn't sure what Linda made of me, this short and slightly cocky cockney pushing 30, who knew a lot and had been around the circuit a few times. But I soon found out. One evening we went to a music gig at the Leadmill Arts Centre, and afterwards we went home together.

A relationship blossomed pretty quickly. We were meant for each other; we had no doubt about that at all. And so it proved. But first we had to work together and that could have spoilt good intentions. 'Warren seemed to be the catalyst for Linda,' Ben Lowe says. 'Initially a bit prone to gloom and despondency, she leapt into life (and often into bed) once Warren came on the scene. Warren gave Linda confidence in her own talent, whether as a writer or performer or otherwise. This is not to say that she wouldn't have been a stand-up without Warren, as she was from the outset a woman with a rare and extra-ordinary wit, wired through with barbed irony. But Warren seemed to instil in Linda a sense of self-belief, and this helped her both as a stage performer and as a writer.'

Linda's sister Barbara can recall the first time she heard the news about Linda and me. 'One evening the phone went, it was Linda, and after a few minutes she said, "Someone wants to speak to you."

'I heard a man's voice and he said, "My name's Warren. Linda's in love again."

'I came off the phone and said to Terry, "Warren. That's a really young name. He must be a kid."

'Linda was absolutely wonderful after that. Warren was

the best thing that ever happened to her. She never looked back. She was a different person and she came into her own with her work.'

It wasn't long before Linda took me to meet Barbara, Terry and Bessie. The Smith family maisonette was at 246a Riverdale Road, Erith, a very long and unusually wide yet nondescript road of small terraces and council houses. This was where Linda and her sister were brought up and where her mum continued to live until her death in 1990.

As I went up a set of outdoor steps, through the front door and into a long hallway divided off by sets of little curtains, I was struck by the late 1950s/early 1960s feel and decor of the place. It reminded me of the upstairs flat my dad's parents used to rent in Stoke Newington, north-east London. Once upon a time the front room may even have been reserved for visitors' weekly use as 'Sunday best'.

At the bottom of the hallway was the old-fashioned kitchen diner, where the refrigerator was always packed with unopened tins of food. However much Linda tried to change her mum's mind, Bessie was firmly of the opinion that keeping the tins cold would ensure that the airtight food within them stayed even fresher. Linda's mum definitely had her eccentricities, and Barbara remembers an amusing episode from one of our early visits to stay with Bessie. Barbara noticed that a spare bed had been made up in the front room, in addition to the one in Linda's old bedroom. The dialogue went something like this:

Barbara to Mum: 'You'd better sit down, Mum: they live together, they sleep together and they have sex . . . they're not married but they live together.'

Mum to Barbara: 'I don't think there's anything like that going on . . . I don't want none of that talk in my house.'

Around the same time I introduced Linda to my parents. They got on famously and Linda was very fond of them. She often referenced our families in her routines and brought the humour out of everyday scenes. Here she is on Radio Five Live's *The Treatment*:

'The received wisdom is that along with potpourri and salad, bleach is woman's gift to man – use it regularly, grasshopper. This isn't my experience, though, perhaps because I live with a Jewish man. Judaism's dietary laws make you more aware of hygiene, I suppose. In his parents' case, obsessed with it. The countryside is a place of fear and loathing for them due to its lack of wipe-clean surfaces, and a snack at their house is a rehearsal for senile dementia: "I thought I left a cup of tea down there, oh . . . did I eat that sandwich? I must have done, the plate's gone; I don't remember though. Nurse, nurse, I'm frightened."'

The group that eventually came together to form Commonstage comprised around ten of us, but with a core of five. It wasn't long before Linda was at its centre. For the first five months we operated from our flats and rooms and the inevitable cafés and pubs dotted along bus routes that traversed the city and linked our home bases. At one point we rehearsed at a premises that had once been the Sheffield Centre Against Unemployment. It was rough, but it had a roof and we were grateful.

We worked on developing topical political sketches, which we performed anywhere from the main shopping street at Fargate to pub venues, trades clubs and the student union. The Conservative government was our main target. I was decked out as the international hate figure and all-round dictator General Pinochet of Chile, and Linda was my counterpart, one Margaret Hilda Thatcher, prime minister of the United Kingdom. My costume was hired, but Linda's 'Maggie' blue twinset was bought at a charity shop. She also acquired a suitable blonde wig, and borrowed a handbag and a string of pearls – from her mum, I think.

Linda contributed to several spot-on scripts and performed her duties impeccably and impressively as Mrs Thatcher. She was very convincing and quite fetching as our beloved premier, playing opposite a young actor from Rotherham called Allan Forrest, who was cast in the role of the equally despised employment secretary and Thatcher favourite, Norman Tebbit. Tebbit was often depicted by satirists as Count Dracula, and I have a press cutting showing Linda peering down at Allan as he lay in a coffin.

It wouldn't be long before Linda could put aside character acting and be herself behind a microphone, but in the meantime there was a lot of mileage to be gained from impersonating the most unpopular politician (or even person?) in Britain in the 1980s. Inevitably she started to build a cult following and worked really hard at voicing the character. We also carried a Queen impersonation in our repertoire – that's the monarch as opposed to the rock band.

I recall two highlights of our group sketch work. Firstly, we were literally last-minute deputies for Red Ladder Theatre Group at the Leadmill, after its van was involved in an accident on the M1. We acquitted ourselves very well, having scraped together a coherent act that included every single idea we had tried out to date. The other was a few months later, when we performed at the main Sheffield City Hall at one of a series of municipally subsidised concerts dubbed either 'Rock Defends Sheffield' or 'Rock Against Rate Capping' – catchy titles both. The headliner was upcoming troubadour Billy Bragg. Admission 50 pence. I kid you not.

These shows were organised as part of the resistance to government plans to curb local democracy, targeting so-called 'high spending' left-wing Labour councils such as Derek Hatton-led Liverpool.

At Commonstage we decided it would be a good time to try and import the New Variety format to Sheffield, as the notion of a variety night was very in keeping with the working men's club circuit. We saw ourselves as pioneers and wanted to prove that variety could work in the new world of non-sexist and non-racist entertainment, and we went off to try and convince the old guard committee at Intake WMC.

What a night. Linda was the only woman involved on either side of the negotiations and I think her presence made them nervous. They were sceptical, but prepared to think about any idea that might be advantageous to the club bar takings on a quiet night of the week. In the end it didn't happen because of Club and Institute Union rules concerning non-members. In years to come we were to meet these regulations in a head-on collision. In the meantime the only way forward was to self-promote at pubs and community venues around the city. But first we had to source a pool of performers that audiences were prepared to pay good money to see. We advertised in the local press for new acts and started holding auditions.

In the autumn of 1983 we tried out our cabaret evenings at the Red Lion, Heeley, with Linda making her obligatory appearance as Mrs Thatcher. Then, to much fanfare in the local press, we brought 'new' variety back to the old Attercliffe district, specifically the Queen's Head pub. We quit there after a couple of weeks because the landlord refused to take down the 'No Travellers' notices in the windows.

Unfortunately, these were a feature of most pubs in this part of the city, a reaction to the travellers' sites nearby.

We returned to town in December and set up shop under our new name, Sheffield Popular Theatre (SPT). Our first production was a special Christmas show at the Royal pub on London Road, Sharrow. It went well and convinced us that we had a satisfying – albeit hand-to-mouth – future as promoters. The following January we set up weekly Tuesday-night shows in the concert room at the Royal. Punters got great value for money, with three acts for £1.30, with reductions for students and the unemployed.

Peter, the landlord of the Royal, was an archetypal golfing, Pringle sweater-wearing bloke whose sour facial expression rarely cracked. Four weeks into our successful run, he suddenly announced an end to the show because he'd discovered that the pub didn't possess an entertainment licence. Thank you, Peter. Determined not to give up, Linda and I secured a good rock-and-roll room above the George IV pub on Infirmary Road, opposite Kelvin Flats. We were also doing one-off shows around the city at places like Parsons Cross and Darnall.

But the theatre group began to fall apart in early March 1984, just as the miners' strike was kicking off. By the beginning of May, personality and policy clashes had led to irretrievable breakdown. The arguments mainly revolved around the direction we should be taking. It was hardly headline-grabbing stuff: 'Theatre Group Splits After Disagreement'! Two members, followers of the Brazilian director and founder of the political theatre methodology, Theatre of the Oppressed, Augusto Boal, chose to follow their own path. And crucially, Linda and I, together with Dave Humphreys, a former colleague of mine from London who'd come up to work at SPT with us, managed to wrest control of the office premises at Star Works, Darnall, which we had been using since January. Even more importantly, we retained the name. To the three of us, this was the real beginning of Sheffield Popular Theatre, and we were set to go on to far greater things.

6

Solid As A Rock

Sheffield to Brampton Bierlow

M ost people have their own version of a 'where were
you, when . . . ?' moment. For Linda and me it was
probably the day we witnessed the march back to work at
the end of the miners' strike on 5 March 1985. The tumul-
tuous year-long dispute had officially ended in South
Yorkshire at 9 a.m. that day. A sea of miners blocked the
main road through Brampton Bierlow village that led to
the Cortonwood colliery. It says a lot about them and their
dignity that they marched in an orderly fashion from the
Miners' Welfare to the Alamo, probably the most famous
picket hut in the world, at the end of the Cortonwood
Pit lane.

Linda, myself, and our friends Ann Lavelle and Mark
'Miwurdz' Hurst had travelled in our orange Bedford van
the relatively short distance from Sheffield to stand shoul-
der-to-shoulder in solidarity with the comrades of our
'adopted' pit. Emotions were running very high in the village
as the march prepared to set off. We joined women, children,
pensioners and many other supporters who lined the streets
as the familiar chant of 'Here we go, here we go' rang out.

But as the miners approached the pit, they came up against
a picket line set up by three Kent miners. The Kent pickets
had voted to continue the strike in support of the reinstate-
ment of 700 miners sacked during the dispute. They wanted

89

an amnesty for all sacked colleagues. NUM officials advised their 850 men not to cross the line. 'The men walked up to the pit gates, turned their backs, and stood in silence. And then they walked away,' recalls Ann.

Two miners took their colleagues by surprise, broke ranks and walked down the pit lane to the colliery, leaving behind a jeering and angry crowd. After half an hour the rest of the miners dispersed, many marching back to the welfare club. They finally returned to work the following afternoon, united and with their heads held high, once the Kent miners had agreed to lift their picket of pits in Yorkshire.

For most mining families, the strike had changed their lives for ever. It certainly provided unprecedented opportunities for a lot of the women from the pit communities. Many of those who supported the strike through the national network of Women Against Pit Closures groups had never gone out to work; they looked after the family and that was the way the miners had traditionally wanted it to be. Then, suddenly, they came into their own at the outbreak of the upheaval. The women found a voice, education and work.

At the same time, Linda too was going through a transformation. It began with a chance meeting in the spring of 1984, when she bumped into Ann Lavelle on Devonshire Green, in front of their favourite second-hand book and record shop, Rare and Racy. Ann and Linda had performed together in *The Diggers* at Edinburgh, the summer after Linda's finals, but they hadn't seen each other for a while because Ann had just returned from a nine-month stint supporting the protest movement at Greenham Common. Now based in Sheffield again, Ann had decided to try her hand at stand-up comedy and made her three-minute debut in a Sheffield pub. She vividly recalls meeting Linda again.

'I said, "I've just had a go at stand-up and it was quite a laugh."

'"Oh, I fancy doing that," Linda said.

'That was it, really. We just started doing it together,' Ann says. 'It was terribly casual, but terribly nice to have a little pal to do it with. We were never a double act. We were two friends supporting each other and it was wonderful to work with Linda, spend time with her and have a laugh.'

Stand-up was a natural progression for Linda, who already felt comfortable filling in the occasional gap or glitch between sketches at SPT shows and New Variety cabaret nights. As she later said, 'Sometimes things would go wrong and people wouldn't be ready, so in between sketches I would start talking to the audience. And I began to find that I really liked it best when I was doing little jokes to the audience.' She worked hard at developing material, and even her earliest routines sparkle with that unique Linda Smith magic:

'As you probably gathered, I don't come from Sheffield. I come from south-east London, or souf-east London as we would say. I don't think they know much about the recession. Things are pretty good down in south-east London. People don't support Margaret Thatcher – they think she should stand down for a stronger leader. And kids are all fully paid up members of "Thatcher Youth". They go to schools like the Oswald Mosley Comprehensive. Their uniform is designer sportswear, gold chains, Lacoste underpants and Aramis perfume . . . furry dice on the skateboard.

'As I say, I go down south and it's like another world. If people actually knew the miners' strike was going on they'd be furious. But they don't tend to watch a lot of news, which is a shame really because you can see some really good things on the news. There's this wonderful new game you can play, a new game show, it's much more popular than *The Price Is Right*. It's actually called The *Return to Work Figures Are Wrong!* It's that much more fun because you can play it every time the news comes on. They give you some absurd figure like "The numbers returning to work at Dinnington pit are actually greater than the population of the United Kingdom.' Incredible things like this and you can write in with the real figures and you can win a night out with Chief Inspector Nesbitt.* Really popular game show that one.'

For Linda and me, the miners' strike threw up a catalogue of memorable times. Often at the centre of these magic moments was a human dynamo called Denise Fitzpatrick. Five feet high and blonde, this irrepressible mum of five managed to keep the wheels going on a typically lively miners' household while finding time to work in the nearby National Coal Board Laboratories as a part-time cleaner.

We had first come across the Fitzpatricks when we offered to put on a free cabaret night at the Cortonwood Miners' Welfare, in the fourth month of the strike. We organised several fundraisers in Sheffield, which many miners' families attended. That evening marked the beginning of a solid friendship, and we started visiting them socially, always calling in at the Alamo picket hut.

Denise became known throughout Britain for her tireless campaigning as secretary of Cortonwood Action Group. She went up and down the land making speeches and taking collections while successfully spinning the plates on the home front. Quite how she did it we never knew. A genuine marvelette. Her house and HQ was in a perpetual state of organised chaos. Everyone knew their role, including the

---

* A familiar figure at the picket lines of the South Yorkshire coalfield.

dog, 'our Butch'. It was an open house overflowing with hospitality, and the base for a group of formidable 'flyers' or flying picketers. During the early hair-raising weeks and months of the strike, the flyers would take off before dawn and lead the combined constabularies a merry dance over county boundaries, circumventing roadblocks and generally outwitting 'Plod' through Yorkshire, Derbyshire, and into Nottinghamshire. Linda and I nicknamed them 'The Flying Fitzpatricks'.

You couldn't invent the Fitzpatricks. They were a far cry from a cosy Friday-night TV sitcom family. Barry, the dad, worked at Maltby pit. He was a gentle giant, provided you didn't cross him. Linda and I thought his Barnsley accent should be bottled and preserved for the nation's pleasure. Boots were 'boits' and toothpaste was 'toithpaste'. Linda and I were fascinated by accents and dialect. In Sheffield, for instance, the accents change subtly as you move across the city. As soon as you head northwards into mining country you can detect the Barnsley inflection.

The older Fitzpatrick sons, Malcolm and Robert, were already mining for a living and well up for saving their jobs. Then came Cheryl, Paul, and the baby of the siblings, 'Little' Denise. I still boast to friends that Denise Fitzpatrick cooked the biggest Yorkshire puddings in Yorkshire – and they were bloody lovely.

Once we went on a weekend trip to Lincolnshire with the whole extended family, staying at a holiday park in Ingoldmells on the outskirts of Skegness. Denise pulled off a sensational three-shift traditional Sunday roast dinner . . . in a caravan. We had to watch our step when we went into 'Skeggy' because of the potential for clashes with Notts 'scabs'. When Denise's mother came to stay, or visitors like stalwart volunteer Mrs Cadwalladar – 'Mrs Cad' as she was known – were in the house, everyone knew to mind their language. Denise's upbringing had been strict and over the years she had developed a concept of 'light swearing', which she employed with great skill in company. 'Chuffin' 'ell' was about as strong as it could get within the confines of those walls, as Denise recalled years later at a tribute to Linda at the Lyceum Theatre in Sheffield. Describing the tensions at the height of the strike, she said: 'One particular day we'd been to Mansfield and the police had been nasty. I was furious and couldn't think of anything bad enough to call 'em. So I shouted – you'll have to excuse my language – "Come here, you black-enamelled bastard!" I kept shouting it.

'When I came back, Linda said to me, "You look like you've had a fraught day."

'"I've had worse than a fraught day," I said. "I've been swearing, real swearing, like."'

'"What have you said?"

'I told her I'd called this copper "a black-enamelled hump-back bastard", and she said, "Denise, what did you call him that for?"

'"Cos it were worst word I could think of."

'"That's not very nice, and there might be someone who is a bastard who is quite nice," she said.

'"I never thought about it," I said.

'"Why didn't you call them 'black-enamelled fuckers'?" she said.

'I said, "God, Linda, I daren't say that! Me mam will kill me." I stuck to bastards, but I often think about that.

'We used to feed everyone that came to our house, and once Warren and Linda came for a meal. Warren's vegetarian, bless him, but when you come from a mining family, you just don't know anything about vegetarians. I got a recipe and bought a rainbow trout and did it in almonds. Warren said he thought you could only get meals like it in a restaurant. After that we took Linda and Warren out for a meal, because we had got a bit of money and back pay.

'So Linda says, "You must come over to us in Sheffield. I'll cook a roast and we'll have a lovely day." So of course we go, about ten of us. Everything was in t'oven and we went out for a drink. When we got back, Linda's serving up a leg of lamb done to perfection, and says, "When you get your vegetables, they're a bit crispy, we like ours crispy."

'They were chuffin' raw! She had either forgot to turn them on before we went out, or she didn't know how to cook them. I says, "Linda, there's cooked and there's chuffin' raw, and these are raw." All in all, they were a very special couple, very good friends to me and mine in strike, and to a lot more families in strike.'

In common with thousands of other lay supporters, Linda and I visited various picket lines during the course of the strike, although we had the good sense to stay away from the mayhem of the 'Battle of Orgreave', when thousands of miners met the full force of the mounted police outside the coking plant. During July and August, with the miners' strike in full flow, we toured mining villages on a 'Summer Measures' scheme for young unemployed people. We dubbed it 'Escape Aid 2' and visited Stainforth, Thurnscoe, Goldthorpe and Brampton Bierlow. We often worked with the breakdance group SMAC 19; they were a revelation wherever we took them. Youngsters turned out from far and wide when word got around that a black breaking crew was coming to their village to demonstrate dance moves and offer basic instruction. This was black and white coming together and sharing against the backdrop of picket-line action.

SMAC 19 were regular occupants of the bench seats of our SPT orange van.

Linda and I became quite addicted to some of the hip-hop classics that we heard around this time, including 'Jam On Revenge (The Wikki Wikki Song)' and 'Jam On It' by Newcleus and 'Planet Rock' by Afrika Bambaataa.

In November, Linda and I decided it was now or never for the push to do a community show. We chose the *Star* and the free sheet *Gazette* to carry our appeals for memories of the old East End and for volunteers to take part in the production. We gave the impression that preparations had already begun for what would become known as the 'Darnall People's Show'. The catchy title 'East Side Story' came a little later.

This free advertising, together with an interview we gave to BBC Radio Sheffield – a wonderful ally throughout our career – triggered a deluge of letters, phone calls and requests to meet up. We had struck a chord. The first wave of replies produced a number of potential volunteers. Soon we had a mountain of historical information to work with and were developing a super core group. Linda grabbed the director's chair and I put on the producer's hat.

As 1984 gave way to 1985 and the miners' strike staggered on, we were aware of the erosion of morale among miners' families and their supporters, and talked about trying to put on more fundraising concerts. Then one day in January I came up with the idea of taking a morale-boosting tour to the South Yorkshire coalfield. Roger Barton, secretary of Sheffield and District Trades Council, agreed to fund our expedition, which would pay for our overheads. The 'Pit Stop Tour' was born.

There was no shortage of sympathetic pros and we recruited performers from the area. We also booked occasional guests from the Smoke, including socialist magician and all-round good egg Ian Saville. From the ranks of our forthcoming community extravaganza came Sheffielder Joy Palmer and Barnsleyite Sylvia Jones, reciting moving verse and singing classics from the miners' songbook. They were stage novices, but hard-bitten and fearless.

We were also boosted by impromptu appearances from 'Big' Bill Ross, a hefty Scot who mined at Maltby. Bill raised money for the Miners' Hardship Fund by selling copies of *Against All the Odds*, a superb anthology of poems from the coalfields. The strike provoked an explosion of working-class creativity, the likes of which we had never previously witnessed and might never see again.

Linda and I had a favourite among the group of early 1980s new-wave self-styled 'ranters', performance poets with an attitude. Forming a mini-movement that had come to the fore during the late 1970s and outlived punk, they were sometimes musicians in their own right, but generally worked with or alongside bands. The best of the bunch that hailed from Bradford was Little Brother – Dave to us. Dave tended to perform in suits, but on the Pit Stop Tour he would often step out in spectacular style, wearing a long black drape coat with leopard skin trim, a white shirt and bootlace tie, and blue suede shoes. In my mind's eye I can see him fancy stepping on the disco dance floor after the show – almost like the Pied Piper – and leading Linda and hordes of people as they got down to the Arthur Conley classic 'Sweet Soul Music'.

We often picked Dave up from Barnsley Bus Station to bring him on tour. Here's gratitude, as he describes his carriage for the night as 'a van, not a big van or a particularly new van, more of a "look at me I'm about to break down on the most inconvenient stretch of road as possible but at least I'm cheap" van.

'Laden to the roof with speakers, props and jolly people, there was just enough room to slot in a then slender poet. One of those jolly people was Linda. The laughter and banter as Warren did his best to negotiate us to our destination convinced me I wanted to be a part of this.'

The Pit Stop Tour was a major breakthrough for the fledgling comedy duo of Linda Smith and Ann Lavelle, otherwise known as 'Token Women'. Ann and Linda came up with the idea for the name early on. 'We were saying it ironically,' Ann says, 'because there were never any women on the bill. It was supposed to be funny, but then we realised that it was a bit of a noose because it was saying that we were . . . not actually any good. It was a nice idea, but it was a bit too clever and actually it didn't really sell us.'

They had very few gigs under their belts before they were thrown into the miners' den. The learning curve was about as steep as it gets, but they survived. 'Some of the miners were lovely and some of them were not. They were dreadfully unreconstructed, very old-fashioned. I think Linda and I were mistaken for strippers a couple of times, or it was assumed that we were singers. What was strange for us was that everything stopped for the bingo, several times.'

As well as the inevitable bingo that Ann remembers so well, there were often interminable fundraising raffles at each show. These could last up to half an hour, but were a vital ingredient in the mix of traditional and 'new' entertainment. They were akin to that scene from the Ken Loach film *Raining Stones*, starring Ricky Tomlinson – one of the prizes always seemed to be a leg of lamb. When you're on strike rations, that's a bloody brilliant prize to win.

Some years later, Linda did a routine about raffles: 'The scourge of entertainment land – raffles. I hate a raffle. And when you do them for political organisations, like the SWP* – I did one in London for the SWP, really nice do – there was this raffle, a massive mega-raffle, which was like Live Aid or something. It just went on and on and on and on. There was a speaker for the raffle and a speaker against the raffle. And what gets me at these dos is the raffle prizes are not like a commercial raffle, where the goods are ordered in terms of how big a consumer item they are . . . like, first prize, mountain bike, fifth prize, nothing. That would be logical. In these dos the raffle prizes are organised in a triumph of optimism over what we know of human nature: "First prize – a pamphlet version of Trotsky's *Theory of Continuing Revolution* . . . in the Cyrillic alphabet. Fifth prize – a new car! And a trip to Brazil at carnival time!"'

The first gig on the Pit Stop Tour was Cortonwood, where we were very warmly received. 'We had the most wonderful nights,' Ann says. 'Massive halls, full of people, with lots of laughter, appreciation and applause; we had the feeling that we were doing something really good. It was an absolutely extraordinary experience. We'd turn up on a midweek evening at a miners' club with our strange alternative bill consisting of a socialist magician, Ian Saville, folk singer George Faux and Mark Hurst, the comedian (Mark Miwurdz as he was known then). A lot of the fun lay in

* Socialist Workers' Party

99

being in a band of travelling performers. I really enjoyed all of that. Games with the police – the sort of cat and mouse thing – it was all very exciting.

'I don't really know what the bemused miners and their families thought of us. We were certainly not the kind of acts they were used to. We were often told, "Whatever you do, don't swear, because the missus is in." We gave it our best shot.'

Some years later, Linda talked profanities with Alison Hurndall of the *Sheffield Star*. 'In life people swear – it is part of our language. Sometimes it can be very funny and nothing else will do. I have tried to take a swear word out of a joke and it just does not work. However, you have to be careful as, especially when you are nervous, it is easy to swear too much and that does not work either. You have to find the right "swearing level".'

Certainly the miners never complained. 'I think they would have preferred the normal line-up of bingo and singers,' says Ann, 'but they gave us the benefit of the doubt because we were there in support of their strike. And no matter how baffled they were by our performance, the evening ended on a high because Warren did the disco at the end of every night. "Solid As A Rock" by Ashford and Simpson always brought the house down.'

'Solid As A Rock' was our top tune, followed by Arthur Conley's 'Sweet Soul Music', 'Free Nelson Mandela' by The Specials, 'Relax' by Frankie Goes to Hollywood and 'Working in a Coal Mine' by Lee Dorsey. Politics were ever present, even at the disco. Usually this lent the evening a positive edge, but occasionally there was trouble. I'm thinking particularly of one occasion at Kiveton Park when a fight broke out between striking miners and those who had gone back to work.

For Ann and Linda, though – as Token Women, later to

be known as Tuff Lovers – there was the altogether separate problem of gender politics to contend with. It was hard enough that the world of stand-up was predominantly male. 'There was Jenny Lecoat, there was Jenny Eclair and probably some other Jenny, I suppose,' says Ann, who ultimately became disillusioned with the scene.

'How anybody can go round the country on their own doing these dreadful gigs is beyond me. They're fun and they're a good laugh, but they can be quite difficult and demoralising. You need transport – and where do you stay at night? You know, two girls . . . you needed to have another friend with you . . . and because very few women were doing comedy then, the audience weren't quite sure if they liked you or not. Still, it was good that we did it together, because it did help us both have a go at it.'

On the one hand there was chauvinism, and on the other radical feminism, which was every bit as intimidating. Ann remembers 'two ghastly gigs' that pretty much put her off stand-up for life. 'The second one was in Sheffield, at the Broomspring Centre. It was a benefit – and that was the bloody cheek of it. You're doing a benefit and you're not even getting any money and they just hate you. We were talking about more than just having boyfriends – but that would be in there too – and all they shouted out was, "TRY WOMEN! TRY WOMEN!" I think I was on first and then Linda, and by the time Linda was on it had all got completely ridiculous. We practically had to run for our lives.'

In the 1980s political lesbianism was a burning issue, and Leeds and Sheffield were on fire with it. Some extremists saw lesbianism as a logical conclusion to feminism. 'But I never thought it was a logical conclusion because I thought . . . well, I'm not a lesbian,' says Ann. 'I'd seen it at Greenham and that was partly why I left, because I thought it had all become ridiculous. The women there were not really unified and it was disintegrating into a war of who was the most oppressed. People donated money to Greenham and it was a case of, "I'm a working-class lesbian, so I should have more money." Then it was, "I'm a black lesbian, so I should have more money!" If you were not lesbian, you obviously were not as high up the needy – the good – list. And if you were a white middle-class heterosexual – well, you might as well slit your throat now.

'It was definitely a fevered time with the radical separatists and feminism. Unfortunately I think poor old Linda and I were a bit like lambs to the slaughter when we went anywhere those women had a foothold. It was hard because we were not really on that trip – we were not being radical feminists. We were having a bit of a pop at that really.'

Eventually Ann decided to head for London, where she temped for a while before embarking on a successful career in TV production. 'I didn't want to do it any more,' she says. 'Linda had more of a feel, a flair for stand-up than me, and that's what it boils down to. I didn't have the stomach to carry on with the hardness of it. Right from the beginning, Linda was a very clever, funny and slightly eccentric person – the way that she walked, the way she had that kind of intensity. When I say eccentric, I mean intensity. There was no artifice or pretence with Linda. It was absolutely what you saw was what you got. That, I think, was part of her talent. She didn't have to put on a persona. She didn't have to become someone else.'

Linda's new-age, stage boyfriend 'Clive' may not have gone down well with lesbian audiences, but he became increasingly popular everywhere else. Clive was a very welcome and timely dig at the dour face of 1980s feminism and the men on the left who allowed themselves to be emasculated by it. His origins lie partly in a book I bought in San Francisco back in 1980.

To this day I can't explain what actually motivated me to spend six dollars on this book, but it was probably the best six dollars I ever spent. My very tattered copy of *For Men Against Sexism* – a book of readings edited by Jon Snodgrass and published in 1977 – is an anthology that reflects the developing consciousness of men profoundly influenced by the women's liberation movement.

Suffice to say that this book could only have been published in the USA at that time. Such penetrating thoughts had not really been committed to print as yet in Britain, or not as far as I knew. Some of the chapter titles are blinding: 'The Socialized Penis'; 'Refusing to Be a Man'; 'Lovemaking with Myself'; if that lot doesn't make you yelp, there are further equally cringeworthy sub-headings.

But not long after my arrival in Sheffield in 1983, I was scouring a noticeboard in a wholefoods store when I came across an item about anti-sexist consciousness-raising groups for men. This was a fringe activity in London but it had spread its wings and reached uptown Sheffield. Soon after I met Linda, she visited my student digs and found *For Men Against Sexism* in my personal library. She was fascinated and alarmed by it in equal measures. I was filled with a mixture of pride and embarrassment. Was she thinking, 'What have we got here?' I was thinking, 'Am I a New Man? Am I on the way to becoming a New Man? Or do I reject this nonsense out of hand and therefore feel that there is no need to reform myself?' After all, I was a plain straight bloke on the left.

Before long, *For Men Against Sexism* left the shelf for a career on stage, becoming a much-treasured prop in Linda's comedy routine about anti-sexist men. Linda drew on another influence for Clive, according to Ben Lowe, the journalist who rented a room to Linda when she was going through her dark days after the end of the relationship with Brian. 'I was the source of much of Linda's material for Clive, an aspiring New Man, active in a far-left political sect, who failed miserably as a New Man and in particular in his relationships with women,' he recalls. 'I was centrally involved in the launch of *News on Sunday*, a short-lived radical Sunday newspaper. According to Linda, Clive loved the *News on Sunday*. He was its only regular reader.'

Wherever he came from, Clive was a winner at being a loser. Here's Linda on stage at the Sheffield Trades and Labour Club in 1985: 'It's driving me mad, the sex. He's into this non-penetrative sex these days. I'm sure there's a lot of women here who are familiar with this allegedly right-on concept of non-penetrative sex. He's been doing this non-penetrative thinking for quite a long time and it's sort of spread to his genitals now and I think it's a complete and utter rip-off – it's just another form of male self-enhancement. It's like, a sort of, "I don't even need to use my prick – my whole body is a prick." I said to him, "Clive, you're literally a dickhead." Another thing he's into is sharing periods with me. I'm sorry, any squeamish boys in the audience, you'll just have to grit your teeth for this bit. He's into it. I think that's fine. So every twenty-eight days I kick him in the guts and charge him over a quid for a box of cotton wool.'

7
The People's Theatre

Broomhill to Darnall, Sheffield

The pressures of living and working together as a couple meant that Linda and I were in dire need of our own space and our own place. However, it wasn't until nearly two years after we met that we finally found it in the form of a charming, if damp, top-floor flat in the delightful oasis of Summerfield in Broomhill. It was our first real home and we relished it.

We never discussed getting married; it just never came up. Neither of us was the marrying kind. But even if we had been conventional enough to tie the knot officially, there's no way I would have carried Linda over the threshold of our new home. It wouldn't have been viable – the flat was at the top of two steep flights of stairs and Linda was much bigger than I was. It would only have worked if she'd carried me.

We'd been homeless a couple of times before we moved to Summerfield, camping out at the houses of a few close friends while we tried to find somewhere halfway decent that we could afford. We had next to no money, so it wasn't easy. For a while we stayed with the poet Mark 'Miwurdz' Hurst and his mother, Kitty, at their home in Broomhall. At the time, Mark had sprung to national prominence as a regular on Channel Four's hit youth music programme, *The Tube*. Meanwhile Kitty was a legendary figure in Broomhall and could usually be found enjoying perfect contentment with her chums at The Hanover pub, her local retreat. We were indebted to them both for their kindness.

We shared a house with our friend and fellow SPT member Dave Humphreys for six months, but when the lease ran out and he moved back to London, we went back to viewing places we couldn't afford. It was very unsettling. It got to the point where the search for somewhere to call home was starting to feel never-ending. Then, Julie Pearn, Linda's great pal from university, heard through a friend about an upcoming vacancy at Summerfield flats, two fine-looking blocks of converted period houses on either side of a sweeping lawn and gardens – originally former homes of steel or engineering barons. Conveniently located in the heart of Broomhill on the west side of Sheffield, the complex was shielded from the street by tall trees and the grounds were beautifully tended by two very friendly caretakers, Ken and Andrea Barlow. The flat was small but the rent was reasonable. We crossed our fingers and hoped.

In the 1930s, John Betjeman described Broomhill as 'the most beautiful garden suburb in England'. By the 1980s this pretty-as-a-picture district had been inundated with thousands of university students, who completely dominated the local economy on the west side of Sheffield. It was all student accommodation, pubs and fast food joints. So I was startled when Broomhill was identified a few years ago as the highest-ranking area outside London for overall wealth. Our meagre wages were certainly not a contributory factor to this statistic when we were living there ten years earlier, that's for sure.

Before you were even in with a chance of renting a Summerfield flat, you had to be recommended to the owner, Mrs Julia Micklethwaite. Once your name was down and a vacancy came up, Mrs Micklethwaite would put you through a formal interview. It was not dissimilar to the screening process employed by the committee at the Dakota Building overlooking Central Park in New York, only this was Sheffield and Yoko Ono wasn't going to be one of your neighbours. Still, lots of arty types had migrated to Summerfield and I think the landlady was quite proud of her artistic colony.

While we waited for a vacancy to materialise, Julie and her partner Araya Reddah generously offered to take us in. It was fantastically kind of them. 'We shared our flat with Linda and Warren for some months,' says Araya. 'They were temporarily homeless and it was a great privilege to share our one-bedroom flat with them. They took the front sitting room as their bedroom and in the time they spent with us there was not a moment's tension. It just felt natural.'

Linda and I had spent a fair number of years living with other people, so we knew how to share space without annoying our housemates. The four of us got on very well and it was a happy and harmonious time, if a little cramped. Working at home wasn't easy, though, and our romantic life felt a bit constrained. We did our courting outside the house; it was like being teenagers again.

We had to wait some time for the flat, but it was worth it. Linda had moved four or five times since coming to Sheffield and it felt good to settle at last. It was the first time she'd been able to put her individual stamp on her surroundings, and she savoured the opportunity. One day, soon after we'd moved in, she arrived home in a state of excitement, 'Come round the corner, quick!'

'What is it?' I asked, slightly alarmed.

She took my hand and tugged me downstairs. About 250

yards from our flat, she'd spotted a skip in front of the local prep school. It was full of discarded furniture and fittings, the best thing by far being a lovely centre carpet with a dark red border and flowery pattern, the sort of thing you'd find in the headmaster's office. It fitted our front room perfectly. We also found some charming old furniture, which we bundled into the orange Bedford van before you could say, 'Stop! That stuff has been earmarked for a house clearance auction!' Linda was great at finding things for nothing, or next to nothing, in skips and charity shops, or at auction houses. Our biggest outlay went on curtains to fit the huge front bay window, partly to help insulate the freezing front room during the very long, cold Sheffield winters.

Nicky Cowan was the first real friend I made in Sheffield and she remains a good pal. We met in the silkscreen print shop of the Common Ground community resources centre on the Wicker in June 1983. Nicky was printing T-shirts to raise money for Eritrea and I was having a go at printing some posters for my first show in Sheffield, the Nicaragua benefit.

Nicky remembers our flat at Summerfield as having an air of gentility. 'It was very Linda. She had a taste for nice things generally, an eye for a second-hand bargain, particularly old china. She had pretty floral patterned plates and teacups, and an old-fashioned cake stand. Linda was definitely the only person I knew, apart from myself, who made tea in a pot, with tea leaves. She also had a penchant for cakes and for teashops that served traditional afternoon tea.' We used to joke about Linda's 'salon de thé'. When people came round, tea would often be a major component of a very stimulating occasion – not any old tea, but various brands of tea leaves in different teapots. Proper tea, no shortcuts.

The downside of our flat was dampness, very basic heating and old-fashioned fittings. But you would set aside your grumpiness – or as Linda would say, 'Mustn't grumble' – about the actual living conditions, because of the grandeur of the location. It was good looking, very convenient and you could park your motor outside your residence. First-time visitors were knocked out; they couldn't believe it.

We were a virtual motel for London-based comedians and theatre groups who stopped over with us if they had a gig in the city – either one of ours, or at Fools Paradise or the Leadmill. We should have kept a signing-in book for guests; it would fetch a few bob on eBay now. Jo Brand, Mark Steel, Jeremy Hardy, Mark Thomas, Phill Jupitus and Hattie Hayridge were among the guests and it wasn't unusual to find a comedian or three crashed out in the front room of a Saturday or Sunday morning. We could provide a mattress, a fold-out bed and cushions on the floor.

Linda loved playing hostess. She was a great entertainer off the stage, a natural party organiser and supreme caterer who loved to try out new recipes on our guests. She was brilliant at preparing for parties, from the smallest event, like an afternoon tea gathering, to a big after-show do. Skilled at setting the scene and getting the music, ambience, decoration and lighting right, she also took total charge of the cooking. If we had eight people round for a meal, she had that innate ability to keep the conversation going while making Cuban cocktails and keeping an eye on how the food was doing. She could be in three places at once, and would never desert her guests.

After some time on the top floor at Summerfield, we leapt at the chance to move into a ground-floor flat with a yard, which was a splendid place to have parties in good weather because we could spill out onto the lawn in front of the flat. Our new flat had large, light, airy rooms with decorative high ceilings. It was wonderful.

'The jazz sounds wafting at Linda and Warren's lunch parties at Summerfield were a new experience for me,' recalls Julie Pearn. 'It felt sophisticated, but at the same time completely comfortable. The parties were held in the afternoon out of consideration for friends who had children. They both loved children and it was quite natural to include them in our social life. I have happy memories of seeing in the New Year at Summerfield, our little boy playing happily in the corner.

'The food was always amazing. Linda and Warren introduced me to freshly made pesto sauce, and Linda's salads were especially distinctive, the pieces being made for giants. She had a particular thing about cucumber. Without the skin and thinly sliced, she found it repulsively slimy. Her answer was to cut it into huge, unpeeled chunks.'

Linda loved associating with people who had experiences far and wide. I'm sure this is partly because her upbringing was very parochial, almost claustrophobic. She was always meeting new people and coming across new interests, from African film to deep soul music. She was a great one for telling stories and anecdotes, and had an immaculate sense of timing, always picking up tales from other comics and retelling them in other settings.

However, there wasn't much time – or money – for partying when we moved into our first Summerfield flat, because the move coincided with the final rehearsal period of the 'Darnall People's Show', or 'East Side Story' as it became known. After six months of intensive research, recruitment, improvisation, writing and rehearsing, we were nearly ready to open the book on the story of the Sheffield Popular Theatre.

Work dominated our lives. It was a bit like running a small business. There was always something to do. The phone would ring, or someone would need picking up. It wasn't all we talked about, but it did consume a lot of our time. We worked a lot in the evenings, either rehearsing or performing, and much of our social life was wrapped up with work, although we also had many friends who had nothing to do with it.

Rehearsals for the show were held in the old-fashioned adult education centre, 'Star Works', in Darnall, situated in a set of former school buildings tended by redundant steel-workers Joe and Mick. The first time I went to look at our headquarters, I was staggered by the urban wilderness that surrounded it. Had Stanley Kubrick not chosen the tumble-down Beckton Gas Works in east London to shoot *Full Metal Jacket*, he could have filmed it there.

If Linda didn't walk across town to Darnall – and it was a long haul – she'd catch the 52 bus, which went door-to-door. But in lousy weather, or if she was in a hurry, she might take a perch on the front-bench seat of our company transport, the ubiquitous, ageing, orange Bedford crew bus.

Linda's knowledge of this patch of Sheffield, with its vast tracts of rubble where old terraced houses had once stood, was vital to our outfit in the early days. She knew all the local pubs, the peculiar opening hours (pegged to work shifts) of the fish and chip shop, the Pakistani restaurants, the Yemeni cafes where you could get the stimulant khat to chew on and so on. The homemade curries produced by local Pakistani women in the café across the playground were amongst the tastiest on offer in the city. At a pound a shot, they were a serious bonus in winter, when we were doing our best to look lively in the frozen rehearsal room or office.

I've already mentioned how we appealed in the local press and on the radio for memories of the old East End and volunteers to take part in the production. Mother of four Joy Palmer was one of our first recruits. Joy's experience of working as both a bus conductor and a cutlery worker was invaluable to the development of the show. Soon after she came on board, we were joined by former nurse and lone parent, Sylvia Jones. 'Sylvia was going to be the wardrobe lady, wasn't she?' Joy says. 'She was adamant that that's what she was going to do. We couldn't move her from that position, could we? And then when we started getting things together, I think she realised that she wanted to be more than that.'

The 90-minute show – trimmed down from more than two hours – depicted the rise and fall of the East End of Sheffield from 1926 until the mid-1980s. It traced the East End from the days when it boasted 37 pits and a thriving steel industry to the onset of government rate capping in the early 1980s. En route it took in the 1930s Depression, the rock-and-roll era of the 1950s and the decline of steel in the late 1970s. It comprised a series of sketches and monologues with poetry, songs, dance and back-projected slides, all linked by a reminiscing narrator.

One day at Darnall Library I came across what at first sight appeared to be vital background material for the show. I had been a compulsive scanner of local noticeboards ever since my days as a cub newspaper reporter, and as luck would have it, among the notices on the wall of the library was an amazing poem written in Sheffield dialect about the Attercliffe of old. Alison Grimshaw, the branch librarian, gave me a copy and I took it to show Linda and Joy. We thought it was just fantastic. The mission was on to find the person behind the words.

Joy recognised the signature of Walt Revell, who had written out the poem in beautiful calligraphy. She put me in touch with him and he gave me the address of the poem's author, one Margaret Barraclough, a sixty-one-year-old retired steelworks crane driver. Little knowing the massive impact she would turn out to have on our lives, I went to meet her at her old-fashioned council house in Woodhouse, at the end of the 52 bus route.

Five foot tall and stocky, with bright, glinting eyes, there was still much evidence in Margaret Barraclough of the tap-dancing champion acrobat she had been as a child. She was a born entertainer and had boundless energy. Had her family not been so grindingly poor – she spent time with her mother in the Sheffield workhouse – she might easily have earned a living out of show business. Instead she went into the steelworks for forty years.

Margaret later told the *Sheffield Star*, 'When I retired five years ago I was looking forward to putting my feet up, taking the dogs out and going to bingo – until Warren came along.' Margaret threw all her energies in to helping SPT get off the ground and become the success story it was, but she still found time to walk the dogs, feed cats in the steelworks, 'clean up' at the bingo halls and lead life to the full with her good-looking husband, Billy. The only activity that had to be abandoned was putting her feet up. A wonderful story-teller, writer and on-stage comic improviser, she went on to narrate the show.

It soon became apparent to everyone – in particular to Linda and me – that we were in the presence of someone very special. Margaret could turn her hand to anything. Off-stage she was writing rhyming verse, comic and tragic sketches and, crucially, the narration, which provided the backbone of the show. On stage she was a ball of fire, igniting the action around her. She stood out as a performer, as a solo commentator and in an ensemble of players, and her off-the-cuff remarks often found their way into the following week's script. She sang in harmony, and even stopped the show as a tap dancer. It was one of those seeing-is-believing occasions, replayed nearly every week for two years.

Linda and Margaret developed a formidable bond. It was a classic director and lead actor relationship, except that Margaret brought her writing skills to the party too. What a bonus. Joy and Sylvia also emerged from the ranks of 'East Side Story' and demonstrated huge stage presence. They could sing, held strong political views and, most importantly, like Margaret they could be very funny on stage. Margaret's epic poem, a eulogy to Attercliffe, where she was brought up and toiled most of her life, became the centrepiece of 'East Side Story' and was requested wherever she went.

'The Death of a District' by Margaret Barraclough

Oh Attercliffe, dear Attercliffe, what 'ave they done to thee?
It breaks my 'eart to see 'er after what she used to be.
From Weshford Bridge to Weedon Street 'er arms were open wide;
She sheltered an' protected us from t' rest o' t' world ahtside.
She 'ad a gret big thumpin' 'eart that everybody felt;
We luvved 'er an' she luvved us back na matter we'er we dwelt.

Remember on t'Cliffe on a Satdy? Thad meet
Dozens o' people tha knew
An' stand laughin' an' jokin' until
tha remembered abaht shoppin' thad promised to do.
If ye dint live down theer then you'll not understand
What the warmth o' these people wa worth;
They dint mek no fuss or use fancy words;
But tha knew, they wer't' salt o' the earth.
If ya a'nt got much money ya dint 'ave to fret;
This allas be summat thad manage to get.
Shopkeepers wer' great an' so understandin';
They knew thad a struggle to pay;
Sometimes the'd seh, 'Tek it owd luv and pay me next week,
I know thall not run away.'
God bless 'em an' keep 'em, they wer' all worth their weight;
Wee aht their 'elp, lots o' kids 'ad 'ave 'ad now't to eyt.
Remember t'owd Attercliffe Palace,
Thid tell jokes an' thid dance an' thid sing;
An' if tha got sat at back o' them pillars,
Thad 'ad it, tha cudn't see a thing.
Remember an' all, all the fun that we'd have
In the Regal, the 'Delph', the Globe an' the Pav;
We dint need no nightclubs, and fancy cafés,
Wid cum aht o't' pictures an' 'ave pie an' pehs.
If tha wanted a pub crawl, an tha could afford,
Thi were pubs ev'ry few yahds on each side o't' roord.
On Saturday nights, the streets would erupt
Foorks sed it were all that stones bitter thi supped.
Yed see 'em go 'aht, lookin' spotless an' neat;
Then cum in black an' bleeding thru feightin' in t'street.
Dear friend I can see, there's a tear in your eye;

Then ya must be from theer like me.
Thiv torn aht that gret thumpin' 'eart that we knew,
An' whose luv we 'ad shared so free.
Na don't get me wrong. We all wanted to move,
The soot an' the grime made life 'ahd.
An' the clouds o' red dust that ed blot out the sun,
An' then settle on t' washin' in t' yard.
We wanted 'ouse wi a gahden an' bath an' fresh air
In us lungs, nothin' moor ('cept for a lavvy in t'ouse,
an' 'ot watter in t' tap an' a few dozen roses round t'door.)
Now that big dirty beast lies theer dyin',
But ya won't 'ear us givin' three cheers,
'Cos we luvved 'er an' we'd like to thank 'er
For all o' those wonderful years.
O we'll miss ya, owd luv, for the rest of our lives
And many's the time that we'll sigh –
Wi got our nice 'ouse wit' 'ot watter in t' tap
But was the price that we paid too high?

'East Side Story' developed through improvisation and writing, informed by in-depth research and interviews. The show was researched, devised and written by the cast under the direction of Linda Smith; ages ranged from 15 to 72, and included six senior citizens. Linda was crucial to shaping the show, injecting discipline into the contributions and storyline and bringing the best out of the cast. 'The cast took over completely and for the first time I got a glimpse of what theatre should be all about,' said Linda.

The first performances featured teenagers from Waltheof Comprehensive School on the Manor estate, recreating the notorious gang wars that were a feature of the 1920s in the east of the city. It was a bit 'Bugsy Malone' but it worked for a while and then became untenable because the kids couldn't get released from the school timetable.

A wonderful feature of 'East Side Story' was its incidental audience participation. It was a joy to hear people mutter in recognition of Margaret's narrative, or sing heartily along to the popular songs. I should add that yours truly played the role of a communist clergyman preaching anarchy and singing 'The Red Flag' from his soapbox with great gusto, before being dragged away by a policeman.

The show leant heavily on the imagined biographies of several characters from the area who were known and recognised throughout the city – 'Long Sammy', the sandwich board man; the 'Duke of Darnall', a deaf mute and dapper dresser who frequently disrupted traffic with his mime displays; and 'Russian Edna', a prostitute who was murdered in 1954. I remember at one show at Darnall Community Centre, an elderly gent in a wheelchair shouted out, 'I've been with her!' Needless to say, this brought the house down and temporarily stopped the show in its tracks. The entire audience and cast were convulsed for several minutes.

The show opened on 5 May 1985 at the modern, single-story Darnall Library. Full-house signs had gone up, the local audience and invited guests arrived in a state of excitement and expectation, and the cast were even more geed up. Linda had met them earlier to put them through their paces, have the proverbial team tactics talk for those who had the sense to listen, and to try to solve a dozen technical hitches with me. The onus was on her to steady nerves in the suffocating dressing room, which just hours before had been a very tranquil staff room. We were as ready as we would ever be. Linda took a deep breath and declared proceedings should begin as soon as Margaret was sitting comfortably on her 'people's throne'. We were off and running. Linda was about to earn her first stripe as a professional director and animateur.

Stephen McClarence of the *Sheffield Star*, now a distinguished travel writer for national newspapers, reviewed the show in his very individualistic style, with the headline 'World Exclusive!'

It was a glittery, celebrity sort of do, what with Mr Mayor in his chain in the front row, and Mrs Mayor in her pastel-flowered hat next to him, and Sheffield's pop poet, Mark Miwurdz, in his braces behind him.

A hundred of us were shoehorned into the library for 'East Side Story, The Darnall People's Show' – the living-memory history of the fall and fall of Attercliffe and Darnall, researched and enacted by the new-wave nostalgists of Sheffield Popular Theatre.

. . . Real community theatre all this, on the 'There weren't half some carrying-on' tack. Slides of the Blitz, air-raid sirens, the night they bombed Marples, 'Run Rabbit Run' sing-alongs, taking your best suit to the pop-shop, the rats nibbling Beryl Reid's knickers at the Attercliffe Palace . . . 'Oooh, it's very true isn't it?' says the old lady next to me, billing and cooing every time they mention High Hazels Park, and tut-tutting lavishly when Russian Edna the prostitute ambles on.

'Is she from Darnall?' asks the man behind me, as Bessie Ridge, one of the pensioners in the cast, starts her song 'Oh yes, just up the road.' All well and nostalgically good . . . and from there it's downhill into the glum political present and Thatcher-bashing and 'the lip-service support' Len Murray and Norman Willis gave the miners . . .

. . . and out we go into the Darnall tea-time, and Mr
Mayor's Rolls-Royce pulls round. 'Oooh,' says a man
in a cap to his wife. 'We've come out before the Lord
Mayor. Shouldn't have done that.' Mark Miwurdz heads
for the 52 bus back into town. 'Sat behind the Mayor,'
he says. 'Dead good.'

The show was so successful that it created a public library
circuit and toured for two years, breaking new ground in
establishing libraries as venues for community theatre. It went
to West Yorkshire several times, to Manchester and Nottinghamshire. The late entertainer and BBC Radio Sheffield icon
Tony Capstick described it as 'Sheffield's answer to *The
Mousetrap*'. Surely there's no greater accolade.

We used to charge a nominal booking fee of £50 so it
was free to the audience – and the proceeds went into a cast
kitty that was paid out at the end of each season in our
equivalent of a Co-op dividend. To help make ends meet,
Linda and I went on the much-vaunted Enterprise Allowance
Scheme, which was made available to encourage people to
sign off and go into self-employment. The star attraction
of the EAS was a guaranteed £40 a week for a year. The
only catch was that applicants needed to prove they had
£1,000 to invest into a new business. We raided our savings
and borrowed some cash so we could show we had the
resources to sustain ourselves and make the necessary investment. This scheme was the making of us. We were firmly
off the dole and could earn fees legitimately.

Linda registered as a writer/performer and I put myself
down as a theatre producer and events promoter. We got
under the bar. We were never going to get rich this way, but
we weren't going to starve. For Linda, who had never had

any money, it provided a delicious, if temporary security. As for me, I'd experienced what it was like to earn a regular wage, but was prepared to forgo that luxury because I loved what we were doing. We both did. They were blissfully happy times; my fondest years ever.

Linda aged one, in a doll's outfit.

Outside Riverdale Road, Erith, with her mother Bessie – note how few cars there are.

Shaking hands with a shy-looking dog.

On holiday in Devon with her parents, Bessie and Ray.

Linda, aged five, playing gooseberry with sister Barbara and brother-in-law Terry, in a speedboat off the Kent coast.

Barbara's wedding with Linda as a bridesmaid, second from the left.

A very rare short haircut for Linda.

Linda, aged seven, on holiday in the Isle of Wight, with her mum Bessie.

Family holiday with her father's side of the family – from left, Auntie Linda, Granny Smith, Bessie and Ray.

Lessness Heath Junior School – Linda aged nine, top row furthest right.

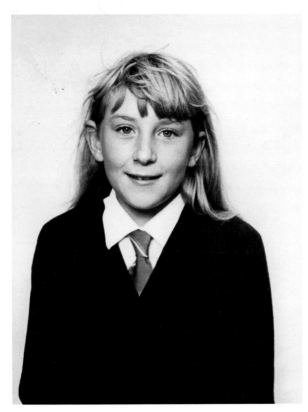

Aged eleven, Bexleyheath
Secondary School.

Erith College of Technology, 1977 – with the cast of *The Real Inspector Hound*.

With her close friend Celia Woolfrey, backstage at the Sheffield University production of *Taming of the Shrew*.

Sheffield University, 1981: Production of *The Taming of the Shrew*: Linda played the father partly due to her height.

With her stand-up partner
Ann Lavelle, overlooking
Sheffield, 1985.

'Coal Not Dole', 1985 – on the beach at Ingoldmels, Lincolnshire with the Fitzpatricks.

Linda with her mum and Auntie Helen on holiday in Devon, 1989 – one of the last photos of these three together, as Bessie died three years later.

8

A Chuffin' History of The Chuffinelles

We will start with a definition of the term 'chuff'.

CHUFF: n. An unrefined, rude, insensitive person, a boor, a vulgarian. Etymology: Middle English chuffe. (Your Dictionary.com)

CHUFF: n. A noisy puffing or explosive sound, such as one made by a locomotive. (thefreedictionary.com)

CHUFFED: adj. Very excited, very pleased, very proud of/about something. (Yorkshire-English phrase book)

CHUFFINESS: n. The quality of being chuffy. (thefree dictionary.com)

CHUFF: Around South Yorkshire the dialect term 'chuff' is really a euphemism for 'F . . .' and a common expletive among older people who would prefer using any word other than the f-word, and so you get 'chuff off' or 'you chuffin' . . .' and inevitably 'chuffin' hell'. (Thanks to pinguicula.typepad.com)

CHUFFOGRAPHY: n. Used for the one and only time by The Chuffinelles for the title of their cabaret show, 'A Chuffography of the World'.

The name Chuffinelles was coined by Linda Smith and myself and was inspired by the frequent use of the expression 'chuffin 'ell' by our friend and activist Denise Fitzpatrick. I'll let The Chuffinelles introduce themselves:

> You're expecting three young dollies.
> But you've got 1930s follies.
> We make the Roly Polys look like Fred Astaire.
> And compared to us, Worzel Gummidge is debonair.

Confused? Well, the story begins with Linda, in the role of Dr Frankenstein in her 'laboratory of theatre', experimenting with the raw talents of Margaret 'Mags' Barraclough, Joy Palmer and Sylvia Jones. Linda put them together in an 'East Side Story' sketch that became known as 'Women at Work'. The result was pure alchemy.

Partly based on Margaret's experiences on the shop floor of the steelworks during the Second World War, as well as Joy's and Sylvia's stories of time spent in various blue-collar jobs, 'Women at Work' was one of the strongest sections of the show. It soon struck Linda and me that Mags, Joy and Sylvia had the will and wherewithal to begin the climb up the greasy pole of show business.

Linda was the creative 'midwife' of The Chuffinelles, known from this point on as The Chuffs. Indeed, this unlikely threesome often referred to her affectionately as 'our mum'. It didn't matter that she was a twenty-seven-year-old in her first professional job. As well as being the mastermind behind The Chuffs, her role was to nurture. Drawing on her many skills, she helped propel a trio of local SPT performers into the national arena. They went on to become the most talked-about women's comedy group of late 1980s Britain. As one

Sheffield journalist wrote, 'What makes them a bit more unusual in the current comedy world is that they are not male, not young, not university-educated and not middle-class.'

'Women at Work' turned out to be one of the most popular sections of 'East Side Story'. There was nothing nostalgic about it. It was very hard-hitting, striking a blow for health and safety and conditions for women in the workplace. These were major issues, so it's no surprise that the sketch gave rise to the idea of doing a whole show about women's experiences in employment. There was plenty of real-life material to draw on. After all, a few years before we met her, Margaret had suffered a near-fatal brain haemorrhage, which was blamed on decades of inhaling factory fumes. She knew all about health and chuffin' safety in the workplace.

The show that grew out of such experiences was 'Gerrin' Worked Up!'. It was an instant success for The Chuffs, who were fronted by Mags Barraclough in the same way as Diana Ross fronted The Supremes. Linda worked with them to develop their range and stretch them artistically, always looking for opportunities to try out new material. As soon as a piece was freshly minted in the rehearsal hall, it was ready to try out on an unsuspecting public. This build-up process continued until a full 60-minute show was ready to unveil to an audience at Darnall Library in 1986. The Chuffs' first promotional leaflet urges potential bookers to 'clock on with The Chuffinelles as they go wild in the crazy world of low pay, health and chuffin' safety, sexual harassment . . . and come out spittin' coloured lights.'

The critics loved it. Bill Harpe of the *Guardian* wrote that 'they address the issues of today with zest, good humour and down-to-earth directness.' The popularity of 'Gerrin' Worked Up!' created a snowball effect around Britain, with arts bookers and women's and trade union organisations requesting a return visit the moment a new show was available. Demand was for a more cabaret-style performance and this proved to be right up Linda's street. In due course, 'Three Go Mad – in Yorkshire!' was delivered off the production line.

In the early years of The Chuffs I arranged all the bookings and tours. More often than not, I was driver and technician too. Until Joy learnt to drive, Margaret was the only driver of the three, and it was considered too demanding for her to do a show and drive there and back in the same day. We used the orange Bedford van for local touring, but it was deemed too uncomfortable for out-of-town journeys. A car was required, which often meant doing a discount deal with a dodgy local car hire firm. But then our friend and all-round good fella Andy Shallice offered us his old car when he bought a new one. We just had to accept this kind gesture. There was only one potential drawback – Andy was the proud owner of a Skoda.

This was a couple of years before the dismantling of the Berlin Wall, so we were still in a period when the mere mention of the brand name Skoda would bring forth guffaws from the gallery. No one in their right mind would be seen driving a Skoda, or a Lada, for that matter. They were a laughing stock. Time to welcome on stage the comedy car from hell! This slightly rusty, lemon-yellow four-door saloon had definitely seen better days, but it was The Chuffs' conveyance during their rise to the top. We grew used to being the centre of attention – a silly car carrying a motley crew.

That car was miraculous and somehow took our combined weight, plus a trunk full of props. Sure, it broke down – often around Junction 29 of the M1, at the turn-off for

Chesterfield. We had a lot of fun and games with all the AA patrolmen who invariably gave up trying to fix it and had us carted home on the back of a lorry.

It would be accurate to say that every outing with The Chuffs had its fair share of laughter and drama. On the last leg of one long return journey, at about two o'clock on a Sunday morning, I was within five minutes of making it to our front door when a police patrol car flashed its lights behind me. The cops made me open up the boot, which contained a collection of very lifelike toy pigeons, eccentric costumes, plastic police helmets, truncheons and – wait for it – a set of replica machine guns. The officers collapsed in fits of laughter. What a story to tell down the station at the end of the shift. I thought, 'Play it straight; tell them about The Chuffs and what we do.' They loved it. They sent me on my way with this concerned valediction: 'Now then, get yourself 'ome, pal. Get some kip. You'll need it if you've got those women to deal with.'

As the legend of The Chuffs began to spread, promoters south of the Watford Gap started to cotton on and book them. They became regulars in London, playing the New Variety venues at Brixton, Wood Green and Cricklewood with the likes of Rob Newman, Attila the Stockbroker and Jo Brand. They went down a storm at the glorious Hackney Empire Theatre, sharing the bill at two packed-out benefits for the London Rape Crisis Centre and International Women's Day, alongside many well-known comedy and cabaret circuit regulars.

The Chuffs had already developed a big following among women, but were also becoming the darlings of the politically active within the lesbian and gay movement. There were a few women-only events where I had to perform my duties as technician behind a curtain, so as not to be seen by The Chuffs' adoring female fans. In a non-theatre space without the attendant technology, this would require quite a bit of guesswork. I could hear, but could not see, so I had to rely on sound cues, which could be a bit approximate. No one seemed to notice, however. The whole show tended to lapse into slapstick mode at the drop of a top hat, anyway. It was very natural and spontaneous, and however unpredictable and uneven it was in parts, the audiences accepted and loved it. The Chuffs' third Hackney Empire gig was 'The Closet's Concert Party', promoted by the all-women production company Twentieth-Century Vixen. Hosted by Lily Savage and featuring the multiple talents of Ian Shaw, Simon Fanshawe, Donna McPhail and Julie McNamara, it was 'a celebration to counter the effects of Section 28'. Section 28, you may remember, was the controversial government amendment that forbade the 'promotion of homosexuality'.

So off we go to big bad London, with The Chuffs squeezed into the back seats, long-legged Linda cramped in the front and me at the wheel. There would be the obligatory stop or stops at motorway services – Leicester Forest East or Watford Gap – depending on the copious amount of tea drunk. It was always an ordeal, punctuated by much hilarity, occasional practical jokes and threats to leave certain individuals behind.

We used to laugh at people's reactions to seeing us decant from the Skoda. What must they have thought as they saw this incongruous group clamber to their feet and shake themselves down on the services forecourt, before preparing to enter the realm of 'Bernie Deathburger', which was the title of a Chuffs ditty dedicated to uncaring bosses of fast-food outlets? To the outside world we must have looked like a dysfunctional family group on a Sunday-afternoon outing.

Perhaps we were two daughters, a granddaughter and her boyfriend taking Gran for tea? The Chuffs, encouraged by mischievous Margaret, would sometimes suggest to strangers, or even venue staff, that I was their pimp.

On the approach to east London, it occurred to me that I should give a potted history of Ian McKellen, so as to avoid any awkward or embarrassing moments when we arrived at the Hackney Empire and were introduced to him. He was very much the man of the moment, a big figure in the arts world who was outspoken about the Section 28 issue. He had actually come out to the general public in a programme on BBC Radio Three, where he debated Section 28 with the conservative journalist Peregrine Worsthorne.

So I explained that he was considered to be one of the great Shakespearian actors of the day, alongside Derek Jacobi and Antony Sher. Silence and then murmurings in the back. It was obvious from their collective reaction that this didn't really register large on The Chuffs' radar. It was a few years before McKellen had begun to establish himself as a screen actor – a decade before his appearance in *Gods and Monsters* and even longer before the role of Gandalf in *Lord of the Rings* catapulted him to global fame. So it's not surprising that The Chuffs didn't know who he was.

Cut to the stage of the Hackney Empire. There we were, the Sheffield posse, chit-chatting away to Ian McKellen like old friends. He made a point of stressing his northern roots, and talked about growing up in Wigan. Linda and I were all a-tremble, but not The Chuffs – not a nerve in their bodies and completely unfazed about meeting a representative of high culture. They were more worried about mislaying a hair-slide backstage. But he was very charming, The Chuffs were charmed, and they too had made a brand-new fan. I remember him telling Linda that the prospect of doing stand-up comedy, all alone on stage with just a microphone as a friend, was the scariest prospect he could imagine, a view-point that has been reiterated to us over the years by some other very distinguished stage actors.

The Chuffs' second show, 'Three Go Mad!', had two sold-out nights at the Crucible Theatre studio in September 1987, as part of the Sheffield Festival. But it was formally launched a few weeks later at Darnall Horticultural Club, when director Linda Smith told the *Sheffield Star*, 'Bits of it get written down on the backs of bingo cards and 10p jotters and we always have to bear in mind that whatever props and costumes we use, the show has to fit into a Skoda, with us in it.'

The out-and-out cabaret format was perfect for The Chuffs. Linda had put them on track stylistically and they stuck to their winning formula. By this stage they were getting a lot of bookings, including prestigious literature festivals at Cheltenham and Ilkley, where the festival director of the latter wrote and told us that The Chuffs were the most popular act of the festival. This was at the height of Thatcher-bashing and The Chuffs' raw energy and uncom-promising stance, plus the fact that they were outrageously funny, made comrade Ben Elton seem a pussycat. For exam-ple, there was the unforgettable Edwina Currie Song:

(Sung to the tune of 'On Ilkley Moor baht 'at')

> What did Edwina say in't Mail? (Daily Mail)
> Say in't Mail
> What did Edwina say in't Mail?
> What did Edwina say in't Mail?
> Say in't Mail

What did Edwina say in't Mail?
We northerners are thick
We northerners are fat
We're thick and chuffin' fat
Silly prat

What do we thick fat buggers eat?
Buggers eat
What do we thick fat buggers eat?
What do we thick fat buggers eat?
Buggers eat
What do we stupid bastards eat?
We're always eating chips
We're always eating chips
We're always eating chips Aye!
And sometimes crisps

When we're not stuffin' our fat gobs
Our fat gobs
What do we thick fat chuffs do?
When we're not stuffin' our fat gobs
Our fat gobs
What do we thick fat chuffs do?
We're always drinking beer
We're always drinking beer
And smoking lots of fags
Silly bags

With 'East Side Story' under way and touring, and once Linda had moulded The Chuffs into a group with a show of their own, it was time to get to grips with our next SPT production. We found a story that we thought would blend local history with international relations and connect with the approaching 50th anniversary of the start of the Spanish Civil War in June 1936.

We asked our friends at Yorkshire Arts Circus in West Yorkshire for permission to adapt their publication, *Tommy James: a Lion of a Man*, by Brian Lewis and Bill Gledhill. It told the story of a leading activist in the South Yorkshire Labour movement, Tommy James, and dramatised his account of his time in Spain with the International Brigades. Once we received the go-ahead to adapt it, we could introduce our new trump card in the form of actor and director Mike McCarthy, with whom I had worked at the Harlow Playhouse Theatre in Essex. Although he hadn't acted for several years, Mike was lined up to take the lead role of Tommy James in an ensemble piece, 'Deepest Red', flanked by Margaret and Sylvia. He was the first professional on stage in one of our locally produced shows. We were aiming to rehearse 'Deepest Red' in April and May and start performing it in June. What with their performance commitments to 'East Side Story' and The Chuffinelles, this meant that Mags and Sylvia were handling three shows simultaneously.

Research, writing and rehearsals started as soon as Mike arrived. 'It was Linda who pulled it together and made it all work,' he says. 'She was the outside eye and she had a really light touch. She didn't impose stuff, which was great and really liberating. It was quite an instinctive and intuitive way of working: "Try this," or, "Why don't we do that?" She could also be quite strong when she needed to be.

'Some directors could be demanding in the wrong way, but with "Deepest Red" it felt as though we were all involved in searching for a way to do it. Linda was good at coaxing Margaret and Sylvia and bringing the best out of them.

They responded very well. There were no concessions made to them; they had to submit to a very rigorous process. It was quite an intensive period of rehearsals, but we got through it.'

This was a coming of age for SPT. We were proving we could put out a professional production and seek a proper fee for it. It was a big breakthrough. 'Absolutely Attercliffe' was the next model to roll off the production line. A sequel to 'East Side Story', it set the weekend adventures of a group of people in Sheffield against the international events of 1956. This was the year Elvis Presley rocked Britain, tanks rolled into Hungary and paratroopers landed in Suez. In Sheffield, it was a time when Caribbean, African, Arabic and Asian people were arriving to settle in the city. Jobs were plentiful, expectations high and leisure booming. People wanted a good night out on a Saturday; they went dancing to the sounds of rock 'n' roll, rhythm and blues, skiffle, trad jazz and the dance bands. The hook was the dance hall in Attercliffe. The politics centred on the Asians and Africans coming to work in the steelworks. It was an attempt to tell a story that would not necessarily be accepted, a challenge to the white working-class hegemony.

I did all the interviews and research for 'Absolutely Attercliffe', unearthing a lot of rich information along the way. Then we wrote up the interviews and began to develop scenes from them. Next we needed to recruit an entirely new cast. This was the real challenge. Could we do it all over again?

Fortunately, we found some amazing people. Following in Sylvia Jones's and Joy Palmer's footsteps came Chris Percival and Dawn Chappell. They were brilliant at managing time, managing family and making sacrifices to do the show. Chris, like Sylvia Jones before her, was a lone parent. Nowadays she is directing an annual community theatre show in Waterthorpe, Sheffield.

The cast got on really well. They were captivated by the material and the idea of recreating the past. People went away to talk to the different generations in their families and communities, which produced a lot of good stories from the period that we could build scenes around.

Mike and Linda worked together as joint directors of the show. 'I was a bit nervous going into it, but actually it worked really well,' Mike says. 'I've tried to analyse it and I think the reason it did work is that I'm quite a big picture person, quite strong on structure and how things hang together. Whereas Linda was much better than me on detail and that brought a real richness to the show. That combination of the big picture and the little picture worked incredibly well.'

Mike remembers Linda having an almost obsessive attention to detail and a passion for authenticity. She would arrive at rehearsals at Darnall Medical Aid Hall with bags full of props and costumes all sourced from a grand tour of Sheffield's charity shops. Determined to get it right – near enough wouldn't do – she tracked down a genuine 1950s feather hat, the perfect floral apron and the most authentically dented tin bath. The whole process, from advertising for a cast to curtain up, took around six months. Remaining loyal to Darnall, we premiered the show at the library there on 14 May 1987. It ran for three seasons and played to packed houses on our libraries circuit, earning plaudits when it appeared for two nights at the Crucible Theatre studio as part of the Sheffield Festival. It became our showpiece, a production that encompassed all ages, was multiracial, drawn from local communities and genuine Sheffield through and through. No one had managed that before. It gave us a real glow.

By now, Linda was spinning several plates – the SPT productions, The Chuffs and her stand-up work. As the stand-up work began to claim more of her time and take her away from Sheffield, Mike started stepping in to take sessions with The Chuffs when she wasn't around. 'She was lead director; I was almost co-director,' he says. 'It was quite a conscious thing. If The Chuffs were going to continue, I had to be drafted in, because it was too much for Linda.

'What I couldn't do, because I wasn't as skilled at it, was generate material with them. That was Linda's forte. She was brilliant at spotting a good idea and building new content with it. Their shows contained a lot of her creativity and material. Although she drew on their raw materials and talent, she was at the heart of the comedy and the comic creation of The Chuffs. Without her, it would never have happened. She knew in the rehearsal process what was working and what wasn't working, and without that they might have done stuff that wasn't very good. She provided that edge.'

In the eight years that The Chuffs existed – between 1986 and 1994 – Linda directed their first two shows ('Gerrin' Worked Up!' and 'Three Go Mad!') – and then remained firmly on the sidelines for the four shows that followed under the direction of either Mike McCarthy or Kate Rutter: 'Too Hot to Handle', 'A Chuffography of the World', 'The Greatest Hits' and 'Life's a Scream'.

The Chuffs were always a trio, with Margaret and Joy as the constants. Sylvia left after the first two shows and the role of third Chuff was filled by Lorraine Gedge, Jane Ashley and Chris Percival. Chris was the only one of those three

women who graduated through the ranks of Sheffield Popular Theatre and was a protégé of Linda and Mike, having been in several of the group's touring productions.

The Chuffs are now an established part of South Yorkshire folklore. Not a bad legacy for a woman from south-east London to leave behind. Their success prompted Linda to write in a birthday card to Mags: 'To Margaret Barraclough, you might be the star of stage, screen and radio, but you're not getting much fuckin' dusting done.'

9

It's Funny Up North!

Sheffield to the Bury Met Arts Centre

Q: At what point did you realise a career in comedy was
   for you?
Linda: When I found out that all the really cushy jobs in
   this country are hereditary. Where's the incentive?
Q: And what was your plan B?
Linda: With a combination of kidnap and self-mutilation,
   to live my life posing as the Duke of Westminster. And I
   would have got away with it too . . .

Venue magazine, Bristol

Linda on the existence of an audience: 'You are the
difference between a performance and an affliction.'

When Claire and Roland Muldoon invited Linda to enter
the Hackney Empire New Act of the Year competition in
the spring of 1987, she performed a brilliant, polished set.
My former colleagues had rescued the Hackney Empire from
a dire fate as a failing Mecca bingo hall, and it was now at
the centre of the alternative comedy boom. They had booked
Linda and Ann Lavelle – Tuff Lovers – for New Variety, and
were intrigued to hear that Linda was now working solo.
She went down a storm. Although she came a close second
to an act called The Two Marks, *City Limits* magazine voted
her 'Top New Comedian of 1987'. It was a watershed

moment, Linda realised. It was time for her to step away from community theatre and directing, and put comedy first. She leapt eagerly into the precarious, peripatetic male-dominated world of stand-up comedy. As she told Oliver Double, a fellow Sheffield comic, in 1989: 'I had been dithering about for ages, keeping up the writing and directing and doing stand-up half of the time and kidding myself that you can do it. But you can't, and the difference is so enormous. Since I said, "Well actually, this is all I do," the difference is immense. So it's almost like I've started again. The main difference is in your head. You perceive yourself as a comedian. You live the life. You are totally concentrated on it. You are not distracted. And it's the only way, I realise now. You drive yourself mad trying to do other things.'

As Linda was lured towards the world of stand-up comedy, Sheffield Popular Theatre became Sheffield Popular Productions, which begat Popular Productions. The famed production line kept rolling on and releasing shows like 'Attercliffe or Bust' 'Brandon' and 'Rip It Up!' onto local, regional and national stages. And the Darnall 'academy' kept producing new faces to adorn those canvases.

It wasn't easy losing Linda from SPT, but there was a sense of inevitability about it. Although she remained an active supporter of SPT, she was often away on the road. Mike and I brought in Janet Bray, who had first met Linda at university. Janet became part of the team and worked with Mike on the community productions and one of the touring shows.

I missed Linda when she was away, but we were grown-ups – I knew she had to do it. It wasn't like I didn't understand what the touring life required. When it worked out – usually at weekends – I'd take her to her shows. If I couldn't take her, she'd go on the train. She loved trains. They were where she did her reading, a lot of thinking and some of her writing.

The period between 1988 and 1993 was the golden age of the independent comedy promoter in the north and the Midlands – a time when many of comedy's current big-name artists were playing smaller venues and agents didn't wield so much power. Back then, Jongleurs Comedy Club was specific to Battersea in south-west London; it wasn't the brand name of a dominant chain of comedy clubs that now tower over the scene in towns and cities beyond the M25. There was already an established London circuit. But now comedy and variety acts from Birmingham northwards were also developing a circuit of pubs, clubs and arts centres, where from time to time southerners were also allowed a chance to prove themselves. It was in these venues that Linda forged her comedy.

At the time, Mark 'Miwurdz' Hurst was seen as the main man of the new northern comedy circuit. Mark broke new ground as a wordsmith and made it possible for a lot of other acts to follow. The other person who was doing the same thing in his own style was John Cooper Clarke – the Bard of Salford – who broke through the music scene in Manchester several years earlier. Linda admired them both and was pleased to count them among her friends. 'I like someone who is a human being up on stage, like Mark Miwurdz, someone you can warm to and not be battered into the ground by,' she told Oliver Double.

Some of the northern comics stayed away from London; they enjoyed being large fish in a smallish pond. But London held no such fear for Linda. As a southerner, her personal challenge was to be accepted in the north. London could wait. A major difference between the north and the south was the variety of acts punters got for their money. London tended to accentuate stand-up, whereas a lot of club bookers elsewhere liked to mix things up and have music, poetry and visual comedy represented on the same bill. This was the same principle that brought recognition to New Variety in London, and is still maintained at the Hackney Empire twenty-five years on.

'Once you get out of London . . . audiences are quite different,' Linda told Oliver Double. 'A lot of the London cabaret scene is quite tacky; the audiences are jaded – they've seen every possible act. The audiences outside of London are fresher. You can be more adventurous with them; they're more prepared for you to try things out. They're not just jaded consumers . . . I suppose it means more to you if you live in Loughborough than if you live in London.'

Oliver suggested that the London scene had stagnated and comedians had started coming north, taking 'the same old shit elsewhere, so that it's more difficult for local things to start'. Linda and I knew exactly what he meant. Several times we'd been completely underwhelmed by comedians who came north and did whole sets about their experiences on the London Underground. Nothing could have been more irrelevant – or boring – to the majority of their audiences.

'Most of the really good comedians don't do the circuit in London now,' Linda told Oliver. 'They've moved on from that and nobody seems to care about it much. It's become a kind of cynical moneymaking exercise for a lot of people – not all – who run venues. They're springing up everywhere; there's so many of them. They can't all be good . . . Hopefully it will be a vibrant enough form to survive this blanding out that seems to be going on.'

And so it proved, particularly in the north, where there

weren't the same comic trends and micro-trends constraining entertainers. In cities like Manchester and Sheffield there was room for everyone, not least Linda's great mate Henry Normal, co-writer of the first series of *The Royle Family*, who helped form the Live Poets Society in 1980s Manchester. (Their motto was, 'Poetry so good you can actually understand it.')

'Henry's a real anti-London, miserable old militant northerner,' she told Oliver. 'He couldn't have grown up to that kind of act in London. It wouldn't have been possible. It would have been, "No one wants to hear poetry, it's finished; that's the old ranty thing, it's gone." I don't think you would develop an act like that in London because you wouldn't have the bottle probably to stand out against the trend. And the advantage of being outside is that you're not aware of all that fashion and trends around you in comedy, so people tend to be a bit more individual. Like Kevin Seisay – he's great, all sorts of people like that.

'I'm really glad that I started developing my act as a comedian and learning my art outside London, because it's a liberating thing, really. Although it is double-edged, because you miss the contact and the crack with other comedians, you miss the debate and the discussion and all that. Although, having said that, whenever I go down there, it's always the f . . . same conversations. It's as though I've just stepped out for a few minutes and come back. Personal bitching, which is always fun, and the left-wing right-wing argument.'

Linda was a regular visitor to the Manchester area over the years, and she had a few memories of dossing down after a night's stand-up work in Henry Normal's Crumpsall bedsit, which was a crash pad for many a visiting comic in the late 1980s and early 1990s. Even so, Henry never thought to buy a spare bed, according to Linda.

In the relatively unconstrained north, Linda was able to give free rein to her individuality and develop her distinctive brand of stand-up. This involved a lot of hard graft, writing and performing. In the world of stand-up comedy, almost everyone writes their own material. It's the be all and end all. Without the ability to write good stuff, forget it! Try another trade. Dawn French asked Linda how it worked.

Dawn: And how do you start the process – what happens?

Linda: I was hoping you'd tell me.

Dawn: I have no answers.

Linda: Torture is how you start and torture is how you proceed. Grand Guignol? It's just a great auto da fé . . . It's almost as though the chair's on fire. I can't sit there. I'm terrible. I really am terrible. Last minute, awful thing, and then writing through the night. I hate those people you read about: 'My day: up at 6 a.m., out for a jog, come back, write for four hours, then they've got the rest of the day free. Oh, what is that?

Dawn: Do you prefer getting up, mooching about a bit, Sky TV, knowing you've got your homework to do?

Linda: *America's Next Top Model.*

Dawn: There's a few of those to catch up on during the day.

Linda: Absolutely.

Dawn: Some biscuits.

Linda: Black and white film comes on.

Dawn: Got to watch that. Now it's time for supper.

Linda: Exactly. Where does it go?

Dawn: The gig's tomorrow . . . and it is like that peren-
nial Sunday-night feeling I used to have. You haven't
done your homework.

Linda: That is exactly what it is. It is like a cloud settles
over you.

Dawn: But when you finally get down to it . . .

Linda: It's on a piece of paper for me, with a pencil.
And when it finally starts flowing, that's fantastic.
When you get a bit and it's really, really going and
you're almost not having to think about it – spirit
messages – that's a great bit as well.

Dawn: Are you the sort of person who carries a notebook
around and writes stuff down as you live your life?

Linda: I should do. I do tend to remember quite a lot
of things people say and do. Funny things. But no,
this is one of my resolutions: start carrying a notebook. I've not done it up to now. But I suppose I have
a little notebook in my head. I have a very selective
memory – it doesn't remember things like where my
keys are, but it does remember a funny thing in a
café that someone said. That's quite handy.

Linda loved 'mooching around' and sitting in cafés and
listening to people. She overheard a lot of funny conversations, many inspiring pieces of stand-up. In an interview
with *Word* magazine she described just one of these splen-
didly funny unexpected moments.

'The other week, I was sitting in my local café and there
were these two young black guys in the full ghetto-fabulous
gangsta style, blinged up, great big trainers like hollowed-
out killer whales, looking really quite heavy. They're sat in
this café, and one of them's got a cake. And the other one

says, "What's that cake like?" The bloke goes, "I could bake a better cake wiv my eyes shut, guy. I'm a bad baker." And so the other one gets him going through all the cakes he can make, Swiss roll, fruit cake, chocolate cake, etc. "And can you make that one with all the different colours?" "Marble cake, guy?" says the other one contemptuously. "That's the easiest one!" That was the least likely conversation you could have expected. Turns out they were catering students.'

From the start, Linda had a clear idea of the kind of comedy she wanted to do – and what she didn't want to do. She definitely didn't want to do gender-specific comedy. 'I tend to think it's quite reactionary to talk about "women in comedy" and until you get away from that ghettoising, then women are never going to get a crack of the whip,' she told Oliver Double. She went on to recall two recent interviews with journalists. 'Both of them said, "What really struck me about your set is that you don't do the sort of thing you expect women to talk about."

'I thought, "That's just your problem. You imagine that women aren't interested in things other than just women's things. Do you expect me to come on and just talk about shaving for forty minutes?" A lot [of men] do talk about wanking for forty minutes. Probably got little else to talk about. If I hear another wanking, or kebab, or "I'm really crap in bed" line . . .'

So what did she want to talk about? She told Alison Hurndall of the *Sheffield Star*: 'Anything is fair game for a joke. It all depends how you deal with a subject, but I think everything in life generally can be funny, whether it is something in the news or personal things. Even death can be funny in some circumstances. I think it is tedious if you get women who do nothing but "women's jokes". If something is funny, then it is funny for everyone.'

Laurie Taylor, writing for *New Humanist* magazine, noted her 'comic antipathy to anything that smacks of authority'. Her comedy, he said, 'depends a great deal upon puncturing big portentous ideas and people, with shafts of ordinary observation. She is not given to large statements.'

'I like to come at big subjects from a very personal angle,' she agreed. 'I'm aware that someone like Jeremy Hardy has so much knowledge and so much information at his fingertips. His satire is informed satire. I don't have that sort of knowledge. I'm not ignorant but I'm not like Jeremy. But I do have an attitude and I know what my attitude is.'

Class was definitely one of those big themes. When Humphrey Carpenter, presenting an edition of *Great Lives*, asked Linda how much the class issue informed her work, she said, 'It definitely is a source, because it's such a preoccupation in this country, specifically in England. You look at comedy of recent times – *Fawlty Towers*: it's all about Basil's middle-class pretensions. *Porridge*: what could be more underclass than people in prison? We are obsessed with it. And it colours a lot of our behaviour and attitudes.'

Politics, too – and while everyone was a target, there were some obvious favourites, among them Thatcher, Kinnock, Major and Blunkett. 'You've got to do what's right for you,' she told Oliver Double. 'Stick to your guns, whatever you think. I'm a big fan of John Hegley. What he does is not directly political but I actually find it one of the most heartening, humanising things you could see, because he's a person, he's likeable, he's eccentric and quirky. I'd put that in the same category as the left-wing people who are directly political like Jeremy Hardy.'

And then there was sport. When I met her, Linda had a passing interest in football, but always followed West Ham's results. Seeing how serious I was about cricket and football encouraged her to get more involved, and over the years she became a keen sports fan. It probably helped that she was knocking around with the likes of Phill Jupitus, Mark Steel and Kevin Day – all absolutely sport nutty. Cricket, football, rugby, golf, motor racing and even Crown Green bowls each entered her routine at one point or another. How many other women stand-ups can you say that about? 'Don't imitate others,' she told the *Wirral Globe*. 'Be yourself and just do things that come from inside you. But I don't think you can really advise anyone on the art of comedy, aside from remembering to turn your microphone on and facing the audience.'

You've also got to be prepared to live out of a suitcase. On *Great Lives*, Humphrey Carpenter asked Linda whether she enjoyed the travelling lifestyle. 'When you first start out, you're staying in terrible bed and breakfasts and touring in old Transit vans,' Linda said. 'I've stayed in hotels where it's been so grim and miserable and cold that at night I've had to get up, get dressed and put my coat on the bed.

'I remember in the morning the manager said, "Did you sleep all right?"

'And I thought, "No, I'm not going to do that English thing and say 'Oh, fine.' So I said, "Well actually no, it was so freezing and miserable that I had to get fully dressed, have a cup of tea just to get my circulation going, and put my coat on the bed."

'And he said: "You should be here in January."'

I reckon there were significant venues, and therefore promoters of new comedy and cabaret, in at least thirty towns and cities, stretching from Birmingham to Newcastle. On behalf of Linda and numerous other acts who 'progressed' from these stages, I salute you all. Most of these people ran gigs from pub, and social club rooms that had been established for years as music venues, for rock, blues, folk and jazz. The few quality venues that operated as municipally funded arts centres ran a similarly eclectic music programme, which took cabaret and comedy under its wing.

These regional promoters kept the scene buzzing and some of them were genuine characters who were regarded with great affection. 'There's one guy [Chris Coope] in Manchester who simply cannot get off the phone,' Linda told Alfred Hickling of the *Yorkshire Post*. 'He's just the same when hosting his shows; his introductions go on so long the performers can't get a word in edgeways. Eventually, he was in such trouble that the Manchester acts clubbed together and arranged a benefit gig to pay his phone bill. He spent the whole of the next day ringing them all up to thank them. There's another one who lives in Blackburn in a house with a large Doberman and boxes all over the floor. Every time the Doberman makes a mess he simply puts another box over it and leaves it there.'

Richard Haswell was director of Bury Met Arts Centre between 1988 and 1993 and must have booked Linda as many times as any other promoter in Britain. 'When I first went to what eventually became Bury Met I was pretty green about running venues – I'd come from a background in 1980s political theatre and run into both Linda and The Chuffinelles a few times on that circuit,' he recalls.

'I also knew Warren at Sheffield Popular Productions from meeting him at Linda's early shows. He rapidly became that rare but necessary thing for a young promoter – an agent you could trust and one with shared politics to boot. We became firm friends. Warren gave me the confidence to develop the embryonic cabaret at the Met and it soon became a core part of the programme. The venue fairly rapidly developed something of a reputation for punching above its weight (Mark Thomas once commented that your heart went in your boots when you saw Saturday night in Bury on the tour schedule, then you went and had a brilliant time) and Linda – who loved playing there – was a really important part of that.

'So gradually I got to know Linda well too – Linda and Henry Normal share the record for the most shows in Bury in the five years I was there (7 each, I think). Over time I took to turning up at Linda's shows every time she was playing locally. The Buzz Club in Chorlton was a regular stamping ground. It was a great period for comedy in Manchester – Steve Coogan, John Thomson, Caroline Aherne and Henry Normal were all at early stages in their careers and all of them played there and at Bury a number of times.

'One of my favourites, though, was Bradford Alternative Cabaret, run weekly by the performance poet Nick Toczek. It was one of those completely mad nights with an open booking policy – if you wanted to play, Nick would book you. One particularly memorable night, Linda was booked to play with a new artist whose show consisted of coming on stage to the accompaniment of deafening rock music and cutting up extremely large vegetables and fruit with a chainsaw. And that was it.

'Linda was far too generous ever to slag off another performer on stage and went on after him and did her set. But afterwards she had one topic of conversation: what sort of person would sit in his lonely bedsit (she had no evidence for this, but you could see the image emerging) thinking up an idea for a show and go, "I know, I'll cut up giant water melons with a chainsaw – that'll slay 'em."

'If memory serves, that was also the night that Nick had booked a punk band, all of whom had Down's Syndrome, to close the night – admirable, but absolutely unlistenable in every respect. But this was the early 1990s and the scene was like that. The corporatisation of comedy had yet to happen.

'Quite a lot of promoters also had an implicit (at the very least) political agenda – we naively thought that comedy had taken over from a failing political theatre movement as a vehicle for cultural change. But there was an anarchic spirit to the programming of what we determinedly called cabaret that allowed things like that to happen. Linda, needless to say, loved it, not least because it provided an endless sea of stories.

'I took to driving over to Sheffield to see Linda and Warren quite a lot, in a rather battered old MG that I had at the time and was inordinately fond of (more material for Linda). I used to stop over at their flat, and inevitably they became ludicrously late nights where we'd stay up telling stories and arguing for hours on end. Linda invariably won.

'She used to drink, but I don't ever remember her drunk (though, like all touring artists I've ever met, she was mildly obsessed with her next meal). Eventually you would just have to submit to the superior – and apparently sober – intellect. One evening, Mark Steel was there too and I chose to try and defend Jesse Jackson (big mistake with either of them), Neil Kinnock (don't even ask), but worst of all in their eyes, Ben Elton, for whom Linda maintained a particularly unreserved level of vitriol. I recall the phrase "sellout" being used once or twice. Then the next day, she'd be up to tramp across the South Yorkshire hills, leaving me to nurse an ailing head and equally ailing car back across the Snake Pass.

'But it's the Bury stories that I remember the most. In a few short years, virtually everyone who became anyone played this slightly unlikely small arts centre – Lee Evans, Harry Hill, Mark Thomas, Bill Bailey, Jo Brand, Frank Skinner, the whole Manchester crowd and many more. But it was Linda we always looked forward to most. Perhaps part of that was that she was one of not many women on the circuit and one of the very few who never degenerated into what we'd now call (but never dared to then) "girly" material – and was all the funnier for it.

'In 1990 we opened a new café bar and venue in the Met, and sure enough Linda was invited to perform on the opening night to an audience of the local great and good. All seemed to go well and the night was a huge success. But the next day, I ran into the head of planning at Bury Council, who had been instrumental in helping us build the new space. I asked him if he'd enjoyed himself the night before. 'It was very good,' he said, 'apart from the woman who came out with all that foul language.' Linda, who had been one of two women on a bill of eight acts, few exactly angels, thought this was hilarious.

'I used to MC most of the shows (for some reason, it was generally accepted then that the promoter was MC, however bad you were). Most of the act was the interval competition (another lost and unmourned tradition), which, in our case, usually consisted of a joke competition to win various bits of merchandise supplied by Thwaites Brewery, our sponsor, with lots of really pretty unsophisticated audience participation. Invariably this bit used to massively overrun, and Linda would end up going on a good ten or fifteen minutes later than I'd told her she would be, having got more and more wound up and nervous. But even that she would deal with by showing admirable courtesy. "Richard," she'd say afterwards, "that bloody competition goes on far too long." And that would be that.'

Linda always got nervous before a gig, but once on stage, her nerves would dissolve. 'It's a weird combination of concentration and relaxation,' she told the *Sheffield Star*. 'Like a heightened version of yourself – yourself writ large. If it's going really well, you don't want to get off. But it varies. You could do a set one night that lasts 45 minutes and the same material the next night can be an hour and the night after that it might be 35 minutes.'

All performers, unless they are walking around in a fool's paradise, have bad gigs. 'Everyone has disasters and anyone who says they haven't is lying,' Linda said. 'Sometimes everything goes wrong and there is only so much you can do to control it. I find technical problems like a faulty microphone much more difficult to overcome than the audience. But it is really strange, as some days you can go out and everything can be shaping up to be a disaster and suddenly everything changes and the audience are with you. I think confidence is 90 per cent of it. As you get more confident, you tend to keep on having good shows as you feel in control. If you are not confident then you are a dead duck. Obviously, I have a life outside and I do not always feel good, but I can usually manage to put that behind me for the length of the show.'

There were some pretty terrible gigs along the way, including a truly awful gig at Teeside Polytechnic in Middlesbrough. She told the *Sheffield Star*: 'It was the worst experience I've ever had. The social secretary seemed to be some tragic victim of Care in the Community and the room was like an NCP car park. I discovered I wasn't going on until after 11.30 p.m. – basically it was a way for 18-year-olds to drink very, very late for 50p. They were all Sid the Sexists. There was a complete expectation that I was going to take my clothes off. There was no other reason I could be up there.'

But nothing could knock Linda off her chosen path now. 'The thing I love most about my job is the hours,' she said. 'It takes me a long time to get going in the morning, but I'm really perky by the evening when I perform. I reckon I was a nocturnal animal in a previous life. I think I have succeeded at what I do because of my inability to do anything like a normal job. I've had the odd one in the past, though – and I was one of the great pioneers of flexi-time. I'd describe myself as conventionally unemployable.

'It is a proper job because you can't just present a lot of old rubbish to people,' she told Dawn French. 'You do have to be professional and work at what you are doing. But on the other hand it's not a job in the way that most people experience a job, where they really don't like it and for too many people their job finances their life and that's where all their energy is. But if you do comedy it's part of your life. It's part of your whole world, so it's not a proper job in that sense.'

'If people didn't laugh, that would be a bit of a trade descriptions problem,' she said in an interview with the *South Wales Echo*. 'When people tell me stories and say, "You could use that in your show!" I think, "Yes, I could if I wanted to be bankrupt and living on the streets." But they mean well.'

When Linda and Dawn French met in 2005 they discussed

whether it was harder for women to have a successful career in stand-up. 'It is a daunting thing to do,' Linda said. 'Let's not underestimate it . . . Not everyone wants to be on display like that. It's a tough one for anyone, male or female, but men are just more used to the idea of everyone looking at them, and having to deliver the goods. That sort of heroic model is one that they've always had from childhood. That's what it is really.'

Linda was continually asked this same question, of whether it was harder for women than men in the comedy world. 'Well, I've nothing to compare it to, really,' she would reply. 'I can't say: "When I was a man it was much easier, although when I was a giraffe it was much harder because you can't get a microphone lead long enough." But, as it's generally harder being a woman in most jobs, I would guess the answer's probably yes."

Sometimes she'd simply say, 'In spite of my doomed attempt to become the Duke of Westminster, I've never been a male stand-up, so I can't really compare the two.'

10

Scaling Arthur's Seat

Sheffield to Edinburgh via Manchester

Any visitors from Scotland in tonight? Yes, one or two. Well, welcome to our Edinburgh Festival. Welcome to it. And I hope you make yourselves at home for the next couple of weeks here. It's very nice. Actually, I did the other festival, Glasgow Mayfest, this year, which is like Scotland's answer to the Edinburgh Festival really, but this one's nice; it's like a party in north London with charades really, isn't it?'
Comedy Boom, Edinburgh Festival, 1988

People used to say that the Edinburgh Festival was just a question of London decamping to Scotland. Everywhere you went you saw your old chums from down south and you got to hang out with them for weeks on end instead of the odd few hours. But for several years, before the festival became a big comedy business, Edinburgh was also like a summit conference for all the weird and wonderful characters on the cabaret circuit. Everyone you could think of was up there doing a show, or taking part in someone else's show. It was fantastic, the pinnacle of the year, especially when you consider that there had been virtually no cabaret shows at Edinburgh ten years previously, as Carol Sarler observed in a festival overview in the *Guardian*. Now there were well over 100 of them.

You can have a tremendous social time at the festival, drinking, dancing and talking all night, night after night, barely sleeping. It's great for meeting people, forging friendships and mixing with allied trades – promoters, agents, radio and TV producers, press and other performers. It can get a bit 'Fellini goes to Edinburgh' sometimes. People seriously indulge and do themselves quite a bit of harm, and then there's quite a comedown afterwards. It's a weird old thing and can really test out friendships as much as make them. Linda always had a lot of fun, but she kept a fairly tight rein on herself.

Edinburgh is very much a proving ground, a place where you can attract the attention of the press and public, and show your peers a thing or two. Peer approval can be a big thing with performers, as Linda admitted to Dawn French. 'I always dread the idea that there are people who I think are fantastic and they would think I was rubbish. That would be horrible. Wouldn't that be just awful?'

Linda's early favourites on the emergent alternative comedy scene included John Hegley, French and Saunders, Billy Connolly and Alexei Sayle. By the late 1980s, she was a huge fan of Arnold Brown, whose humour she described as 'witty, urbane and intelligent'. Kit Hollerbach, Jeremy Hardy, Mark 'Miwurdz' Hurst and Arthur Smith were other favourites. She also admired Chris Lynam and said of his work, 'It's the sort of thing that fails or works extremely well . . . It's as though you've given Max Wall millions of acid tabs . . . Inspired lunacy. Incredible.'

Linda debuted at the Edinburgh Festival in 1988 with 'Linda Smith and Friends', which played for two weeks at the Comedy Boom in Picardy Place at the top of Leith Walk. It was a very convenient venue for us, because we were staying at the bottom of Leith Walk. Having said that, you had to walk the length of it to get to Leith, which was fine when you were sober, but a trial when you'd been going at the lemonade for hours.

The Comedy Boom was a small but atmospheric basement in a pub, booked and run by Ivor Dembina and Addison Creswell – the latter rapidly emerging as *the* comedy agent and supreme promoter, the force behind Off The Kerb Productions. This was also the beginning of the fly-poster wars that were waged between Off The Kerb and the new boys on the block, Avalon. Comedy was about to go big-time.

Linda was in good company at the Comedy Boom. The shows preceding her slot featured the comic female trio Sensible Footwear, and hardened circuit mates Mark 'Miwurdz' Hurst and musical comedy duo Skint Video. Linda had eighty minutes at 11.30 p.m., which she split with a different guest each week – Marxist magician Ian Saville for the first week and comedian Ian McPherson, a *Time Out* comedy award winner, for the second. Her show qualified as a 'late show', but only just. As any Edinburgh regular will tell you, 11.30 p.m. local time is the equivalent of 8.30 p.m. normal time, and shows continue well into the early hours. Linda would do the second half and, in spite of some smallish week-night audiences, often drunk, she did well and received some glowing reviews.

'The *Scotsman* said that we both had "stage personae displaying that apparently embarrassed, self-deprecating warmth which is like gold to a comedian", recalls Ian Saville. 'I'm not sure that Linda was actually embarrassed, but she certainly displayed her golden qualities. While I just did the same old cabaret stuff that I was doing for quite a long time, I was amazed at how much new material Linda produced from the first day onwards. Topical, fresh and relevant to an Edinburgh audience: she worked hard at her art and it paid off.'

Ian may be referring to this section of her first set at Edinburgh: 'I've been taking in a few shows at the Fringe. I love these people who busk the queues trying to drum up support for their show. There was a bunch today, women, young women, juggling, fire-eating, acrobatics, face-painting, and then one of them shouts out, "And if you'd like to see more of this, come and see our show about the poet Sylvia Plath." What's that then? Perhaps this is a lost episode in Sylvia Plath's life that we don't know about. Perhaps this explains her later manic depression – you know, during her lost years as a circus acrobat she had a blow to the head or something.'

Or this: 'Fascinated by those Morningside ladies in Jenners Tea Rooms – those posh ladies. They sit there like badly upholstered armchairs, tweed from head to foot, and they sit there ritually slaughtering Dundee cakes and they always have those pursed disapproving lips. It's as though they were rouged cats' bums rather than mouths. I don't know how they force the tea through them actually. Quite dodgy really – a drip to the arm would be easier.'

A counterpoint to these posh tea-drinking ladies were The Chuffs, who proved that they could hack it with the big girls and boys by pulling off two weeks at Pleasance One and one week at Viewforth Centre, Gilmore Place. Twentieth-Century Vixen had approached us for permission to act as their producers for a run at the festival and, although it was a little bit last minute, it worked out well. At 65, Margaret reckoned she was the oldest performer on the Fringe that year. What a time for Linda – a festival debut with her own

show and her Chuffs wowing the crowds under Mike
McCarthy's direction.

The following August, she decided to return to the same
venue, but this time to share the billing and overheads with
her friend Jane Baker, who had turned to full-time performance with her character Betty Spital. Their show was entitled,
'The Seriously Funny Guide to Love, Death and the Co-op'
and comprised two separate acts, loosely linked. The good
reviews and creditable audiences gave us the confidence to
take it on tour for the next year under the revised and
catchier banner, 'Sex, Death and the Co-op.'

Linda's co-combatant Betty Spital was at the heart of the
action, and she could be very rude and outspoken. 'The
show was ostensibly an AGM for SPLAF – the Sheffield
Pensioners' Liberation Army Faction,' Jane says. 'We handed
out a numbered agenda to everyone, which also acted as a
raffle ticket. Then Betty lectured the assembly on the SPLAF
manifesto, which included the immediate and unconditional
release of Nelson Mandela (achieved!) and a minimum standard dying age of 87. She also spoke of how she'd liberated
tea bags from the Co-op and such matters as "Youthanasia",
or a pensioner's right to choose which of their offspring to
have put down. And then Linda was introduced and came
on and did her routine. She was billed on the agenda as
"Youth Wing" in very tiny writing.

'It was the contrast that worked so well, this cantankerous
old campaigner and Linda, upright and sparkling, although
Betty acted as though she'd only brought Linda along as
part of her education. At the end we had the raffle and,
although everyone thought they might win the Ford Fiesta
in Rabid Red with go-faster stripes, Linda always managed
to look surprised when Betty won every night. We took this

show all over the country, but we had to tone it down a bit for places like Basingstoke.'

Watching the show every night was Elb Hall, a tour, stage and technical manager who was a regular crew member of Sheffield Popular Productions. Elb was running the Comedy Boom with Jane McMorrow during the festival. 'There were three shows per night: Linda and Betty, Mark Miwurdz and Tony Allen,' he says. 'Linda and Betty hadn't brought any music for pre or post show, so I offered them free rein of my cassettes, which were in Jane's car. I remember Linda being quite taken with the Ramsey Lewis Trio's live version of "The In Crowd", which starts with about five seconds of healthy applause. I was instructed to play this every evening when Linda left the stage "just in case no one claps". It was a worry that turned out to be unfounded, but the absurdity and downright cheekiness of playing your own applause at the end of the set was perfect and always got an extra laugh as people were getting up to leave. I still have that cassette; it still has a torn bit of masking tape on it with "Betty and Linda – End" written on. I don't know where the Ramsey Lewis Trio recorded it, but it does sound very similar to a smoky basement on the corner of Broughton Street.'

Douglas Fraser's review of the show in the *Scotsman* was very complimentary. 'Linda Smith, honorary member of SPLAF's youth wing, is a Londoner showing healthy traits of northern ancestry,' he wrote. 'Her stand-up sparkles as she toys with a mane of blonde hair and she lopes cheerfully through her performance with warmth, charm, and sharpness.'

'You know, it's that "lope" that I love,' says Jane Baker. 'If ever there was a loper, it was Linda Smith. I remember that vital energetic lope as she strode up Leith Walk in

Edinburgh. I could never keep up with her. She had to keep stopping. She loped through life – Linda the Loper. Lovely.'

This was the year that Linda had her first crack at BBC national radio, when Arthur Smith told listeners to Radio Four's *Aspects of the Fringe* to get ready for some jokes from a relative newcomer. Linda made the most of her few minutes of airtime.

'Hello . . . thank you. People tend to stereotype you because of where you come from . . . It's lovely to be in Scotland – home of the curly perm . . . No, it's true. People think that if you're from the south of England you must be rich . . . you must be – stupid word – a yuppie. I've met people who think you're a yuppie if you've got your own teeth. Oh dear. Actually, I'm staying in Leith . . . where I think you *are* a yuppie if you've got your own teeth . . .

'But I've moved out of London into the commuter belt. To Sheffield. Which is nice. The only drawback being – all my mates from London coming up to see me . . . They don't really want to see me, they just want to wet themselves over the house prices. It's a kind of pornography for them. A house-buyers' red-light district. The decision for them, really, is . . . "What do you think, darling – shall we try that new Tandoori restaurant, or shall we buy a three-bedroom semi-detached house? Oh, let's go mad – and have a meal!"

'Because they're excited now – they're off kerb-crawling around the estate agents. Pressing their snouts against the window, going "Look, darling, look – Chatsworth House . . . one pound ninety-nine! Look, look, look – if we got rid of that timeshare on that bird-bath in Hackney, we could buy Manchester! Look, my man, here's all the loose change I've on me – give me Barnsley with four hotels on it."

'Different culture though, the north – from the south . . .

there's no getting round it. Of course, the main difference, really, is . . . the further north you move in Britain, the more unwilling the local people are to accept the idea that it's bloody well freezing! What is it? It's like a shameful secret, isn't it? It's like . . . "We're moving a bit further north, it gets a bit colder . . . Aye but don't tell bastard sootherners." As if you won't notice . . . Because in a northern town, you can always tell the southerners and the students and the tourists and the people who work at the Town Hall, because . . . it's winter, there's a bit of snow on the ground and you think, "Oh, I'll wear a coat."

'Cockney pervert – obviously. There's the local lads, Friday night, several degrees below freezing . . . underpants! "Cold, pal? Never 'eard of it. Anyway, are them tha teeth? Stitch that, tha yuppie!" If it gets really cold, they'll add a tattoo . . . Girls are just the same. You'll be waiting at a bus stop, middle of January – three girls come along . . . white shorts – gooseflesh on their legs you could grate nutmeg on. Well, I've done it before . . . "Just dangle over this rice pudding, love, would you?" Normally I'm just coming from Marks and Spencers . . . because I'm a busy woman – or I have been up to now . . . And I can't mess about cooking . . . I use those ready-meals. The Marks and Spencers "Lazy Bastard" range. Quite reasonable really, aren't they? Chicken dinner – 65 quid!

'That's all from me. Thank you, goodnight.'

Three weeks of self-enforced festival imprisonment presents few opportunities for daytime release – a maximum of three days off from performing, and some years it was just one day. All performing days are dedicated to recovering from the night before and getting into a routine that prepares the mind and body for the evening to come. So for us those precious hours off would be spent at the Portobello seaside, or strolling in contemplation among the still of the beautiful Botanical Gardens, or scaling Arthur's Seat, the famous peak in the middle of Holyrood Park. There, at over 800 feet, the pure air helped cleanse the lungs after the battering they received from passive cigarette smoke inhaled over nights in venue bars. We loved to sit and take in the panoramic view of Edinburgh at festival time, although we only seemed to manage to reach the summit every other year.

In 1990, Linda and her pal Henry Normal came up with a plan for a two-hander show at Edinburgh, to be called 'The Therapy Sessions'. The press release must have been a product of Henry's penchant for word play – it included this absolute diamond of a paragraph: 'Jung, Freud and single, or just under the Web(b)er? Don't despair, this show is the Reich stuff. As you can see, these two get up to semantics. They've got a way with words; well, they've got away with a few here, hopefully.'

But as is the case with most Edinburgh productions, Linda and Henry were forced to arrive at an artistic compromise, because putting on a show is an expensive business. I can't remember what it cost in 1990, but if a performer has a reputation to protect, an outlay of up to £10,000 at today's prices wouldn't be unreasonable for three weeks. Then, participants would struggle to raise the cash to pay for the expedition north of the border. What's more, it required a major investment of time – the other great evil empire – as it would take months to work up and write a brand-new show. So Linda and Henry's two-hander inevitably turned into two separate comic acts coming together on-stage at the start and the end of the show, when they did a couple of routines together, in the same way as Linda and Betty Spital had done the previous year. That's as far as the togetherness went. Linda was preparing some new material and would also be including some of her older stuff expertly recycled. She spoke to the *Sheffield Star* just before she headed off to begin a 21-night run of shows: 'It is very exciting and a great experience to work every night, as it sharpens you up as a performer – you come out of it match-fit!'

I would normally have driven Linda up to Scotland, but I was detained back in Sheffield with the daily grind of producing and marketing shows for the autumn touring season. I couldn't hit the high road until a few days later, so Elb Hall took the hot seat in my place. He was going to be working on 'The Therapy Sessions', so it made sense for him to drive Linda north.

'I was looking forward to the scenic drive up the A1 through Northumberland,' he says. 'Sadly, all thoughts of tea shops on Lindisfarne were cruelly dashed when Henry Normal's grasp of geography and vehicle capacity intervened. We were summoned to "pick him up on the way" from Manchester. (I still maintain that Manchester isn't really "on the way" to Edinburgh if you're going from Sheffield . . . it's something to do with the Pennines being in the way.)

'It was always going to be a bit of a squeeze getting us all into my ageing orange Volkswagen Variant, along with a month's worth of luggage, plus various boxes of leaflets. But imagine our surprise when we arrived in Crumpsall to find Henry bringing his very own leafleteer – the insanely good-natured Chris Coope! It was an uncomfortable journey but, thankfully, only a matter of hours.

'Linda's unexpected acquaintance with Chris was to last for much longer. If she was surprised at the fact that he was going to be sleeping on their floor for the foreseeable future, she didn't show it. When we arrived at Edinburgh, I dropped Linda, Henry and Chris off at their digs, which were somewhere towards Haymarket station, and took my by now much roomier car to where I was staying in Leith.

'Now I don't know, because I wasn't staying in the same place as them, but what with the unexpected presence of the "Publicist of Lunacy" and the washing machine exploding upstairs and resultant flooding incident, I think it's safe to say that whichever Muse is responsible for overseeing Edinburgh Festival accommodation, she wasn't smiling on Linda in 1990. I bumped into Chris Coope a couple of times during the festival and later he got the train back to Manchester. I heard that Linda paid towards his ticket.

'The show was at Marco's Leisure Centre, one of those unlikely venues that are appropriated for the duration of the festival and with a bit (but never quite enough) of black tat, some squeaky staging and half a paint-spattered scaffold tower are converted into a quick-turnaround performance space. It wasn't on the established comedy circuit, it wasn't very easy to find either, but when you did, you would be mystified by the fact that it was still operating as a leisure centre and populated by Scots indulging in a bizarre cocktail of fitness activity, alcohol and deep-frying. Linda's performance would be underscored by wafting chip fat and muffled music from a nearby aerobics session, but it was worse for Henry doing the quieter poems.

'A lot of trouble was caused one evening by my casual (and innocent) remark that there was someone in the audience who looked like Spike Milligan. This escalated out of control and within minutes Henry was a nervous wreck, muttering about being in the presence of a comedy God. It was, of course, just some bloke who didn't really look like Spike Milligan.

'One night we were in the bar at "Late & Live" in the Gilded Balloon, and as was customary at about 2 a.m., I bought a copy of that morning's *Scotsman*. There was a review of "The Therapy Sessions" in it and I hurried over to Linda to show her. Big mistake. It wasn't a bad review, but it did include the word "twee", which infuriated her beyond measure. I was tarred with being the bringer of bad tidings, and held responsible for ruining the whole evening. Mark Hurst was also there and, hugely enjoying my discomfort, suggested that in future I should let the performers buy their own newspapers and, moreover, in the cold light of day. This turned out to be some of the best advice I ever had. That and never to mention Spike Milligan.'

Radio Four's *Kaleidoscope* sent Tom Robinson along to 'The Therapy Sessions' and he did a piece highlighting Linda's work. He thought her delivery was a bit tentative, but her material was strong and she was extremely entertaining. It was just unfortunate, he said, that the venue where she was performing was a 'breeze block bunker not conducive to atmosphere'.

He played this clip from the show: 'There's so many things that aren't right. These days I think I wish I could be Salman Rushdie. I wish I could be him, because no one in that man's life is ever going to say to him, "Don't you think you're being a bit paranoid, mate?" How can you be paranoid? People say to me, "Linda, calm down, calm down, just because we don't know what Iraq's nuclear capability is, it's not the end of the world."'

Our friend and leading north-west comedy promoter Richard Haswell, of Bury Metro Arts, always went up to

Edinburgh at this time of year to scout for comedy, theatre and music acts. He was very much in evidence at the 1990 festival and shared a flat with Henry, Linda and me. He was my main buddy when it came to going to see shows and whiling away the drinking hours in the bars of the Gilded Balloon, Pleasance and Assembly Rooms. Here are his sober memories of that particular festival: 'Linda wanted time on her own to prepare for the show, and Warren and I used to meet up with her afterwards in the Gilded Balloon for "Late and Live" (my memory says that Skint Video were on every night every year, but I'm sure that can't be true). But it was the (very badly hung over) mornings that stick in my mind.

'Every day the same ritual – someone going out and getting literally all of the papers, and Linda, Henry, Warren and various friends round the breakfast table, going straight for the reviews. One day after the usual exchanges – "Where's my review?" "Look, so and so only got one star!" "Do you think he'll get a Perrier nomination?" and so on – someone finally turned to the news pages and commented, "Blimey, there's a war broken out." Saddam had invaded Kuwait – and in our Edinburgh bubble where nothing else existed apart from the festival, we'd all missed it. Needless to say by that night Linda had a routine about it in the set. Henry's response was a bit less sophisticated: 'I only got one bad review. It was in all the papers' – a line that stayed in his set for evermore.'

There remains a select group of talented comic performers who have always tried to honour the 'spirit of the Fringe' by working tirelessly to serve up a brand-new show every year, based on a novel idea. Two that deserve special citation, and who were very much heroes to Linda and me, were Arthur Smith and John Hegley. And so I dedicate this chapter to the innovation and charm of those two gentlemen and, dare I say, veterans of the festival.

I first met Arthur when he and his former comic partner, actor Phil Nice, auditioned for New Variety in Cricklewood in 1983. Since then he has brought us so many unforgettable gems. Among them are: the 'Arthur Smith Sings' collection – notably, 'Leonard Cohen' and 'Andy Williams'; his highly individualistic takes on *Hamlet* and *Swan Lake*; and the much-acclaimed 'Live Bed Show' with Caroline Quentin. Somehow this favourite son of Edinburgh manages to embody everything the Fringe has come to represent, while relentlessly taking the mickey out of it.

Linda and I took ourselves on a couple of Arthur's legendary 'Alternative Tours of the High Street'. These involved after-midnight marauding through the Old Town in the company of the ultimate comic tour guide, plus dozens of complete strangers who were jolly enough on Scottish stout not to worry what they got up to. There were shimmies up lampposts, strips on pillar-boxes, songs sung out of tune through a megaphone and below-window serenades of sleepy-eyed residents with Robbie Burns poems. Madness, lovely madness, and even better when the local cops got roped in. Only Arthur could get away with it in such style.

Performers like Arthur and John Hegley seem to thrive in Edinburgh, but for a lot of people it can be quite a masochistic experience. Linda performed at the festival seven years in a row and the thrill eventually wore off. In those early years, it had a certain magic, but it was hard work without much reward. The money side of Edinburgh is definitely not funny. People get seriously burnt there, even if they're successful, because they can end up paying for a publicist, an agent and a promoter, the venue and advertising.

It's expensive to stay there and you're shelling out all the time on meals, drinks and taxis. It goes on and on.

It's a weird experience, and can be quite disheartening. Of course, it's also full of the unexpected. Someone might see your show and commission you to do a TV or radio show, just like that. But generally, it's expensive and tiring and can leave you feeling quite jaded. Several times at the end of the run we'd look back and realise that we could have gone on holiday three times over with the money we'd got through in those three and a half weeks. In later years it didn't seem worth putting ourselves through it.

Often we'd use the festival as a launch pad for an autumn show, which meant leaving Edinburgh at the beginning of September, taking a holiday immediately afterwards and then starting a tour at the end of the month. It worked well, but as time went on it felt too much like a non-stop existence. Inevitably the lure of all-night festival drinking and indulging ebbed away. 'Forget Edinburgh – let's just go on holiday!' we'd say. Then, instead of feeling exhausted when it came to starting an autumn tour, we'd come back to work feeling energised and inspired.

11

Farewell to Erith

Sheffield to Erith and Bexley

In the early days of commuting from Sheffield to the hurly-burly of the London club circuit, Linda would telephone her mum to say she was coming south to do some gigs and might be able to visit her in Erith. Linda thought nothing of using the term 'gig' in conversation. After all, it was and is the common trade parlance of musicians and comedians. This telephone communication between Linda and her mum went on for quite a while. Bessie would ask her daughter how she was getting on and if she had a lot of work. Linda would casually reply, 'Yes, lots of gigs.'

Bessie would respond, 'That's good.' Then one day she dropped a bombshell. 'Plenty of gigs, Lin?'

'Yes, Mum.'

'That's good. By the way, what *are* gigs?'

Linda had always been something of an enigma to her relatives. As she told Helen Fox at *Northern Star* magazine, 'If you took any member of my family and asked them for a million pounds to say what Linda did at college, they couldn't do it. They thought it was odd and for a long time I was seen as a very strange person. It was only when I began to be moderately successful that they understood, and only in terms of it being a living.'

At the time, Linda's gigs were very varied, mostly solo, others double-headers with Henry Normal or Betty Spital.

They would stretch from a Liverpool comedy club to the very cultured Ilkley Festival and then down for a short set at the Hackney Empire in London, her favourite venue of all. She always wore a suit for the Empire shows, insisting that you should look good when you were framed by a proscenium arch. Privately, she was dismissive of performers who treated it like any old scruffy club or pub gig and turned up in a T-shirt and jeans.

The genial and generous Arthur Smith would often compere at the Hackney Empire and he once suggested that he and Linda do a show together under the title 'The Smiths', just to confuse the punters at a time when the band of the same name had split up. I think that would have made Morrissey very morose.

While Linda gigged up and down the country, Mike McCarthy and I continued to put together and tour new shows with Sheffield Popular Productions. Linda and I did our best to synchronise our movements as much as possible, and whenever I could I'd drive her to gigs, but we were both all over the place – literally. Apart from Edinburgh, our only regular gig was Christmas in Erith and Bexley, which had been a fixed point on the calendar from 1983 onwards. We often stayed at Linda's mum's place in Erith, a few minutes' drive away from Barbara and Terry in Bexley, but there were times when we pitched camp at Barbara's and completed a full house of members of the Smith/Giles clan.

By the late 1980s, Barbara and Terry were doing well for themselves. They were enjoying the fruits of prosperity, or so it seemed to us. We were diametrically opposed on the party political front. They admired Margaret Thatcher and benefited from her time in power, while we had worked towards the woman's demise. There was always a lot of banter and baiting during our stay. Our journey south would culminate in a splendid Christmas dinner with all the trappings and trimmings. Places would be set around the dinner table for Linda's mum, aunt Helen, Linda, me, Barbara, Terry and the boys, Scott and Austin. I always seem to be singled out for attention as the only non-meat eater in the party. Barbara afforded me full-on hospitality and a specially prepared dish of salmon, which garnered admiring glances and comments from the turkey enthusiasts surrounding me. Once I'd fended off the predictable and harmless gags about vegetarians, it was plain sailing through to the divine Christmas pudding. And although we were fit to burst, within hours we'd be faced with another round of delicious Christmas food and drink.

Sadly, Christmas 1989 wasn't as jolly as the previous Christmases had been. Bessie had been very poorly during the year and was being treated for cancer; throughout our stay she was uncharacteristically subdued. We all tried our best to carry on with business as usual, for everyone's sake, but I don't think we were feeling too optimistic about the future. Linda was travelling to London for shows quite a bit, so she managed to pop in on Bessie fairly frequently. When Bessie was up to it, Linda would take her out for something to eat. One of these meals spawned a particularly delicious anecdote, which Linda recounted in an interview for *Word* magazine more than a decade later.

'My mum had a funny way of dealing with the family. I took her out to a restaurant and asked – as you would – "Any news then?"

'"No news," said my mum. Then halfway through the meal she said, "Oh yeah, Uncle John died." Her brother. Oh right!

'He was a miserable old sod actually. He wouldn't go round to his son's for Sunday lunch; he made his daughter-in-law bring his lunch round to him and he would eat it on his own. One day, she knocked but he didn't come to the door, so his son came round because he had a key. He found he'd gone to the toilet and, Elvis-like, had a heart attack on the toilet and died.

'I said, "Oh God, how terrible!"'

'My mum said, "Oh no, he had clean pyjamas on."'

From 1990 until 1992, Linda would often commit herself to a very hectic twelve-hour shift on a Tuesday, catching the train down to London to take her seat as a regular member of the Comedy Store's *Cutting Edge* topical comedy team. It was mentally and physically challenging, but she loved doing it. She went on to become the only female regular on the team of this weekly political satire show.

'You have to be specially gifted as a woman to break into and be accepted by the inner sanctum of the boys' club that has always been the mainstay of stand-up comedy,' fellow comedian and close friend Arnold Brown says. 'Before the Comedy Store started in May 1979 (as an antidote to the sexist, racist Bernard Manning/Jim Davidson ethos), there was only a handful of stand-ups doing intelligent, observed material: Billy Connolly, Dave Allen and Jasper Carrott, and on the horizon coming up in the early1980s was the sole woman who could compete with these major talents, Victoria Wood. However, even in the early days at "The Store", with its testosterone-fuelled, late-night drunken atmosphere, it proved hazardous for female performers to display their worth, despite using the shield of characters, as French and Saunders went on to do.

'By the mid-1980s, as the comedy progressed and politics

became more controversial, happily audiences grew more accustomed to receiving informed ideas from both sexes – and the dilemmas of the poll tax and the miners' strike threw up issues that Linda innovatively began to explore in her adopted town of Sheffield. Here she really took off and started to shine as one of the new breed of comedians such as Jo Brand, Helen Lederer, Jenny Eclair, Hattie Hayridge and Jenny Lecoat, all of whom had a refreshing feminist perspective, both on world events and the minutiae of everyday life.'

In *The Very Best of Linda Smith*, Mark Thomas paints a vivid picture of Linda playing 'gag-tag' at the Comedy Store. 'In the beery haze of the Store, Linda seemed completely at ease amidst the rising tide of testosterone and bad puns. The subject of gag-tag might be the Royal family, so the boys head for the in-breed jokes, ranting about the Windsors being German and sponging off the state. Up onto the stage amidst the smoke Linda would jump, shouting, 'Tag!', flicking her long hair back, and with a disarming look of innocent confusion calmly utter, 'Princess Diana – so thick and yet so thin.'

Cutting Edge was the perfect place for Linda to hone her improvisational skills, as quick-witted ad libs were the main requirement for a show that was based on the week's events in politics. The playful format also suited her down to the ground. On the train down to London she'd read the papers and write notes in preparation for her appearance. By now she was used to producing topical material at the last minute; often it could only be used once or twice before it passed into comedy obsolescence.

Just after Terry Waite was freed from captivity in Lebanon, Linda spoke to Stephen McClarence at the *Sheffield Star* about writing up-to-date jokes. She was in the process of thinking of a few gags about Waite for a show that evening. 'No good doing topical stuff if you're not on the ball,' she said. 'The topical stuff you do has a very short life indeed – a week and it's gone. When Thatcher was overthrown, even that only lasted a week. People also like to hear about the little things that *they've* observed as well.'

The last train from St Pancras to Sheffield left at a ludicrously early hour, about 10 p.m. So as to make it home the same night after the show, Linda would have to make a dash from Leicester Square and hurl herself onto the leaving train, sacrificing the after-show drinking session.

I, in my capacity as lead driver of 'Waz Cabs', would be parked up at Sheffield Midland Station, ready to collect her Ladyship at the time posted on the network timetable. Inevitably, the stationmaster would be making apologies around 1 a.m. for points failure on the 'Bermuda Triangle' section of track between Derby and Chesterfield. One unforgettable bitter winter night, I and a bunch of other family members, partners and friends of passengers, including a taxi driver from Barnsley, were cared for by a very hospitable station platform worker, who provided us with shelter and hot drinks until the train finally came crawling in about an hour late. Imbued with the true spirit of the Blitz and tons of British stoicism, it was worthy of an episode of Tony Hancock.

When Linda wasn't prepared to sacrifice the after-show element of the evening, then she would resort to kipping down on a colleague's sofa bed. Jenny Lecoat recalls one such evening of revelry. 'It must have been around 1990, a time when Linda and I worked together fairly regularly doing the *Cutting Edge* show at the Comedy Store. One night we'd been working with Bob Boyton, and after the gig the three of us decided that we wanted to go on for a drink somewhere.

'This was before the days of private members' clubs and late-night bars in town (unless you were a Groucho Club member – yeah, right!) so it was quite hard trying to find places that would serve booze late. But boy, did we find 'em that night: little underground drinking dens with concrete floors and beers served straight from the cash 'n carry wrappers; Greek "restaurants" that would keep serving wine provided you ordered a plate of olives between you; rooms above places; rooms under places; bars where you couldn't hear yourself speak for the music; and bars where you thought you might get stabbed if you looked at another customer the wrong way. We went from place to place, drinking copious amounts and talking non-stop – God knows what about, but I know we all laughed the whole time.

'Eventually, about three o'clock, Linda and I suggested moving to another venue. Bob announced that he was arseholed and needed to go home. Linda looked him up and down: "You fucking poof. Come on, Jen, you got any booze at yours?" And that is indeed where we ended up, drinking disgusting white wine and talking about life, the universe and everything till gone five. I can still see Linda in my old second-hand armchair, legs tucked under her, her wine glass weaving dangerously through the air as she used it to make a point. The following week we bumped into Bob Boyton. He looked at us with fear in his eyes and declared that he was never, ever going out with the two of us again.

'That night will always stay with me, because sadly I never got to spend much time with Linda after that. We did a few more gigs together, but she was getting more involved in touring and radio work just as I was pulling out of the live circuit to concentrate on writing, and despite a dozen promises that we were going to get together, we never did. But we'll always have that night – one glorious rip-roaring night when we got to know each other and sealed a friendship.'

Around this time, Linda was beginning to emerge on regional TV. This was back when local commercial stations still had an identity; they were learning that stand-up comedy was cheap to produce and would pull a new audience – young people seeking televisual pleasure after pub hours. Granada TV led the way with *Stand Up* and Linda recorded an edition on the second series. Kevin Day, Sean Hughes and Rob Newman all did sets on the same edition. Linda made it onto similar formats – at Tyne Tees with *On The Edge* and LWT's *First Exposure*. Her first national TV was around this time – *Paramount City* for BBC1. (Strangely, the series also featured another comic called Linda Smith, from the USA.)

Linda had always discouraged her mum from coming to see her live. Among other things, she was worried that she would disapprove of the swearing. But she couldn't prevent Bessie from watching her on the box and, as it turned out, the first time Bessie saw Linda on TV, her objections had less to do with the swearing than the adverse comments about those two sacred icons, Lou Beale from *EastEnders* and the Queen. She wasn't best pleased when Linda sent her a card with a doctored photo of the Queen and Prince Philip on the front either. They were covered in warts, which didn't go down well at all.

Bessie had been living with Barbara and Terry for six months when she was admitted to the Brook Hospital in south-east London for tests in April 1990. At the time Linda was on a mini-tour of Scotland with Henry Normal, but she managed to fly down to see her mum the following Sunday, before flying back in the evening in time for a show. The next day the dreaded call came through asking her to return to the hospital as soon as possible. She got on the next plane. Bessie died on the Monday, some hours after Linda had arrived. Barbara, Terry, Scott, Linda and I were all there at the hospital to say goodbye.

Linda was exceedingly upset by her mum's death. It affected her for a long time afterwards. I think it brought back the particular horrors of her childhood. She felt very alone: her mum had died; her dad was gone. Barbara and aunt Helen were the only close relatives that remained. She got on with her life and work, but it was a very emotional time for her.

It was now that she got the bug for gardening and began to develop a fascination for gardens. Her great friend and confidante Jane Baker, aka Betty Spital, definitely had a hand in the evolution of this new interest. Jane had a superb garden backing onto the formal Botanical Gardens in Sheffield. It was a place where we would take tea on summer days, and if Linda wasn't at home when I got back from my office, there was always the chance she would be round at Jane's, gossiping about the world in general, but gardening in particular.

'I think I just re-awoke an interest in Linda for gardens and plants,' Jane says. 'Our relationship regarding plants started when her mother died. She was so upset and it was a case of diverting her attention from sadness. I had the feeling that her memories of plants and gardens were somehow associated with her mother and happy times.'

Linda's first garden project involved the conversion of the

tarmac backyard of our ground-floor flat in Sheffield. She made an impressive rockery by importing wheelbarrow-loads of soil and muck, and borrowing stones from the Derbyshire countryside. She then put together an assortment of pots for plants that could survive out of the ground. Her planting repertoire included: big day lilies – Golden Trumpets; white and pink hostas; blue Echinops – globe thistles; lavender; rosemary; cranesbill geraniums; oriental poppies; flame-red honeysuckle; wild strawberries; blue delphiniums; ragged robin; night-scented stocks; and pink roses.

'After many long journeys to and from gigs discussing plants we loved and gardens we desired, one day Linda told me on the phone that she was creating a garden in the yard,' Jane recalls. 'Oh yeah, I thought. Only an amateur would try and make a garden there – better get an allotment.

'When I saw what she was up to – asphalt up, soil imported, encyclopaedia and reference books – I was amazed, but shouldn't have been really, as she never did things by halves. It was only a matter of time before she was putting me right and introducing me to new plants. I'd never even noticed dogwood, for instance, not until she did. It's such a good colour, especially in winter when there's not much colour about. She loved the old favourites, lavenders, delphiniums and plants usually referred to as cottage garden plants. She became really knowledgeable about gardens and was always putting more plants in, stuffing her little corner with them. "There's always a little bit of room for a few more," she'd say.'

Our friend Sarah Broughton has fond memories of that garden. 'Linda took me into her bedroom so that I could smell the scented stocks outside the windows,' she says. 'Flowers that you could only smell at night – how fabulous.'

Not content with contriving a garden out of nothing, Linda also wanted to cultivate an allotment for vegetables and flowers. She secured a totally overgrown patch of land with a sweet derelict shed on it, on a suntrap slope in the Rivelin Valley on the western approach to Sheffield. It was managed by an allotment society but owned by the city council. We put a lot of back-breaking effort into clearing the site before winter, so that it would be ready for planting in the spring. But we returned some months later to find that a gentleman of the road had been sheltering in our shed, so we did the right thing and left it to him.

Linda's enthusiasm for planting her own garden soon led to an interest in other gardens. 'Discovering Hodnet Hall Gardens in Shropshire was very exciting,' Jane says. 'It was a total accident. We were coming back from a gig in Cardiff – a hell of a drive – and we were tired and half-heartedly looking for an afternoon tea when we spotted an "Open Garden" sign.

'What a find. A beautiful wooded garden, a lake with black swans on it, streams and waterfalls, idyllic. Wild flowers everywhere and iris and rare species usually considered too tender for this climate. Oh, and not forgetting the teashop. Heaven. We sailed home after that, no problem. Then when we got back to Sheffield, Warren would say, "Good gig?" and Linda said, "Not bad, but a fantastic garden."

'One time when I went to pick Linda up for a show, I didn't have a car and I borrowed a pick-up truck. When I called to collect her you should have seen the gleam in her eye. We had always been limited by the height of the car but in a pick-up truck the sky was literally the limit. So off we set to Barrow-in-Furness or somewhere, and by the time we got there, the truck was full of plants and a weeping fig tree for Linda's sitting room. On our way back across the Pennines it started to snow, so we had to stop, get out Linda's coat and wrap it around the tree, because we thought it would get too cold.

'Even after we'd stopped working together, if she spotted a good garden she would send me a picture postcard of it. That is how I discovered Mottisfont near Southampton: very pretty, all pink and blue and white, best in June, famous for its roses; alliums also good. The postcard of Mottisfont is so over the top it looks unbelievable and on receipt of it we left home immediately to have a look. Not such a good afternoon tea, as I remember it . . .'

Gardens and gardening provided Linda with a soothing outlet for her grief over her mum's death. She also threw herself into work, gigging relentlessly around the country, night after night. Linda was picking up a lot of press coverage as she dashed around the UK, so we must have been doing something right.

As decision time approached for registration for Edinburgh in 1991, she decided against the toil of a three-week run and considerable cash outlay – also without the material for a brand-new solo show – and opted for a fun-filled week savaging the stories behind the headlines at the Gilded Balloon, as part of the *Cutting Edge* crew up from London's Comedy Store.

'Everybody in the team – Mark Thomas, Bob Boyton, Pat Condell, Richard Morton, Linda and I – all took turns in compering and running the various topical games we played,' says Dave Cohen, a longtime regular. 'Only Richard and I did the music. On the first day of our run, at 10 a.m., nine hours before show time, news came in that there'd been a coup in Russia. Frankly, our Gulf War material was already starting to sound a bit creaky, and all those jokes about George Bush invading Saddam's Iraq to get hold of his oil would have to wait another twelve years before enjoying a revival.

'So we had nine hours to produce an entirely new show. And that meant everyone had to do everything, including joining in with some of the songs. Now, as fans of *I'm Sorry I Haven't a Clue* will testify, singing was not Linda's strongest suit. However, she threw her heart and soul into 'Mikhail Gorbachev sings Elvis Presley' and it came into its own as the week progressed.

'At that time, I was popping down to Leeds at every opportunity to visit my mum, who was by now very ill with cancer. Linda, whose own mum had died recently, was a great source of comfort. Indeed, over the next twelve months, as I came to terms with my mum's subsequent death, Linda was one of the main people to see me through that time. Although she was still living in Sheffield, she came to London most Tuesdays to perform with the *Cutting Edge*, and sometimes she stayed overnight in my flat in Balham. We would talk about our families, or rather I would probably talk at Linda for hours on end, and she would offer sympathy, and advice. I always felt she was there for me.'

Popular Productions (formerly Sheffield Popular Productions) pulled off a neat coup in 1992 when John Connor, the producer of *Cutting Edge*, gave us the green light to promote the regular show for two nights at the Sheffield Festival, its only dates outside of London that season. The event was part of an extensive programme imaginatively entitled 'Hotter Than July' – our contribution to the festival. And so it was that a proud Ms Smith took her place on stage at Crookes Working Men's Club with teammates Kevin

Day, Steve Gribbin, Dave Cohen and Phill Jupitus, who provided a feast of topical gags, sketches and games.

After the show, *Sheffield Star* showbiz writer John High-field summed up Linda's significance on the comedy scene by calling her 'the first lady of South Yorkshire alternative comedy'. *Cutting Edge* led directly to Linda being invited onto the red-hot new BBC Radio One show *Loose Talk*, fronted by Mark Thomas and Kevin Day and produced by comedy wizard Armando Iannucci. I remember going with Linda to one recording at the historic Paris Studio in Lower Regent Street, London – truly the temple of radio comedy. I spent a while just staring at the walls of the stairwell leading down to the auditorium. They were plastered with stills from *The Goons*, *Round the Horne* – you name them; all the great series.

'It is very popular with prisoners,' Linda told the *Sheffield Star*. 'We get a lot of letters from people in jail. They send us jokes, which we broadcast. One lot sent us a letter telling us their pet mouse had died last week. It was really sad.'

Quite out of the blue, in November it was announced that Linda had been nominated for the 'Stage Newcomer Award' at the second British Comedy Awards. With characteristic wide-eyed bemusement, Linda told the *Sheffield Star*: 'I had never heard of this award until I had been nominated. No one could be more surprised than me about it.' She wasn't just being her modest self; we were both genuinely ignorant of the existence of the British Comedy Awards.

Nevertheless, we made the journey down to London on a wintry Sunday afternoon in December, just days away from Christmas. The journey was made all the more interesting because we would be travelling in a new car. That's new to us, because it wasn't ours, and new to the actual owner, because she had only just taken delivery of it. Credit must go to our friend and neighbour Valerie Marks for being prepared to lend us her new Lada – the latest model – because our Ford Transit van was not the kind of vehicle that award organisers would be expecting us to arrive in. That's right; I'd actually made it from Skoda to Lada in just a few short years. The invitation to the ceremony at the London Studios was clearly marked 'Carriages at 1 a.m.', not 'Ladas at 1 a.m.' Nevertheless, the deal was that we would go to the ball and drive back to Sheffield by daybreak, returning the car as we found it, so that Valerie could drive it to work a few hours later.

We didn't own a car, and I didn't have a tuxedo. I was far more a jeans and cords kinda person then – not the sharp suit wearer I am now – so I had to hire a tux for the weekend from a Pronuptia wedding dress shop on Ecclesall Road. Linda was always up for buying a tasty bit of new gear and an invitation to don formal evening wear was the perfect excuse for her. She went to a designer label clothes shop near Barnsley and returned with a wow of a costume, confirming the shop's reputation as the best between Manchester and Leeds. You couldn't get a good piece of clobber in Sheffield at the time – not for a woman of substance under the age of 35.

If Linda was nonplussed at the nomination, she had no expectations of winning, especially not against Jack Dee, or upcoming northern club comedian Billy Pearce. It was just great to be singled out. After all, she had only been a full-time comedian for three years.

The second British Comedy Awards in conjunction with the Writers' Guild of Great Britain were broadcast on LWT, bringing to mind our comedy chum Henry Normal's great joke, 'London Weekend Television, three overrated concepts'. The first awards had been hosted by Michael Parkinson at the ornate London Palladium; that the second had decamped to the London Studios on the other side of the Thames was a clear signal that there was change afoot on the television and radio comedy landscape. The old school was declining; the new wave had arrived and required a new venue. 'Parky' was replaced by the now ubiquitous Jonathan Ross.

We arrived for the early-evening reception quite hungry, foolishly expecting a buffet. Big mistake. We had signed up for a marathon, with nothing but drinks supplied until after the show. Such a dangerous mixture of comedians and alcohol on empty stomachs fuelled the feeling that anything could happen any time. But we sat at a table with Steve Punt and Hugh Dennis and their partners and we were all very well behaved.

Finally it came to time for the announcement we had been waiting for. The camera picked out all the nominees. I know this because my mum later told me that she saw Linda and me, and moments later, our friend Jack Dee skipped up to the stage to make his acceptance speech.

Two hours later, it was done and dusted and we headed off to a back lot where there was a funfair with old-fashioned carousels at our disposal as after-show entertainment. It was all good and lively stuff – lots of gossip, food (finally) and plenty to drink. Of course, I had to stay sober so that I could drive our carriage the 150 miles back home, and in that situation I tend not to risk even one glass.

Linda's nomination and appearance at the ceremony consolidated her status as someone to watch, and there would be other awards and prizes: the Radio Four listeners' poll; Test the Nation; and a radio Sony Gold for *I'm Sorry*

I Haven't a Clue. But Linda was never fussed about accolades. She enjoyed her work and was very content to be circulating with comedians and writers.

There has been posthumous recognition of her impact. The Chortle website presented me with an award for Linda's outstanding contribution to comedy, and I was honoured to be invited to the Savoy Hotel by the Radio Academy to witness Linda's induction into the Radio Hall of Fame. Fifteen years on from Linda's first unexpected nomination, I must admit I experienced a sense of déjà vu. As with the British Comedy Awards, I'd never heard of the Radio Hall of Fame until the invitation plopped through the letterbox.

Perhaps, though, Linda's former comedy contemporaries are better at assessing her comic abilities than any panel of judges. 'Her unique talent – in any medium – was a gift she had for personalising the great issues of our time in the context of mundane domesticity,' says Arnold Brown. 'This can no better be summed up than in her classic comment on Weapons of Mass Destruction: "They have looked every-where – they'll be in the last place they look, won't they? I'm like that with scissors. Of course the difference is, I know I have some scissors." A joke I would have killed my Granny for,' Arnold adds. 'Thank you, Linda.'

12

How Cable TV Changed My Life

Sheffield to Cuddington, Bucks

In the autumn of 1991, Linda and I spent a weekend with my brother and his then partner at their chocolate-box thatched cottage deep in the heart of Buckinghamshire. It was an unlikely place to start a love affair with America's most dysfunctional family, but I guess it had to happen somewhere.

Up until that weekend, Linda and I believed that *The Simpsons* was nothing more than a kids' cartoon series – over-hyped and over here. But as darkness fell over Bridgeway Cottage, Cuddington, and the log fire flared inside Tony and Melissa's rural haven, we saw the light. Or, more precisely, we took a rather different view of this garishly yellow family.

More than a decade later, in an interview for the documentary *The World According to 'The Simpsons'* on Channel Four, Linda recalled how it all began. 'My boyfriend's brother worked at Sky and the Simpsons were his ray of light in this really grim regime at Isleworth – as soon as you went in there, there was less light in the world. It was a very, very grim regime and the thing that kept them sane was watching and talking to each other about *The Simpsons*.

'"You must watch this; it's so brilliant," he urged. I didn't really believe him at first, but we were staying at his house one time and he just got a stack of videos and said, "You must watch at least one," so we watched one. Several hours later – early hours of the morning – we were still watching and just creasing up laughing and thinking, "This is the best thing we have ever seen in our lives. Ever." It hooked us from the opening credits.

'To begin with we were just getting tapes off him. Eventually we had to make the decision to go with Sky TV, which we'd always resisted because of Rupert Murdoch. My – sadly – late friend, Paul Foot, had a similar dilemma about the cricket and he agonised about it for ages, not wanting to get Sky but wanting to watch the cricket. Eventually he rationalised it by deciding that he loved the cricket more than he hated Rupert Murdoch – and that's how we rationalised it for *The Simpsons*, really. In the end, we loved them more than we hated Rupert.

'We became evangelical about them . . . so we'd make tapes from our connection at Sky and sort of leave them around, like Gideon's bibles, I suppose. We'd give them to people and say, "No, you must – this is the way, this is the future, this is the word."

'And it really caught on among the comedians, not surprisingly; they all loved it. Phill Jupitus was a huge early *Simpsons* fan and he does some very good impressions. He does Chief Wiggum particularly well, actually, and was much in demand in dressing rooms – "Give us a bit of Wiggum!"

'I just thought it was the best cultural product that I'd ever seen. It was wonderful, everything about it, from the opening sequence. The Danny Elfman music is so fantastic. It harks back to the great days of American TV sitcoms, when you had the great exciting show tune type music. Like *Your Show of Shows*, *Jackie Gleason* or *I Love Lucy* – a big orchestral sound, very Broadway influenced . . . exciting music, which builds in that way of classic American theme music.

'All the characters' personalities are outlined in the opening sequence and before the show's even started, you've got jokes: Homer at the nuclear plant with the plutonium down his shirt; Bart on the blackboard – always great – 'My homework was not stolen by a one-armed man'. I think that was one of my favourites. There are loads of visual gags, little signs on the hotel in the background – 'COCKROACH AND SILVERFISH FREE FOR THREE MONTHS'. The animals are always doing interesting, funny things. You could watch them several times and find visual gags that you've missed before.

Krusty the Clown is a big favourite of mine, because he just epitomises that dark heart of show business. There's a wonderful scene where Krusty's just finished a bit of the show and he's laughing and the curtain's coming down and you can see his eyes get progressively deader as the curtain drops. And he ends up with one of his: Urrrrrrr – that bombed!

'There's a wonderful moment before he starts a show where he's in something a lot of performers will recognise – a sort of pre-show melancholy and he's standing looking really hangdog and he pats his chest and goes, Urrrrr that brisket just ain't fitting right!

'You could talk for ever about how brilliant the script is. It is an astonishing script – I can't think of many live-action comedies that have anything like the same laughs per minute. I imagine the writers to be very much like the sarcastic comic-bookshop guy, both physically and in their persona, really. I imagine them being pretty geeky and really compulsive with just enormous brains and a big, big internet habit.'

The characters are the lifeblood of *The Simpsons*. There's an amazing gallery of personalities and Linda had a view on almost all of them, from major to minor.

'Homer will always be utterly stupid, utterly greedy,' she

said. 'Very basic child-like emotions really, not beyond that oral-fixated stage in life. So when he goes into the witness protection scheme, obviously he wears a T-shirt saying, "WITNESS PROTECTION SCHEME". There's a wonderful bit where the FBI are trying to explain his new identity to him. The agent says, "So you're not Homer Simpson any more. This is your new name: Mr Smith. So when I say, 'Mr Smith', that's you." And Homer just sits there blinking. That thing he does – that Homer blink, that uncomprehending blink.

'The reason we love Homer is that in all of us, however sophisticated we might think we are, there are elements of Homer. When someone explains something to him that he's not really interested in or it's a bit complicated, he's looking at them and listening and his brain is going, "Doo-di-doo-de-doo-doo."

'We all do that. I personally do it when people are telling me their names. I'm thinking, I'll remember that name another time; I'm not going to listen to it now. Then there's the greedy thing, which is totally exaggerated, but everyone has elements of it. With Homer it's everything. When the mathematical theory of Pi is mentioned, he says, "Mmmmm, pie." When pie falls on the floor, "Mmmmmm, floor pie." Everything is enticing to him. He's the advertiser's dream – as we all are to some extent.

'The writing's so honed – there are beautiful turns of phrase that come up all the time. For example there's an episode where Bart is at Sunday school with all his friends and the Sunday school teacher's telling them about hell and how terrible it is and Bart's saying, "Wouldn't it be like a hot bath – you eventually get used to it?"

'"No, you never get used to it throughout eternity."

'Martin suddenly pipes up, "And how might we avoid this abode of the damned?" So beautiful.

'I think the verbal comedy is very appealing to a British audience. We love those brilliantly honed gags, that cleverness with language; it's what we love in other American comedians and film-makers – for example, the good Woody Allen films. What we love are those fabulous gags and the turn of phrase. I also think the satire appeals to us greatly. The satire is not obviously topical because the episodes are made far in advance, but themes in American life and in world events, big themes – religion, education, capitalism, show business – are always in evidence.

'The main target for the satire, really, is consumerism – capitalism itself. There's a film, *Supersize Me*, where a guy lives on McDonald's, every meal for a month. He's Homer Simpson, really. Homer's been doing that for years and we've seen the results of that. The gluttony, the excess . . . all the outlets, the Krusty Burgers, the Do-nuts . . . this incredible piling up of rubbishy foods. For example, there's an episode where they go to a medieval fayre and Homer says, "I've eaten four different meats; I'm a real renaissance man." It parodies absolutely this excess.

'Kenneth Tynan famously said that he couldn't love anyone who didn't want to see *Look Back in Anger* and I feel that I – not that I couldn't love them – but I can't imagine having a really close friendship with someone who didn't get *The Simpsons*.'

Approximately eighteen months after the arrival of *The Simpsons* in our lives, Linda and I again found ourselves at the high altar of TV comedy, Bridgeway Cottage, Cuddington. As we took our all-too-familiar seats in the cosy living room, Tony said, 'I've got a bunch of tapes of this new

American comedy series which has yet to air on British TV. I think you might like it.'

Might like it . . . Linda instantly fell in love with it. She said soon afterwards, 'I think *Seinfeld* blows every sitcom out of the water . . . this is ground-breaking comedy.' It was a show like no other, 'a show about nothing', as paranoid, self-loathing, selfish, neurotic George Costanza (played by Jason Alexander) put it. He was possibly Linda's favourite sitcom character of all time.

Seinfeld was a comedy about a bunch of selfish, unsentimental New Yorkers constantly fretting over the minutiae of life. Set mainly in an apartment block in Upper West Side, Manhattan, it starred Jerry Seinfeld as an eponymous, fictionalised version of himself, and his three friends George, Elaine and Kramer. Cynical and mature, it revolutionised sitcoms. Not for Linda the sickly gooiness of *Friends* – in *Seinfeld* you would never hear those hideous 'oooohs' and 'aaahs' when the main couple made up after a fight, or someone said, 'I love you' or 'I missed you' or something equally sweet and yucky. Indeed it is said that the Seinfeld writers' mantra was, 'No Hugging, No Learning'.

Linda went on to consume every *Seinfeld* episode ever produced. Unfortunately, to her disgust, ridiculous late-night scheduling in the UK meant it never really took off this side of the Atlantic. But perhaps the current DVD box-set craze will lift it from being viewed as just another 90s American sitcom so that it can take its place in the comedy hall of fame, perhaps as the best comedy series of all time.

The Larry Sanders Show was another favourite. Larry Sanders is much beloved of British comedians and comedy writers. Linda and I worshipped it and made a point of enthusing about it to our friends outside of the comedy world. I reckon we must have watched every episode at least half a dozen times.

Much imitated but never matched, it took us by storm when it first aired in 1993. There was a lot of high-risk language, which explained why terrestrial TV didn't show it much before the midnight slot. Then it sometimes got paired with *Seinfeld*, which has no swearing.

A spell guest-hosting in Johnny Carson's seat on *The Tonight Show* inspired stand-up comic Garry Shandling to create Larry Sanders, a talk-show host with a strong line in vanity who felt perpetually undermined by the people who worked for him and everyone who appeared on his show.

Perhaps it should be a three-way tie for second place behind *The Simpsons*. For *Curb Your Enthusiasm* was Linda's last great TV comedy love. By the time she had viewed the first four series she was a committed fan, watching re-runs to further analyse plot lines that were finessed to the point of perfection.

And last in the pantheon of Linda Smith's all-time favourite US comedies is *King of the Hill*. First seen on Channel Four and still showing on FX cable channel, where Linda would devour it every day as an early-evening hors d'oeuvre, *King of the Hill* centres on the everyday workaday lives of the suburban Hill family living in the fictional Texan town of Arlen. Hank Hill is a salesman of 'propane and propane accessories' and is a traditionalist struggling to maintain his moral standards in a sea of modern trends. His many catch-phrases include: 'I'll tell you what'; and, about son Bobby, 'That boy ain't right' and 'What has the MTV done to you, son?' Linda adopted them all with glee.

Her other great TV love was crime. It seemed she was never more than a few paces away from *Columbo* and its eponymous central character. If she was at home of an afternoon, not writing or gardening or on the phone, she would spend well over an hour in the company of the most famous fictional homicide detective in the Los Angeles Police Department.

Lieutenant Columbo had his own distinctive uniform: white shirt; dark tie; crumpled suit; very crumpled beige trench coat; and chewed cigar. His most recognisable catchphrase was 'just one more thing', which was always uttered as his signature farewell. It often took the suspect by surprise and levered out another crucial shred of evidence.

What attracted Linda to this series was its formula – what was known in TV crime circles as an 'inverted detective story'. In *Columbo*, the TV audience sees the build-up to the crime, knows who did it and how it was perpetrated. The hook for viewers on the couch is spotting the clues that will lead Columbo to a successful prosecution of his theories.

Linda was always fascinated by the leading actors and actresses who turned up as special guests, mainly playing baddies. Patrick McGoohan (*Danger Man* and *The Prisoner*) led the way with four episodes and also directed several; Robert Culp (*I Spy*) and Jack Cassidy both appeared three times as murderers. Obviously *Columbo* was a series actors were delighted to have on their CVs.

I thought there were hundreds of episodes, but I'm assured that there were only 69. Linda must have seen all of them, and some many times over. Apparently, and Linda would have known this fact, *Columbo* was parodied twice by *The Simpsons*; reassuringly for the folk of Springfield, police chief Wiggum boasted he was 'able to solve an episode of *Columbo*'.

Linda talked about her '*Columbo* thing' to Sian Pattenden of *Word* magazine in 2004: 'Getting cable television installed is the road to hell. I reckon I've watched every episode of *Columbo* ever made, and they made them for about forty years. It's not chronological – you have this weird sensation, watching Peter Falk age and grow young, age and grow young. By the time you're finished he must have been 93 and retired from the LAPD. I got cable telly for the murders. Like George Orwell says, there's nothing like an English murder. On *Midsomer Murders*, the body count would raise eyebrows in South Central LA. But it's not accompanied by a shred of annoying tension as to who has killed or why. There's no thriller aspect to it. It's entirely restful. What isn't murder is Nazis on cable. There's about 500 history channels, all completely obsessed with the Third Reich. You can watch UK Nazi Gold for about twelve hours a day, marvellous shows like, *My Top 20 Nuremberg Moments*, with Stuart Maconie and Lemmy from Motorhead.'

Linda's best '*Columbo* buddy' was Simon Nicholls, fellow popular culturalist and former producer of *The News Quiz*. He had the bug big time as well. 'I was a big fan of *Columbo* and Linda and I would discuss it at great length. And she, like me, knew episodes word for word. If I watch an episode of *Columbo*, in the first five minutes I can tell you exactly how Columbo finds everything out.

'She said, "If you like *Columbo*, you should watch *Monk*." For me, that's Linda. On the one hand you've got the incredibly intelligent intellectual, and on the other hand you've got someone who's obsessed with trash. One minute she could be talking about some amazing poetry and the next minute *America's Next Top Model*. I've got a very eclectic mind and I take in everything. I think Linda was that kind of person.'

It's true. Linda's tastes were wide-ranging. But her preferences leant heavily towards crime. She (and I) thought *The Sopranos* was the greatest piece of TV drama ever. The arrival of each episode was met with a level of anticipation that no other programme ever commanded in our household.

She loved the film *Goodfellas* and could recite whole passages of dialogue from it – mind you, we must have watched it on TV and video a couple of dozen times. In an interview with Andrew Collins, Linda confessed: 'I could probably enact every part in *Goodfellas*. I think I know every frame.' *Mean Streets*, *Casino*, *Taxi Driver*, *Raging Bull* and *Cape Fear* were also big favourites from the Martin Scorsese canon.

In case I give the impression that Linda was engrossed only in dark materials, there were just as many forces of light among her favourites. Our friend and keen moviegoer Sarah Broughton recalls, 'In Sheffield one Saturday afternoon, Linda and I dressed up in fifties clothes to celebrate the wondrousness of Audrey Hepburn. Linda had arranged an "Afternoon of Audrey" where we watched *My Fair Lady* and *Breakfast at Tiffany's* on video and then had afternoon tea. A perfect Audrey afternoon.'

13
Flight of the Plant Pots

Sheffield to Forest Gate, London

Q: Who or what is the love of your life?
Linda: Warren, my boyfriend (plus my work and gardening).

L inda and I rarely argued, but she would occasionally get cross with me if I was behaving selfishly, unthinkingly or being plain stupid. In our early years, what really provoked her was unexplained lateness. She would get worried if I didn't show up when I said I would. I don't remember arguing over any other thing.

'You said you'd be back early evening! Why didn't you ring?'

'I'm sorry.'

'Well, phone next time.'

Linda would never go 'girly' on you. She just wasn't like that. I don't think she ever liked to display vulnerability, certainly not in public, and not at home, really. There would always be a sense of decorum. She would make her opinion known, but it wouldn't turn into a tiff or a quarrel.

I didn't read much into it back then, but now I wonder if her anxiety around my lateness was linked to what had happened to her just before we met. She'd been dumped on from a great height, first by her dad, and then by her boyfriend Brian. Perhaps there was a subconscious fear that I'd disappear, as they had done. Looking back, perhaps I was careless of her feelings. I didn't have the same worries. I came from a very stable family and my parents were together for life, without any question – and so were their friends and contemporaries. That was also my expectation.

When it came to timekeeping, Linda was allowed to be late. It didn't work both ways. Other men might have fretted about their partner still being out in the West End of London at two or three o'clock in the morning after work – after the Comedy Store – but I trusted her implicitly in all respects. In the time before mobile phones, I just had to hope that she was safe and that nothing untoward was happening. Of course, this was also the case once mobile phones were around, because Linda didn't use one.

She had a whole network of friends in comedy whose places she could stay at, but by now she was spending more time in London than she was in Sheffield. There was a huge amount of travelling to and fro. 'This is silly,' she said finally. 'I'm going to have to get a place in London. I can't keep sleeping on people's couches, or at your brother's place.'

I agreed in theory, but I wasn't ready to leave Sheffield. I wanted to stay; there was more great work to be done – and what about our fantastic social life? How could we leave that behind? At the same time, we both knew the move back to London was inevitable. Linda's work was going from strength to strength, and London was the focus. 'Let's get to the point of packing up, at least,' she said. So, gradually, we began to box up our possessions.

Aside from our community and touring theatre work, which gave rise to The Chuffinelles, we will be remembered in Sheffield for providing six glorious months of the Route 52 cabaret club. The opening night on 31 January 1992 was hugely anticipated and did not disappoint its 400-

capacity full house. Linda was pivotal to the success of this venture. She took on the mantle of resident compere, while Suzanne Phillips and I looked after booking the acts and promotion. The spadework had been done by two DJs we knew who ran the Ju Ju Club, promoting world music. The Ju Ju Club set up a night at the concert room of the Crookes Working Men's Club on Fridays – and we came to an agreement whereby we alternated Fridays with them and put out a joint mailing list. Legend has it that local rock heroes Def Leppard played at Crookes in 1979.

The club was subject to the arcane membership rules of the Club and Institute Union, which reduced women to passive supporters. They were there courtesy of their husbands or boyfriends, not in their own right. So although the set-up was ideal in every other way, we were always going to be on a collision course, no matter how cute we were about trying to navigate our collective way round the sexist statutes. It was a little local detail that Linda would exploit to the full when she got to the microphone.

Route 52 took its name from the 'Eager Beaver' bus route 52, which linked the Crookes area with the city centre. South Yorkshire Transport even put in a little bit of sponsorship and merchandise, including a set of one-off Route 52 beer mats. A lot of beer was sold at the bar at very reasonable prices, which must have been a boon to the club's finances. What's more, if members of the audience drank too much, they could leave their cars and head up or down the hill on a number 52 bus. It was one of the most reliable services in town.

The winning format was an update of the New Variety-style show I had imported from London. What was different was that several regular performers like Linda, and a house band fronted by vocalist Jane Ashley, provided more of a club feeling. Linda and I had always wanted to introduce a band. The aim was to play tunes from Duke Ellington to Motown, along with a specially composed Route 52 theme.

Linda reiterated our long-term commitment to the New Variety format to Alfred Hickling of the *Yorkshire Post*. 'A lot of favours have been called in, but myself and producer Suzanne Phillips like to think of Route 52 as unique among comedy clubs in that it will not present a series of stand-ups exclusively. We hope to draw in many other types of entertainment. With the six-piece house band, we aim to create a feel akin to that of the Steve Nieve band on the Jonathan Ross show. Let's face it, they're the only reason I watch it.' (Steve Nieve was Elvis Costello's bandleader.)

The first night of Route 52 hit the spot with a new and exciting cocktail of comedy, music and variety, headlined by Mark Steel and ably supported by Betty Spital, Kevin Seisay and Claire Mooney. With tickets at £5 and concessions £3, it was tremendous value for money, even if you did have to shell out another £3 in advance to buy membership to the three clubs: Crookes, Ju Ju and Route 52.

'Route 52 was a phenomenal success,' says Mike McCarthy, 'but first you had to get past Derek the doorman, whose main mission in life was to turn away as many punters as possible unless they had parted with a membership fee. I remember looking out of the front doors and seeing queues snaking out of the car park down the road. We never had a bad night there. It caught the public's imagination.

'Popular Productions was making a conscious effort at that time to move away from theatre – hence the name change. We didn't know where we were going, but we wanted to explore stuff that wasn't totally theatre-based. This coincided with the realisation that we just wouldn't get the level of financial support – grant aid – for the theatre work to allow us to operate at the level we wanted to. We were getting severe headaches from banging our heads against that wall.'

You could definitely get your kicks at Route 52. It was a fast-moving variety show with a mix of acts drawn from South Yorkshire, the Manchester area and often a bill topper from London. The burgeoning Manchester comedy scene supplied Caroline Aherne, who performed both of her best-known characters, Sister Mary Immaculate and Mrs Merton. Steve Coogan spilt lager all over the stage as Paul Calf, and John Thomson gave us a rendition of his non-sexist club comic, Bernard Righton. On the very last night people were literally dangling from the rafters as they hung onto Eddie Izzard's every word. He served up a magnificent one-man show over two and a half hours that final hot July evening.

We had a large hardcore of regular supporters. Some came especially to hear Linda in her anchor role as compere. Frances Gray, local resident and Linda's former university drama lecturer says, 'One occasion I can recall vividly was the day after the Labour election defeat by Major in 1992, when Linda did a gig at the working men's club. 'Monster Raving Loony Party did well, didn't they?' she said. 'Never thought they'd win.'

Maria de Souza, one of the city council's arts and festival co-ordinators, also remembers that night. 'I always loved Linda's line at Route 52 just after Labour's election defeat in 1992. "Kinnock, you useless slaphead – the Hezbollah could have won!"

Twelve years later, when she came face to face with Neil Kinnock on *Have I Got News For You*, Linda was able to question the former Labour leader about this ignominious defeat. 'In 1992, do you think you'd have won if, instead of campaigning, you'd just pissed off on holiday for three weeks? Just gone away, kept your gob off the telly, maybe replaced yourself with, say, a lovely little kitten. A ginger kitten, if you wanted to be a bit rebellious. A jar of ginger marmalade. Something like that. Do you think you would have sailed in? I mean, I realise you were up against the mighty charisma of John Major. That's a tough old one, isn't it? The man who ran away from the circus to become an accountant.'

Out of sheer curiosity, and comradeship for our socialist magician friend Ian Saville, Linda went along to a Labour Party rally in Islington on the eve of the 1992 general election. Ian had been booked to perform on stage, but was sidelined to a roving role around the hall. This was the election that Neil Kinnock thought he couldn't lose. Having seen off the left of the party, he had begun a process of reform that was to lead to New Labour.

According to Ian, all politics were expunged from the event, and a couple of people who started singing 'the Internationale' were hustled away by the security guards. At the end of the event, Neil and Glenys processed down the steps like a regal couple, and after Neil had made his vapid speech, the party workers dutifully threw their streamers (as the little printed notes on each table told them to) while balloons fell from the ceiling.

A few days later, Mike McCarthy and I filled two seats at the massive Sheffield Arena, where Kinnock's electoral machine had set up a bizarre eve-of-poll rally. Kinnock's message to the people was: 'We meet here in Sheffield on the threshold of a great victory. It's time for change. It's time for Labour.' Only ten years earlier he had emerged as *the* person most likely to lead a left-leaning Labour Party, not one set on the path to hounding out the left.

Kicking off with a ludicrous orchestrated ceremonial march into the auditorium, complete with heavenly gospel choir, colliery brass band and some of the finest soul, R&B and jazz voices in Britain, this event was destined to be a political shambles. The press mocked it and Kinnock. Poorly thought out and woefully lacking in atmosphere, it reeked of defeat. The sparsely attended event reflected the subsequent dearth of votes for Labour and ushered in another five years of John and Norma and their pea-eating circus. Things could only get better.

Linda's politics were always quite hard to pin down. Most people would think of her in terms of being a socialist, but the following statement made in an interview with Laurie Taylor for *New Humanist* magazine is about as near to a personal definition as she ever got. 'I'm left wing, but not in an organised way. I'm personally left wing. And there's also something of the working-class anarchist about me. I like to throw a little spanner in the works.'

She was an anarchist in her own way, always pushing against authority and rules. In a Q&A for another magazine she confessed to admiring freedom fighters, disliking fascists, censors and puritans, and said that she would quite like to have been Trotsky or Lenin during the Russian Revolution. She resisted all overt and covert approaches to join a party, and proudly claimed that she had never been a card-carrying member of any political organisation or grouping. But she did flirt with friends who were active members of the Labour Party, Young Socialists, Militant, Socialist Workers' Party and Big Flame. She wasn't a great wearer of political badges,

The Chuffinelles.

Linda with Betty Spital in 'The Seriously Funny Guide to Love, Death and the Co-Op' at the Edinburgh Festival, 1989.

With Henry Normal (left) and Chris Coop, on their way to Edinburgh, 1990.

The Cutting Edge Team, 1991.
L-R: Dave Cohen, Bob Boyton, Linda, Richard Morton, Kevin Day, Mark Thomas, producer John Connor.

Christmas dinner with Bessie, Barbara and family.

Hattie Hayridge and Linda backstage at Edinburgh, 1994.

Linda and me on
holiday in Cuba, 1991.

Linda and me on the
beach at Whitby, North
Yorkshire, 1993 – we
didn't actually build
this sandcastle.

Linda taking tea in the garden she created from scratch in Sheffield. This was a typical pose for her.

Portrait of Linda, by Martin Jenkinson, 1993.

With fellow patrons of the Spit Lit festival – clockwise from left, Bonnie Greer, Jo Brand, Yasmin Alibhai-Brown, Linda, Dame Helena Kennedy.

With friends Sarah Broughton and Suzanne Philips and me, at Sissinghurst Gardens, Kent, on one of Linda's last trips out, 2005.

Linda sitting in for Robert Elms at BBC Radio London, 2004 – the only photo of her on air that I have ever come across.

but she assisted a sizeable list of causes by appearing at events and demonstrations.

Linda appeared at dozens of benefit concerts, for both international and domestic campaigns. These ranged from striking and sacked miners to the striking Liverpool dockers and Hillingdon hospital workers. She swung behind solidarity movements from Cuba to Nicaragua, helped raise funds for medical aid for the victims of torture and fundraised for medical supplies for Palestine and El Salvador, for the welfare of people in Tigray, Ethiopia, and for Women's Aid refuges in Britain. The list is endless. As a paid entertainer, she appeared at dozens of social events for the trade union and Labour movement until that kind of work literally dried up.

Unfortunately, Route 52 came to an end when a young Crookes club member took a swing at Eddie Izzard. We moved the concept to the city centre Ponds Forge swimming complex basement space for the autumn season and renamed it 'Splash Club', but it was never the same. The venue didn't have the right atmosphere and the acoustics were lousy. Linda began touring a new show and was unavailable to host. We really missed her pizzazz.

The sun was setting on the empire, but we refused to accept that the best days were behind us. Meanwhile, our Popular Productions agency was representing Linda and several other comedy and music acts. We were also booking out tours such as Steve Coogan's new show, 'In Characters', which he was trying out before going to Edinburgh. He went on to win the Perrier Award that year with his Manchester buddy John Thomson.

Although Linda was often away on the road, she and I did our fair share of gallivanting around together. Music was a huge part of both of our lives, and we were jazz fans.

Whether it was grooving in a pub room, sophisticated Soho club or formal concert hall, if the music was good we would be sky high for days.

Possibly the best holiday we ever had anywhere was our trip to Cuba in early 1991, when we signed up for the annual Ronnie Scott's jazz club pilgrimage to the Havana Jazz Festival. At the time, the global picture was not pretty. The US air force was carpet-bombing Iraq and hostilities were hotting up in the first Gulf War. This was the backdrop as we arrived to join our fellow jazz enthusiasts gathering for a flight from London to Shannon in Ireland, before switching to a shambolic Aeroflot plane and the tortuous flight on to Cuba. We all got drunk on Guinness – the nerves needed calming after the Aeroflot crew had ordered us off the plane twice so they could get on with repairs before we left.

Cuba had sided with China at the United Nations and opposed western action on Iraq. It was also beginning to reel from a chronic petrol and diesel shortage since the calamitous break-up of the Soviet Union, its main political and economic ally. It marked the end of the vital oil-for-sugar arrangement and the country was awaiting delivery of thousands of bicycles from China. Most of the fuel-guzzling old American cars were parked up on bricks, as their owners had neither fuel nor spare parts to keep them on the roads.

The festival director, the great pianist Chuco Valdes of Irakere, had broken a hand, so he wouldn't be playing. This did not augur well. American musicians such as Dizzy Gillespie and Wynton Marsalis had to turn back and reluctantly observe the US government blockade, or they would lose their passports. As soon as we entered our room at the Hotel Presidente we spotted a cockroach in the shower, so another room was prepared. Let's just say nothing ever went to plan and it was complete mañana. But we loved every minute of the concerts, the jam sessions, the rum-filled open-air nightclubs, spontaneous parties in strangers' flats, smuggling goods to locals from tourist shops and the decaying glory that was old Havana.

Linda often said that the most memorable gig she saw was Nina Simone at the Winter Gardens, Blackpool, during the jazz festival in July 1992. I remember it vividly. We both loved her music but were worried about Simone's famed artistic temperament disrupting the concert. I'd never seen her live but Linda had – at Ronnie Scott's in the early 1980s – a gig that turned sour because the diva went 'off on one'.

There was a big but apprehensive crowd gathered, waiting patiently for this great symbol of contemporary black music; a woman who had been a child prodigy and desperately wanted to make her mark as the first African-American classical pianist. Her dream unrealised, events in her early life fuelled a hatred of racial injustice in the United States and led to her development as a seminal figure in the civil rights movement of the 1960s. I apologise to the memory of the late Nina, because she rightly didn't like to be categorised. That night we were treated to a compilation of jazz, R&B, gospel and soul by the 'High Priestess of Soul'. There, now she's gonna put a spell on me.

Later Linda said of the gig, 'She was a tricky customer, I must say. It was a great concert, but there was just this strange fear through the audience because she demanded the amount of applause you'd expect to get at the end of a five-hour opera, after every number.

'And there was a kind of psychic understanding between us as an audience that if we didn't clap hard enough, if we didn't clap our hands bloody, even when she announced what song she was going to do, she'd just walk off. So it was a strange relationship to have with an artist. Terror, really. The first time she announced a song she was going to do and a couple of people in the audience clapped, and stopped, she said, "Yes," implying, yes all of you, please, clap now. A bit like, "You, boy."'

Linda's other favourite jazz gigs included: Pharoah Sanders at Dingwalls; Mingus Big Band at Ronnie Scott's; Ruben Gonzalez at Ronnie Scott's; Betty Carter at Ronnie Scott's; Jimmy McGriff Quartet at the Leadmill, Sheffield; Sun Ra and his Arkestra at Sheffield University. Her favourite jazz venue was 'Old' Ronnie Scott's, not the place it now is, under new management. Her least liked venue was the Jazz Café.

Both Linda and I were 'vinyl junkies' until the last. We gave way to buying CDs long after most of our friends and the rest of the western world had surrendered. Linda began her vinyl collection in earnest with raids on Rare and Racy in Sheffield; I spent far too many hours in the basement of Dobell's Jazz Shop on Charing Cross Road raking through the second-hand section. Linda's favourite jazz albums were: Dexter Gordon, *Our Man in Paris*; Chocolate Armenteros, *En Sexteto*; John Coltrane, *A Love Supreme*; Miles Davis, *Kind of Blue*; *Ella Fitzgerald Sings the Cole Porter Song Book*; Nina Simone, *Baltimore*.

Around that time, Linda and I got the bug for 'Deep Soul' music from Dave Godin – one of the most brilliant, erudite, entertaining and passionate human beings either of us had ever met, and certainly the first Esperantist. He was manager of the only UK civic cinema – the Anvil in Sheffield – and made some of the boldest programming decisions in British picture-house history, including, for one night only, on

Linda's birthday, arranging a special presentation of *Baby Doll*, one of her favourite films.

Linda went up to Edinburgh for the last week of the 1992 festival to perform at the first 'Women In Comedy' festival, presented by the Gilded Balloon in association with the *Guardian*. This celebration of funny females played to packed audiences in the main house in the prime 9.30 p.m. slot. Among Linda's fellow performers were Lynne Ferguson (compere), Caroline Aherne, Hattie Hayridge, Jenny Lecoat, Jenny Eclair, Maria McErlane, Gerry McNulty – and from the USA, Thea Vidale.

She spent the latter part of 1992 working on a new and original sketch comedy show with Steve Gribbin, formerly half of the defunct Skint Video double act. Sponsored by the trade union NALGO (now Unison), 'Hello Cruel World' was a riotous guide to world history, including: Martin Scorsese's version of the English Civil War in the style of *Goodfellas*; the Marx Brothers' *A Night in Eastern Europe*; and star nightclub comic turn, 'The Pope'. Written and performed by Linda and Steve, the 90-minute show was directed for Popular Productions by Mike McCarthy and toured until the following summer.

'I enjoyed it,' Mike says. 'It wasn't really like directing theatre; it was more like providing an outside eye for performers, to advise them on what was working and what wasn't working. I was observing more than directing. I think I provided the safety net. It was great, the fact that Steve and Linda were constantly generating material for it. Really turning it out, funny stuff. It was interesting for me to watch the process by which comedians work, the way they would happily throw stuff out, the constant rewriting.'

Linda and I should really have moved to London in the

summer of 1992. The best work in Sheffield was over by the late summer, although I went into another round of cabaret in autumn 1992, which wasn't brilliant. Mike had moved away and was about to start another project. Suzanne Phillips was now my partner, but after a year she decided she wanted to go into TV directing at BBC Wales and moved to Cardiff. I was faced with the slightly daunting prospect of finding another work partner. Our theatre work had run its course over ten years and there was no more funding in prospect. What's more, I'd done my best work on the cabaret front. The truth was, if I wanted to keep running the agency, I could do it in London. Linda really wanted to go, but I held back, umming and ahhing. I kept thinking something might come up. If I was as decisive then as I am now, we would have gone a full year earlier than we did.

It made Linda none too happy that I was dilly-dallying. She was pressing to move because it made a lot of sense for her life and work. She'd been in Sheffield four years longer than I had – 14 years in total. Sheffield had taken a big slice of her life and she'd run out of steam there. Her work was now in London and around the country. Sheffield was simply where she lived. 'There's a lot of pressure to move to London as a comedian, and as a Londoner it makes a lot of sense, but I won't move away,' she told the *Sheffield Star* in 1989. But by 1993 she had changed her mind completely. 'I wish we had moved a year earlier. It would have been better for both of us,' she said later.

People in London were saying to her, 'Hold on, we're going out for a drink and you're rushing to get your train back. And it's going to take you three hours to get there. Why are you doing that?'

She was right and I was hanging on for something that

was never going to come. 'You know it's the end,' she said
to me. 'You've done your very best here. You can't trump
it. So why not just say, "That's it, clean break, goodbye?"'

I was being a bit head-in-the-sand, but finally I accepted
that it was time for a change. So I started to look for jobs
in the arts in London. I was after something that would pay
me a reasonable salary; it didn't have to be in theatre or
comedy, necessarily. That summer I got a job as an arts
manager and fundraiser in Hackney, so I moved down to
London.

Linda couldn't move at that point because she was about
to do a whole season in Edinburgh. At last she had taken
that final, bold step and made all the correct preparations
to present her first full one-hour solo show. She loped out
on stage on Saturday 14 August at the Music Box in Victoria
Street, a new venue to her, but one that had an impressive
roster of acts promoted by the aptly named Curious Productions from Glasgow. It was branded under the Fool's Paradise
banner, the same as the club in Sheffield, and was produced
by one of the ubiquitous Evans brothers, the one known in
the trade as 'Evans Below'.

A curious business it turned out to be. I didn't go up for
the first few days, as I couldn't really get away from my new
job in London. Shame on me! If I had, there is no doubt
that Linda would not have mislaid her opening night on
Friday 13 August! She told me on the phone later that she
had genuinely thought it was starting on the Saturday. The
whole run seemed plagued by venue apathy and was probably
her biggest disappointment at Edinburgh. It should have
been the year she really got noticed, but things just didn't
go her way.

She consoled herself in good company. Our pal Mark

Steel was in the slot following hers for the whole three weeks, and we struck up a friendship with punk poet legend John Cooper Clarke, who was doing the early-evening show for the last week. To look at him – tall and ultra slim in the tightest pair of jeans imaginable – people would think he hardly ever ate a meal. Not true. We went out dining with him after midnight on a few occasions and he had the biggest appetite of all of us. He also had the best rock 'n' roll stories we'd ever heard. Talk about a national treasure – he's flaming brilliant.

Finally Linda and I moved in with Ian Parsons and Gail Elliman at their house in Forest Gate, east London. We arrived as paying guests from Sheffield and left eighteen months later as lifelong friends. We moved about a mile away but still remained solid mates. We just clicked on first meeting. We shared politics and a distinct liking for most matters cultural. The only other time this had really happened to Linda and me was when we had first met each other. So Ian and Gail became our constant companions to jazz gigs at clubs like Ronnie Scott's, to comedy shows, movies and film festivals.

Linda's next foray into BBC radio coincided with our move to London. She was hired as an on-air contributor for *Windbags*, a series co-hosted by Jo Brand and Donna McPhail. Hailed as a new (female) format for new wave comedy, political satire and chat aimed at metropolitan women, it went out on Radio One. During one episode, she took a gentle swipe at our new living environment.

'My local paper, *The Newham Murderer*, is a fine publication. It's about 20 pages of assorted murders and the weekend TV in the middle – which is quite handy really, 'cos you're not going out with all that going on – and I love the small ads in it. It's got all sorts of personal services in it, like kissograms and grannygrams. I don't know what the hell grannygrams do – I suppose they burst into family parties and say, "You're not putting me in a home!"'

In 1995 we finally moved into our own home – not rented, but bought. We weren't ever fussed about mortgages in Sheffield – renting was fine – but in London we got to the point where we decided we needed to be settled. We bought a former railway worker's cottage in Stratford, east London and – joy of joys! – Linda finally had her own garden. She set out to transform it, although she couldn't do anything about the somewhat challenging dimensions: 100 feet in length and 10 feet wide.

After we moved in, we went out to inspect our new 'Garden of Eden' and found a shocking dog's toilet courtesy of the former owner's Alsatian. That clearing and cleaning-up job was nowhere to be found in good gardening manuals. We filled several skips with debris, including hundreds of frag-ments of broken glass and other remnants from Second World War bombing raids. We levelled the ground, intro-duced tons of new soil and then I went about building a winding yellow brick path. We dug and constructed a pond. It was a big hit with the local frogs. A builder acquaintance called Andrew (Linda sneaked him into a character in her radio sitcom) did all the heavy-duty work, laying a bona fide York stone patio sourced from street workmen in Hack-ney and Enfield. He also brought in railway sleepers to edge the patio and bank the flowerbeds – quite fitting for a railway cottage (and a railway worker's daughter).

Linda's work on the garden coincided with Geoff Hamilton's creation of his Artisan's Cottage Garden on TV, which he achieved on a very small budget. Geoff's garden epitomised his approach to gardening. Like Linda, he crammed in the plants and allowed them to do their own thing in what seemed to be organised chaos. She admired his style.

Linda's planting regime relied heavily on producing a riot of colour, starting with a mass of white roses over the wooden patio frame – a Mme Alfred Carrière – then red oriental poppies, cardoons, alliums, hostas, iris – yellow and blue – very tall sunflowers, box plants in the ground and in pots, achillea, aquilegia, euphorbia, sweet peas, tulips, *Verbena bonariensis*, peonies, chocolate cosmos, night-scented and Virginia stock, larkspur, nigella, black ornamental grasses, other roses – white Iceberg, white Mme Hardy, white Gloire de Dijon – all a nod to the Sissinghurst White Garden. Linda also planted tomatoes and vegetables, having great success with courgettes and potatoes.

Our friend Liz Kneen is a professional gardener. 'Strangely enough, I didn't talk too much about gardening with Linda, but we exchanged plants,' she says. 'When we did discuss stuff it was clear that she belonged to that large and select band of English women gardeners, usually self-taught, who obsess about their plants, have very specific tastes and take endless trouble, experimenting with commitment and flair. She once remarked that there should be a sort of masonic guild for garden obsessives, The Order of the Muddy Boot.

'The first time I saw Linda's garden, it was the middle of winter. Warren and Linda had taken up residence with Ian Parsons in Forest Gate and were looking for a place of their own. Arnold (Brown) and I had been invited over for Sunday lunch and we had a fantastic meal, a gorgeous chicken stew (Warren must have had something else!) followed by something I'd never had before, a homemade chocolate cake called

Diplomatico. Later we went out into Ian's garden and Linda showed me her temporary garden, a mind-boggling array of hundreds of labelled pots of all sizes, housing most of her plants transported from Sheffield. They were Linda's dormant favourites waiting for . . . destination unknown. This was a woman who clearly did nothing by halves.

'The next time gardening came up was when Linda and Warren arrived for supper at ours (about three hours late) rather hyped up and distracted. They had been chopping up space and landscaping their own virgin Stratford garden, which we saw later on that summer. It was exceptionally long and narrow, but Linda made some good decisions to enhance the rectilinear space – beds in a zig-zag configuration edged by upturned bricks with a path leading down to a pond.

'The garden was filled with the plants that gardeners love. Beautiful peachy roses, vibrant pinks, phlox, penstemons, campanulas, hellebores, wild strawberries – invasive but too appealing to miss out on, was her reasoning. There was morning glory on the fence and in one bed, on its own, a lovely plantation of sunflowers that she had organised in rows. "The better to see the way they turn their enormous heads towards the sun during the course of one day," she said. That was her take on the whole thing. It was worshipful.

'I remember we talked about the fact that certain plants had square rather than round stems, but why? We decided it must be something to do with the plant's best way to absorb maximum sunlight. We used to laugh about horticultural snobbisms. Dahlias were all the rage at the time. Of course they had been good old boys' show favourites in gardens and allotments for decades ("Some as big as your head!") and now they were reclaiming their rightful place in smart gardens. But never the lemon yellow ones, we agreed. Then we all sat down to a whole barbecued salmon. They sometimes go together: fabulous cook, fabulous gardener.'

Gardening became a major passion of Linda's. She loved it for its own sake, but it also complemented her work. When she was writing, she would often go out into the garden first, with a cup of tea, and get picking and weeding. Then maybe an hour or two later she'd come in and do a little bit of scribbling. Once she'd written down whatever it was she'd come in to write, she'd go out again. That's how she often worked, in little spurts. She'd think of something, sort it out as she gardened, come in, write it down and go back. It was one of her places for thinking. The garden – and gardening – inspired her. It also provided a haven from her packed work schedule, which was about to get a whole lot busier.

14

Linda and Her Beloved Auntie Beeb

'When I first started doing *The News Quiz*, funny how it happened really – I wasn't meant to be a panellist. I was a between-stairs maid at the BBC and I'd just come into the studio to black lead the grate and bring fresh laudanum for the panellists. I think how it came about was a bet between Alan Coren and Francis Wheen who, as you probably know, is 17th in line to the throne of England, and they had a Pygmalion-style bet between them. Alan said, "I bet you, Wheen, that I could have this little scullery maid making light-hearted comments about the news like a duchess." And that's how it happened. That's how I got to be on it. Of course, I say Alan Coren; it wasn't the Alan Coren we've got now – there have been several Alans over the years, obviously, because he would be about 500 or something.'

Ever since her teenage years, Linda had been a keen listener to radio comedy and drama; as an adult she was among thousands of people who have Radio Four on morning and night, even when they're not at home! We lived in a divided house: Radio Four in the bedroom, the living room and the garden; Radio Five Live in the kitchen. We would achieve a diplomatic balance in the car, depending on the time of day or evening, and what was on.

For Linda, Radio Four was the promised land, a place she

never imagined she would reach. She hadn't had the kind of 'good start' in early life normally associated with many people in the professions, particularly BBC radio broadcasting. There have always been a lot of people from working-class backgrounds in the world of entertainment, but when you get into the rarefied atmosphere of BBC and radio, it's very heavily weighted towards Oxbridge, and that includes performers as well as producers.

Then there were all those people who had been there for ever: veterans like Barry Cryer, Tim Brooke-Taylor and Alan Coren. The thought of one of them shifting over and saying, 'Come and sit next to me' was outlandish. Surely it could never happen. For many years, at least, the idea that one day a BBC Radio Four producer would offer her a guest slot on *The News Quiz* was as remote as Erith being named European City of Culture. Either possibility would have provoked that characteristic look of bemusement that Linda became so well known for.

On the other hand, we'd be in the car, listening to the *The News Quiz* or *I'm Sorry I Haven't a Clue*, and although neither of us would say it, we'd both be thinking the same thing: it was obvious that Linda would shine on either programme. But it was one thing to know that, and another thing altogether for it to happen. We should have realised that, in fact, Linda's progression to Radio Four was inevitable. They were made for each other.

Her first brush with the station had come at the Edinburgh Festival, when she had performed her few minutes of stand-up in an edition of *Aspects of the Fringe* hosted by Arthur Smith. Then in 1991 and 1992 she guested several times on Radio One's *Loose Talk*, presented by Mark Thomas and Kevin Day. In 1993 she was hired as a contributor to

Windbags on the same station, alongside Jo Brand and Donna McPhail, and soon afterwards she and Mark Steel provided the funnies for DJ Michelle Stevens on *Morning Edition* for Radio Five, as it was then.

Eventually, the call did come from Radio Four, in 1995, when Linda was invited to join the line-up of *Late Edition*, a new weekly night-time programme with a comic slant on current affairs. *Late Edition* had a regular panel comprising Kevin Day, Francis Wheen, Mark Steel and Pete Bradshaw. It was this series that cemented Linda's position as a top-class topical radio comedian.

The following year she began to appear on *The Treatment* on Radio Five, which took an irreverent look at the week's news. Presented by Stuart Maconie, it was a mix of journalism, discussion and sketches and featured a regular pool of guest comedians and media pundits. These included Kevin Day, Jane Bussman, Mark Steel, Jo Caulfield, Steve Punt, Rob Brydon, Fred Macaulay and Vicky Coren, plus the fictional Derek 'Robbo' Robson, sport's most opinionated columnist. Recorded in front of a live audience of about 30 people every Friday evening, in a small studio at Bush House in the Strand, it aired on Saturday lunchtimes and quickly achieved cult status. Between 1996 and 2000, Linda appeared on *The Treatment* 40 times.

'She had one of the fastest minds I've ever encountered – dazzlingly quick and witty,' writes Stuart Maconie in *The Very Best of Linda Smith*. 'But she was also an elegant craftswoman with words: she understood the music of scripted speech.'

Linda's remarkable memory meant that she had an extraordinary breadth and depth of cultural reference at the ready. This was strongly evident in some of the subjects she tackled for *The Treatment*. One minute she'd casually reveal her wide knowledge of literature while tackling the thorny subject of the aftermath of the death of Diana, Princess of Wales: 'From repression comes great art, thought Sigmund Freud; Thomas Hardy, guilt-stricken upon the death of his unloved wife, channelled his remorse into great poetry. Similarly placed, Prince Charles just looks even more like a bewildered haddock than usual.'

The next minute, when called upon to explain the origins of April Fools' Day, she'd cite Hammer House of Horror and *Beadle's About*, while giving the nod to Bram Stoker: 'It's a little-known fact that the feast of April Fools originates in medieval Transylvania. On the night of St Anorakus of the Internet, Vlad Beadlecula, the evil count, lured a hapless village wench, April, to his ancestral home, Castle Bouncy. Then, for a laugh, he mashed her up with custard and served her to his mates for pudding. Thus the wretched girl (played by Ingrid Pitt in the Hammer biopic – wasn't she a good sport?) became the first April Fool, and to this day we eat strawberry fromage frais in her memory – and once a year let bastards play tricks that aren't clever, or grown-up, or big in any way.'

One of the writers on *The Treatment*, comedian and scriptwriter Dave Cohen, remembers how desperately the programme needed someone like Linda. According to Dave, 'Producer Cathie Mahoney was shouting despairingly, "Where are the funny women?" At the risk of offending Cathie's humanist beliefs (and Linda's), her prayers were answered by Linda's arrival.'

The BBC is a small place and word gets round quickly if someone's brilliant and funny. But there was still an obvious reluctance to embrace Linda in mainstream Radio Four.

There was a grudging acceptance in the BBC that there wouldn't necessarily be riots on the boulevards of Tunbridge Wells if the occasional presenter sounded like someone normal – on Radio Five. On Radio Four, the occasional woman's voice was tolerated (for goodness' sake, ladies, you get a whole hour every day to discuss childbirth and knitting patterns), and the occasional working-class voice was allowed to sneak in. But a working-class woman?!

Nothing was written on paper and no one gave specific feedback. There was just a sense, coming from somewhere, that this was not the sort of voice that listeners should expect to hear at 6.30 p.m. on a Friday evening on Radio Four. By early 1997, Linda was exasperated enough by this situation to write a personal letter to a producer in Radio Light Entertainment. Yes, she finally dared to dream! It was unlike her to be so forward, but her friends and colleagues were urging her to push for what was rightfully hers. Absolutely everyone who knew her – and many who didn't – felt intuitively that she would be the perfect guest on *The News Quiz*. Everyone, it seems, except the producer she approached.

She received no reply to her letter for two and a half months. When an answer finally arrived, it was patronising in the extreme, and the tone was distinctly bored. ('I will add your name to the list of possible guests . . . I am aware of your work . . . However, it is a slow process getting on *The News Quiz* . . .') But unbeknown to its author, it contained some absolutely fantastic news. A huge admirer of Linda's, Jon Rolph, was about to take over as producer of the show.

Jon had seen Linda on stage in the early 1990s, at Nick Toczek's gig at the Spotted House in Bradford. 'I think I was doing the door at the Spotted House for Nick, for a fiver, or possibly for nothing if he'd paid the acts the whole of the door takings and had none left over,' Jon recalls. 'Linda was great – funny, assured and clever. Certainly the best female stand-up I'd seen, before or since. I used to co-run a comedy night in Leeds then; we never had any money, so the headliners were almost always unknowns (a 17-year-old Ross Noble) or favours (Dave Cohen was my co-promoter's cousin). I can't remember why we never booked Linda. I think we had a vague sense we probably couldn't afford her.' Now he could afford her (after all, no one does radio for the money!) Jon Rolph was quick to book her – in mid-February 1998 – and then book her again, because 'so much of the secret of success on Radio Four is the audience's familiarity.'

Jon's faith in Linda paid off in spades. 'The first of Linda's great, glorious, memorable moments on *The News Quiz* was the week that Ron Davies resigned after his 'moment of madness' on Clapham Common. The BBC's chief political correspondent John Sergeant had been summoned to hear Davies' confession, and I had already booked John to appear on the programme that week alongside Linda. 'Linda was given the question about Davies and generously gave way to John, who laconically sketched in the bones of the story. Davies had happened to be walking on the common when he was approached by a man he described as a 50-year-old black Rastafarian with dreadlocks. Davies agreed to go with him for a meal, and was mugged.

Linda took over and delivered the perfectly straight-forward, perfectly executed dissection of Davies' ridiculous excuse that Simon Hoggart recounts in *I Think the Nurses are Stealing My Clothes*. Linda said: 'You know what it's like. You go for a walk, you think, ooh, aren't I doing well;

I'm in the cabinet, I'm about to become the first prime minister of my homeland. On the other hand, I could murder a dish of rice and peas.'

Jon recalls, 'That was the first really huge, long laugh-and-applause Linda got on the show, the ones that last so long you have to cut them down in the edit or the audience sounds stoned and hysterical. It was the moment I knew the audience in the Radio Theatre at Broadcasting House had fallen in love with her, as they already loved Alan [Coren] and Jeremy [Hardy]. Thereafter she appeared as often as I could fit her in.'

At first Linda was intimidated by the challenge of *The News Quiz*, as she admitted to Dawn French. 'It was quite a gentleman's club, really. You felt like, you know that scene in *Mary Poppins* where David Tomlinson brings his son to the bank to invest his tuppence and there are all these doddery men in black, and he wants to run off and buy that birdseed? Well, I wanted to buy that birdseed. It was daunt-ing. "You don't want to sit there – that's Mr Coren's chair."'

It didn't take long for her to find her feet, though. 'You realise that this format is so tried and tested that you don't even have to think about it,' she said. 'It gives you confidence to know that you are not trying to make something work that doesn't work. You are part of a group of people who want it to work and want you to do well. So you start to relax into it. Once you feel that, it's like a little sitcom, and you know what they'll all be like. Alan will be grumpy and Andy will go off on tangents and Jeremy will do his Jeremy thing and you slot in. You've got your role. So it's about getting comfortable with it. But I do like that riffing thing. You know, stuff off your head. Jazz, man.'

It was the spontaneous side of her work that really

intrigued Dawn French. 'Maybe you are allowed to do a little bit of preparation, but you mainly have to rely on your wits. I cannot bring myself to do that. Can you explain what it feels like?' she asked.

'I'll tell you what it feels like to me. No homework!' Linda said.

Former *News Quiz* producer Simon Nicholls remembers Linda being a little nervy in the beginning. 'When I first took over the programme, she refused to go at number one and get the opening question. She was either too nervous or too shy. But then one week I said to her, "Can you go at number one?" She was reluctant but she did it and was fantastic, and after that I quite often opened the show with her. I think the audience really enjoyed hearing her voice first.'

It's interesting to note that the producers very rarely allowed two women to guest on the show. When it did happen and, say, the wonderful Sandi Toksvig was permitted onto the same show, Linda would joke, 'It'll turn the milk sour.' Most shows had a similar unspoken policy, as comedian Jo Caulfield points out. 'Two women are never allowed on the same show in case the world spins off its axis.'

Simon Hoggart, chairman of *The News Quiz*, remembers 'a sigh of happiness' every time he introduced Linda as a panellist, 'or a slight, courteous, Radio Four-listener frisson of displeasure if I didn't'. But it wasn't always that way. When Linda first broke into the ranks of the show, there was a steady flow of complaints about her. Some older (and, dare I say, bigoted) listeners could not tolerate her voice, others her south-east London accent. They saw her as a gatecrasher – at 40, she was younger than some of the regulars, plus she was a woman, and she had a working-class accent. It was just too much to take in one go. As the

panellists on *The News Quiz* always say, 'There'll be letters!'
And there were.

But there was no changing her. 'I've never known anyone
who had the ability to be so utterly confident in herself and
in her place in the world and never have to pretend to be
anything else,' says comedian Chris Neill, a former producer
on *Just A Minute* (*JAM*). 'Never upped the level of working-class roots, never downplayed them either.'

There were not only letters; there was hate mail. One
correspondent kept writing things like, 'Why don't you get
back into the gutter where you belong?' As Linda told the
South Wales Echo, 'The thing about accents is that it's like
swearing – people hear it around them all the time, but
somehow when it gets broadcast they seem to un-know that
fact, and convince themselves that it's a problem.'
Conversely, she was much loved among the erudite, more
liberal listeners to *Word of Mouth*. And listeners raved
about her appearances on *Booked*, a literary quiz
programme for which she wrote some hilarious fictional
'Dear Diary' entries by classic authors like Charlotte Brontë
and Henrik Ibsen.

So many things interested Linda, and she loved to chat,
as Simon Nicholls recalls. 'I'd ring up all the panellists on
the Wednesday, just to check that they were OK for the
following day's recording, no one's pulling out, check they've
read their papers and all that kind of stuff. And with Alan,
it was always a brief, sort of formal, "Are you all right?"
"Yes, good. Who's on the panel . . . am I with Jeremy? Oh
God!" And then I would ring up Jeremy . . . "Are you all
right, Jeremy?" "Yeah, I'm 42 and I'm still alive." And then
I'd ring Andy or Francis and they were all lovely, but we
always had quite brief conversations.

'But my conversations with Linda would start at about 12.30 p.m. and we would still be nattering until about two o'clock in the afternoon. Initially I was ringing her to check she was all right and chat about some stories, ask whether Wozza (Warren) was coming with her – "Shall I put him on the guest list?" – and very quickly it would turn into a right old gossip, then she'd get a right hump about Tony Blair or someone and go on about that for half an hour. It was always a really fun chat.

'She never answered the phone, never. You'd say, "Hello Linda, how are you?" and then she would pick up the phone and come out with some bullshit excuse about being on the loo or having the telly on loud. But she ran out of excuses after a while. Still, I always knew to leave thirty seconds of message until she said, "Oh hello . . . I've just walked through the door." I used to leave messages saying, "I know you are there, pick up!"

'My first outside broadcast was at Cheltenham. I was wet behind the ears and did not know what I was doing. I booked Linda, Alexei Sayle, Jeremy and Alan. When I rang Alan to tell him the line-up, he said, 'Are you joking?' Because it was like a Socialist Workers' episode of *The News Quiz*. The red flags were on the stage instead of the Radio Four flags. Iraq was the first question. So Jeremy, Alexei and Linda just went for it and it got completely outrageous. The next thing I knew I was on *Feedback* explaining why I had booked Jeremy Hardy, Alexei Sayle and Linda Smith all on the same show. Linda was a huge fan of Alexei and they had long chats afterwards.'

For Linda, the regulars on the show became like family, especially her fellow panellists. They bantered on air with that kind of familiarity – and off air Linda and Jeremy

Hardy called Alan Coren 'Dad'. Linda's dream team was Jeremy, Alan and Andy Hamilton, who also became a close friend. She goes down as the only female regular panellist to date, and sometime team captain.

'*The News Quiz* is a bit like a gladiator fight,' says Simon Nicholls. 'It's like being at the Colosseum. You've got these four people who are all highly intelligent and all want to do their thing and get laughs. Linda was like that too, but she was also very giving. Occasionally you'll get a battle of egos, when someone starts something and then someone else suddenly starts talking on top of them. It's quite competitive. But Linda was always generous, a team player, and she would let other people have their say. In that way she was great.'

From *The News Quiz*, Linda went on to her first appearances on Radio Four's other big shows, including *Just A Minute* in 1998. 'It's amazing to think that I'm doing a show that Kenneth Williams used to do,' she told the *Manchester Evening News*. A grateful listener once sent Linda this cutting to read out – I can't recall if she did, but I found it in our archive and thought it would have been just perfect for her. From the *Hendon Times*' classified section: 'Hamster cage, door loose, recent bereavement forces sale, £13, also one cat unwanted.' What a gem.

Linda began to appear on *I'm Sorry I Haven't a Clue* in 2001 and so became one of the elite few who appeared on all three of the BBC's gold-star comedy programmes, along with Jeremy Hardy. 'Humphrey Lyttelton comes across on radio as lovely, urbane, witty and subversive in that posh way, like Sergeant Wilson in *Dad's Army*, and he's exactly like that,' she told *Word* magazine. 'All that lot (Barry Cryer, Graeme Garden, Tim Brooke-Taylor) are like elderly delinquents, big kids who live this brilliant life larking about, smoking and drinking all day, then doing the show at night. What's lovely about doing those shows is that you do feel like you're part of some institution, part of British comedy culture.

'The first time I did *I'm Sorry I Haven't a Clue*, I was thinking, "I'm in this chair that Willie Rushton used to sit in, and these people worked with Kenneth Williams!" It's the same with the newsreaders; they don't disappoint, either. Peter Donaldson, one of the chief announcers there, just has this wonderful voice. You believe everything he says. If he turned to a life of crime, he'd be unstoppable. He'd sell you anything: "Why, these timeshares will pay for themselves in six months!"'

Chris Neill produced *Just A Minute* at one time. 'It was so nice to introduce Linda into *JAM*,' he says. 'She was immediately very at home. That's that thing about fame happening slightly later in life – you've had time to find your voice. It doesn't have to be developed in the public gaze in the same way. It's almost as though she had always existed on Radio Four, whereas rather tragically, she was a regular for only eight years.

'Linda was always very relaxed about doing *JAM*. Everyone on the show liked Linda; there was never any difficulty. She played the trickier members of the team well. She was charming with them, very clever at it. She found a very good way of playing the game and often made political points. I remember when we did the show in Newcastle, she managed to get the subject of closed shipyards into a bit about doilies. She had that knack of reducing quite big things to small things.

'Panel games are a strange beast. You think that just because you are a funny comic, you will be good at panel games, but it's not always the case. You have to find a balance between certain things – that's why certain people who aren't comics are always good on panel games, like Boris Johnson, and certain comics who are really funny, but always want to do their material, are not. I think Linda understood that. She had a distinctive voice; she wasn't just *the woman*.

'That was one of her great achievements – she stopped being seen in that tiresome way as *the woman on Radio Four comedy games*. No one was saying, "I booked Linda – that's the woman done." It's been a real failing of Radio Four, well not just Radio Four, but all producers and commissioners. This idea, you know, it used to go: "It's either Stephen Fry or Julian Clary – you don't need more than one gay on the show, surely." One gay, one woman, and the rest would all be white middle-class heterosexual males.

'I do think Linda suffered a bit from the Radio Four "quota". I think she was really pissed off when she was taken off *The News Quiz* because Radio Four said, "We need other women on the show." They seemed to be forgetting that there were three other seats. Why not fill one of those seats with a woman? I don't think Linda was ever grand about it. She never felt she should be on the show because it was her rightful place. But why this fuzzy logic, that it should be a woman replacing a woman – that they couldn't possibly have two women? It really irritated her.

'She told me that when she first went into that green room, there was a degree of snobbery about her voice, as well as the fact that she was a woman. She had to resist that and she really carved her own path. So she quite rightly felt resentful when Radio Four said, "Now you've blazed a trail for women to be on the show, would you like to step aside while we try some other women out?" She wasn't interested in carving out a niche for women. She wanted to be on the show because she was good on the show. It wasn't her job – it was a producer's job, and Radio Four's job – to get more women on it, and certainly not in place of Linda. 'I don't think most listeners would say, "Oh my God, there are two women on *The News Quiz* this week! I'm turning off now." There might be some, but they are probably the same people who turn off when there is one woman on the show.'

There was another point to be made when it came to the gender agenda, as Chris acknowledges. 'The other side of this problem is that Radio Four have commissioned shows from women who, if they had been male, wouldn't have got on the network in the quantity they have. (I don't count Linda in this.) On one hand, they are not allowed to have too many women on a certain show; on the other, they say, "We need more women!" Some things frankly shouldn't have seen the light of day and have been allowed too much exposure. Terrible stuff, some of it. But if you made the playing field level, you wouldn't have to make this strange kind of compensation measure later on.'

Despite such obstacles, Linda was hugely in demand by the early noughties. The offers were coming in thick and fast. She had an established reputation and so it seemed like a good moment to put her head above the parapet and venture out on the road again. By now she was hardly performing live gigs at all. It was time to see whether there was public demand for a full 90-minute solo Linda Smith show. Would enough people turn up? Could she sustain a whole evening performing on her own in front of 500 people? Linda agreed that it was worth testing the water.

We had discussed the possibility before, in bursts of

frustration. Linda had finished with the London comedy circuit years earlier because it no longer offered an artistic challenge. She had been keeping her hand in for a few years with split-bill outings with other comics, where each would do 40- to 50-minute sets with an interval dividing them. But even these had declined and she had involuntarily 'retired' from live work. However, she knew as well as anyone in full-time comedy that if a comedian can't cut it on stage then they are struggling to justify their membership card as a comic. Now her success on Radio Four had brought her a whole new mass audience that probably had no idea she had done years of service as a foot soldier on the comedy circuit. We both knew this was the perfect chance to test out her newfound fame and gauge her popularity in terms of seats sold at theatres and arts centres.

The turning point came in July 2000 with a gig at the University of Surrey, Roehampton, for the annual conference of the Social Policy Association. It was a small and intimate social evening, but no less important for it. In accepting the booking, we had decided to see if Linda still had the nerve to get up and do it. First, intensive preparation was required in order to get a credible set list together. Linda began by sifting through old material and selecting and rejecting pieces. Next she set about creating new stuff that could join the timeless pile if it worked on its first outing. Finally she needed to drop in some topical and political stuff about New Labour and Blair. She was nervous before the gig, but she rose to the occasion and overcame her fear of prolonged absence – one that had threatened to condemn her to the stage comedy scrapheap. The gig went well and Linda redis-covered her appetite for her craft. Now, more than anything, she wanted to go on tour.

So much depended on the response to the first big mail-out, which I sent in autumn 2000, with a view to starting the tour in spring 2001. Still, we didn't have to wait long to find out if it was make or break. The response was superb, as I had suspected it would be. We were in business. But as the months flew past, I couldn't help asking her: 'Linda, how are you getting on with thinking about that show?'

Tick, tick, tick. 'Mmmm,' she'd say, with a slightly faraway look in her eyes. She was so busy, doing loads of radio – and then something else came along to crowd her schedule. Radio Four commissioned her to write her own radio sitcom and the pressure was on. There was no escape clause.

The 'Linda Smith Live' tour (or, more appropriately, 'Back From the Wilderness') was set to begin on 23 April 2001 at the Thornbury Festival near Bristol, before proceeding at pace to a lot of other towns. But first Linda needed match practice. And what better way to do it than invite seventy of your friends to come and witness your rebirth as a stand-up comedian? So I organised a gig at one of London's most respected and long-standing basement comedy clubs, 'Downstairs at the King's Head' in Crouch End.

Linda had played at the King's Head many times, so it was an apt place to return for her resurrection as a live stand-up. But she wore a pained expression of supreme self-doubt as I drove her from Stratford to Crouch End on the night of the gig, a few days before her tour started. 'What have I let myself in for? Why did I agree to be party to this?' she asked me. I just kept on driving.

Miracle Number One was that Linda managed to navigate her way through a set that verged on the chaotic. It was like the uninhibited freeform of an improvising jazz musician. The longer it went on, the funnier it became as she cut loose and threw caution to the wind. Notable as the first time Linda deployed very personal material – stuff about her family and her upbringing – it lasted around an hour, spliced by an interval. The personal routines went down really well and stayed in the extended set from then on.

'With the live stand-up show you have to find your own framework,' she told *Time Out* comedy critic Malcolm Hay. 'The one I use tends to move from the general to the specific. The first half probably deals more with the outside world. In the second half it's more personal. It's about me. I doubt whether I've ever done so much personal stuff before about family and so on. In the past I tended to dismiss that sort of thing. Now I really like that part of the show.'

Miracle Number Two occurred five days later, when Linda stepped out to huge applause in front of a packed hall near Bristol. She proceeded to present a 90-minute show with such composure and poise that the audience would have thought she'd been doing this same performance for years. How did she make that great leap forward, not only calming the chaotic nature of her warm-up gig, but also finding an extra thirty minutes of material? Knowing her as I did, I can confidently say that the secret lay in her ability to improvise. She had this innate ability to compose comic material on her feet. Nevertheless, she had been nervous beforehand, and it was a huge relief for her that the gig went down so well. She was back in the world of stand-up, and this time she was running her own show.

15

A Perfect Weekend in the Life
of Linda Smith

Journeys across the Metropolis

Occasionally, Linda and I would clear our work and social diaries to make space for a purely selfish weekend of indulgence in London. The idea of this was to pack in as much cultural activity as possible without feeling mentally and physically wrecked by Monday morning.

Our hectic thirty-six hours of cosmopolitan fun would start on Saturday morning and finish on Sunday evening. It could only happen if there were no gigs or recordings on Linda's itinerary on the Saturday or Sunday. It would be a close call if she had to work on the Friday night, particularly if she went out of town. There was a risk that she would feel drained and might not be up to the first half of Saturday's rigorous schedule.

For our perfect weekend we needed a completely clear run at our objectives. These would vary: sometimes we might take in more than one film at the expense of another indoor attraction, such as an exhibition. Our priorities outside of food and drink tended to be movies and music.

Sometimes we preferred using public transport: London Underground and late-night buses. But for the weekend described here, we've opted for the car, with me behind the wheel. The advantages of driving at the weekend are: no congestion charge and free meters/parking.

So sit back and enjoy this imaginary whirl around some of our favourite distractions in London Town. Although based on actual events, I have disregarded the dates so as to make the journeys seamless and timeless, blending them into a perfect concoction. If this chapter were a drink, it would be a mango lassi. I hope you enjoy it. We did.

Saturday:

The *Guardian* is strewn over the bed and Linda sits up to consume mugs of Yorkshire tea and rounds of toast. The order in which she reads the various sections rarely varies – *Weekend* magazine followed by *Review*, then *Travel* and the newspaper itself . . . *Sport* finds its way to me . . . *Finance*, *Family* and *Work* would go straight to the recycle bin.

Maybe a quick glance at TV, perhaps hoping to catch a classic Claudia Roden programme about Middle Eastern cooking on BBC2 – or more likely an item from the 'geezer cook' Gregg Wallace. (Gregg is later dropped in favour of Antony Worrall Thompson, whom we can't stand. Gregg is now fronting *MasterChef*.)

Then a brisk stroll through our local Wanstead Park, owned and maintained by the Corporation of London. Wanstead Park was formerly part of the historic Wanstead House Estate, which in the early 19th century boasted one of England's grandest houses, and formal gardens comparable to Versailles. We settle for the humble duties of feeding stale bread to the ducks and swans as we wander along the banks of the various ponds.

We make our way towards our first gastronomic stop of the tour, to the Forest Gate end of Green Street. We mosey along east London's liveliest shopping street, perusing its bewildering selection of sari and jewellery shops, food stores and pavements stacked high with the finest mangoes from the Indian sub-continent. In the crossover season of late spring/early summer, you can buy the highly perfumed small Indian mango (Alphonso) and the much larger, sweet-as-sugar Pakistani (Honey) varieties.

We arrive for a light lunch at the Mobeen, a consistently excellent, value-for-money Punjabi canteen-style restaurant in the high street, where you order at the counter. Here they serve the finest mixed vegetable curry, masala fish and pilau rice in east London, and it is delivered to your table. There are also very good Indian vegetarian cafés on Green Street, although the best in the area is the nearby City Sweet Centre on Romford Road.

Then on through the City for a quick fix of London's oldest food market at Borough, trading for over 250 years on the site next door to London Bridge and Southwark Cathedral. Borough Market is fantastic for the freshest and broadest range of seasonal fruit and vegetables, fish, meats and breads, and we always hit the Spanish goodies at Brindisa. Friday and Saturday are the best days; the rest of the week the market opens primarily for the wholesale trade. Many shops have grown up around it, such as Neal's Yard cheese and dairy products.

Next we'll take a quick spin along the South Bank to catch the Edward Hopper retrospective exhibition at Tate Modern. Linda was a fan of Hopper's truthful and poignant portraits of everyday American life, from iconic streetscapes of New York to isolated figures of ordinary people, as seen in *Nighthawks*. Indeed, the Tom Waits album *Nighthawks at The Diner* was Linda's favourite. Sadly, she never made it to the States to see Manhattan.

Crossing Waterloo Bridge, we make for Soho and tea at Maison Bertaux in Greek Street, serving real French pastries since 1871. It's a bit faded and old-fashioned, but full of character. And there's nothing quaint about their top-of-the-range croissants, coffee, cakes and chat. You'll find bags of ambience in the room upstairs, which still attracts a goodly crop of Bohemians, literati, and discerning comedians, such as Linda and Arnold Brown (who, in his words is, 'the ultimate teashop kinda guy').

Turn the corner and you're in Old Compton Street, where you can raid the equally divine Patisserie Valerie before lurching on to the mummy of Italian delis, Camisa. At Brewer Street we add to our stockpile of seriously good fresh pasta and sauces (we love the green pesto), cheese and olives. Linda always finds time for a flying visit to American Retro in Old Compton Street and a slightly off-the-wall gift to herself.

We slide into Leicester Square, to the huge Empire cinema, for a large-screen special Director's Cut of Martin Scorsese's *Casino*, the final part of his gangster film trilogy after *Mean Streets* and *Goodfellas*. Starring Robert de Niro, Joe Pesci and Sharon Stone and based on a book by Nicholas Pileggi, it follows the American mafia through the 1970s as it wrestles for control of the Las Vegas gaming industry.

Only one place to go after a movie like that, an American-style deli-diner that could feature in any of Scorsese's New York movies – except this one is on Charing Cross Road and is Israeli, not Italian. Gaby's is another tried and trusted central London cheap eatery; lots of thespians, musicians, comedians and tourists hang out here. It is handily placed for the many specialist and second-hand bookshops, and is favoured in our circle as a rendezvous after protest marches that end up in Trafalgar Square. Gaby's does no-nonsense

Sephardic Jewish food: lentil soup, falafel, mixed meze – the joint is also renowned for its salt beef sandwiches.

Staying in Linda's much-loved Soho, we head for a night out at 'Old Ronnie's', the world-famous jazz club Ronnie Scott's – not to be confused with the current club, which reopened in 2006 under new management. The original was fashioned by the late saxophonist, bandleader and racing car enthusiast Ronnie Scott and his partner, former saxophone player and booker of worldwide talent, Pete King. We are here with old jazz pals Gail and Ian to experience the inimitable sounds of the Mingus Big Band. Linda saw the Mingus Dynasty group in 1982 in Sheffield, a gig that sealed her interest in the music of Charles Mingus.

It was Mingus himself who said of Ronnie Scott in 1961, 'Of the white boys, Ronnie Scott gets closer to the negro blues feeling, the way Zoot Sims does.' It was a fitting tribute to one of the standard bearers of British post-war modern jazz. Ronnie regularly acted as master of ceremonies, and was famed for his repertoire of jokes, asides and one-liners. The cornier they were, the better. If you went regularly you would look forward to hearing him retell the same set of gags. When he didn't, you felt robbed!

The Mingus Big Band is a fourteen-piece jazz outfit based in New York City, and it specialises in the compositions of the late Charles Mingus. Managed by his widow, Sue, it plays weekly in Manhattan and tours frequently to Europe and elsewhere in the world. Linda and I literally wore out our copy of *Gunslinging Birds*, released in 1995, which featured such great players as Randy Brecker (trumpet); Ku-Umba Frank Lacy (tenor sax); Craig Handy (tenor sax); John Stubblefield (tenor sax); Chris Potter (tenor sax); and Kenny Drew Jnr (piano).

After a great evening had by all, we'd tumble out late into the night air and stumble across to Bar Italia for a quick shot of espresso. Not so much a coffee shop as a London institution, this authentic Italian café is like a little piece of Rome in the heart of Soho. Even in the middle of the night you'd be lucky to find a vacant red leatherette stool at the long counter.

En route to home we stop off at Brick Lane Beigel Bake, where we join a long peak-time 3 a.m. queue. We line up behind taxi drivers clocking off, Shoreditch and Hoxton clubbers chilling out, central London casino gamblers heading back to Essex and sleepless market traders who will soon be setting up their stalls in Houndsditch and Middlesex Street. Open 24 hours a day and baking through the night, it serves us crispy beigels and platzels filled with smoked salmon and cream cheese, accompanied by a piping hot cup of tea. This is the place that invented the salt beef beigel. And by the way, that's beigel pronounced 'bygel' not 'baygel' – who wants the soft American version when you can have the hard Cockney one!

We'll be back on this patch within hours.

Sunday:
We start with a similar routine to Saturday's, but substitute the *Observer* for the *Guardian*.

Up and dressed, we won't forget our indispensable plant carrier bag, produced especially for the traders of Columbia Road Flower Market. We zoom off to Bethnal Green for our usual weekly excursion to one of London's best specialist street markets. The likes of Michael Rosen, Ben Keaton, Josie Lawrence and Patsy Palmer obviously agree, as we spot them down there from time to time.

Linda used to say, 'If gardening is the new rock 'n' roll, then Columbia Road flower market must be its Memphis.' What a beauty of an expression. This area has a resonance for me. My dad was born and brought up in what were tenements off Virginia Road, at a point where Bethnal Green meets Shoreditch. It was once a hive of light industry, with dozens of small factories and workshops turning out hand-made furniture. My paternal grandfather was a Russian immigrant cabinet-maker around here.

We join the hustle and bustle of a crowded street market, packed with anxious punters jostling for position to grab the best bargains from the fifty-odd stalls. This is where you find colourful and exotic flowers and every plant under the sun. Linda paces the length of the street before marking out her territory. She has her favourite pitches and knows where and when to pounce. She normally goes with a mental shopping list and a strategy – as always with her, timing is everything. The market closes at 2 p.m., so bargain hunters are out in force during the last hour or so, when prices are slashed and frankly can hit throwaway levels – but you've got serious competition from them that knows!

There is always a cessation of activity for a few minutes, to pause, consider and review. That's when refreshments are taken – a glass of freshly squeezed orange juice and a just-right cappuccino from the man with the mobile coffee-making machine. If it rains you've got around thirty garden, furniture and trinket shops and cafés where you can while away the showers.

Next I go to the car and Linda heads for her supplier of organic compost. We meet around the corner to load up a couple of bags. She does the buying and I do the driving – that's how it works. We scoot down the road to a parking spot about a quarter-mile from the old Spitalfields Market. This attracts thousands of people from across London and the world. We usually make a beeline for the organic fruit and vegetable stalls. First there's the perusal and then the choosing, after which we're off to cruise the rest of the market for oddments. These could include CDs, a distinctive item of clothing, knick-knacks – it's a great place to buy presents. You're guaranteed to meet someone you know, inevitably someone you've been actively hiding from for months, or years. Then it's time to rest up for a delicious lunch at the Mediterranean organic café.

Back to the motor, we hit the road and make for the Marylebone High Street shopping area, north-west of Oxford Circus, first of all seeking out Daunt Books. This is a dream bookshop specialising in travel books – arranged country by country. It stocks every kind of guide, novels and non-fiction books. Light, airy and ornate, it's acknowledged to be the most beautiful bookshop in London and is also good for gardening, cookery and interiors. Allow yourself lots of time to browse in its very relaxed atmosphere. We rarely leave this establishment empty-handed.

It is the obligatory drill to walk up and down the parades of tempting shops on both sides of the road, nearly always taking in Cath Kidston, cashmere stockists Brora and the wondrous scented emporium of L'Artisan Parfumeur. Enough. No further time to ponder. We must be off up north.

Rendezvous with friends at Marine Ices opposite Chalk Farm tube station. This place is synonymous with the best Italian ice-creams and sorbets. Countless afternoons of strolling across the greensward of Hampstead or ambling through Camden Lock Market have started here. They've been serving a bewildering range of ice-creams for over seventy-five years, but you can be excused if you are like us and go for simplicity – the finest vanilla, or coffee, or pistachio flavours. If your eyes are bigger than your stomach, as my nan used to say, go for the famed Sundae Vesuvius – a blend of vanilla, chocolate and Marsala ice-cream with crushed meringue, cherries and sponge soaked in Marsala wine, with a double portion of cream. You can always walk it off.

Back into the car for a short hop to Highgate and a long traipse over Parliament Hill, at the western edge of Hampstead Heath. This also has boyhood memories for me – of playing sports, mainly cricket, on the fields on special days out from east London. We never tired of a stretch over here. The air is always fresh and you've got the year-round distraction of people plunging into the bathing ponds, with one especially reserved for ladies. What good form. There's woods and Kenwood House at the top of the hill.

When you've had enough cardiac exercise, you can retire to Café Mozart across the road in Swain's Lane to top up your cholesterol with hot beverages, savouries and pastries. This place is an authentic Viennese coffee house that serves a great brunch or afternoon tea. It is a haven where you can read newspapers, listen to peaceful classical or operatic music and watch the world go by, outside if the weather allows.

We head across to Hampstead to the Everyman Cinema – one of the capital's special and long-standing independent cinemas, which is also very comfortable and welcoming. This is a treat – a special showing of *A Great Day in Harlem*, a film about the day Art Kane shot a black-and-white group portrait of 57 notable jazz musicians, including Charles

Mingus. They gathered early one morning in the summer of 1958 between Fifth and Madison Avenues in Harlem, New York City. Made by radio producer Jean Bach, the film was nominated for an Academy Award for Documentary Feature in 1995.

And then we round off the day with a meal at a long-time haunt of ours, the Mangal Ocakbasi in Arcola Street, Dalston, *the* best of the small but perfectly formed charcoal grill eating houses in this pocket of north-east London, where Turkish and Kurdish cafés and restaurants abound. Just take your pick along Kingsland Road or Green Lanes; you'll never be disappointed with this healthy and tasty food.

'Home James, and don't spare the horsepower!' And so to bed. The curtain comes down on a jolly good weekend.

16
Work, Rest and Play

Palma to Deià, Mallorca

For many years, Linda had suffered from the common gynaecological condition of endometriosis. In most cases it is considered benign, if periodically very painful. So, when she began to feel increasingly unwell in the late summer of 2002, she at first attributed it to the endometriosis. We will never know if it contributed to her cancer.

We had to postpone the autumn tour that year because Linda just wasn't up to it. In December, after some frustrating, unnecessary delays, she was diagnosed with fairly early stage ovarian cancer. She was one of the exceptions among sufferers of the disease, rather than the rule, because she was under 50.

To start with, the prospects were reasonable. There was a possibility that Linda was going to come through the illness and make a full recovery. In the spring of 2003, she underwent a course of chemotherapy at Bart's Hospital in London, followed by a hysterectomy, which went well. After the surgery, there were more tests and regular check-ups. In June, we returned to Linda's specialist hoping that there would be no evidence of cancer cells remaining. It was a terrible blow to learn that, although they were barely visible under the microscope, the cancer cells were still there. That's when we realised that we were in it for the long haul. I always sat in with her and the consultant. I only missed two of her appointments in three and a half years, when I wasn't well, and her sister or a close friend went with her instead.

Linda's consultant told us that the disease could be managed, but there might not be a cure. In other words, unless some radical treatment could be obtained that proved successful, she would have to live with the disease.

'What do you mean, managed?' we asked.

'These days, women are living for between five and ten years after a diagnosis,' he said.

I remember thinking, 'Which women? What age are they? You've almost got to interrogate the consultants – never let them off the hook when they say something.

Linda wanted to know everything. She would be very tenacious, a bit like her favourite TV detective Colombo. When she was about to walk out the door and the doctor thought he was in the clear, she'd say, 'Just one last thing . . .' She would be completely charming about it. She always managed to get what she wanted – whether it was a referral or information – without being offensive about it.

Doctors like to retain a mystery. People who work for them are there to protect them. It's like a class structure within the health system, almost a caste system, where nurses, no matter how wonderful and educated they are, are deemed to be the servants of the doctors. Ancillary workers, too. Then you get the agency staff, who sometimes leave you screaming in agony because it's time to clock off. Linda saw – and experienced – it all.

Nevertheless, she remained faithful to the National Health Service. It was how she was brought up and what she believed in – free state medicine for the citizens of Britain. However – and it's a terrible thing to live with now – if we'd gone to a private specialist, she would probably have been seen by an expert much more quickly than she was. We might have had a quicker diagnosis and, perhaps, dealt with her illness months before. I'm sure we could have found the money somewhere. Linda had a lot of friends.

But, from the start of her illness, we had decided there was no need to broadcast the fact that Linda had cancer. In any case, we believed it was treatable at that stage and we would eventually overcome it. So we kept the news within a small circle of family members, very close friends and a handful of people in the comedy world.

In the spring and summer of 2002, Linda had been working flat out on all fronts. Aside from touring her stand-up show and recording *The News Quiz* and other panel games, there was also the small matter of writing and recording the second series of her own Radio Four sitcom, *Linda Smith's A Brief History of Time Wasting (ABHOT)*. The writing process proved to be a hot and sticky business. I remember many warm nights with Linda sitting beside me in our top room, she devising, formulating and dictating the scripts as I typed. Sometimes it was torturous, mostly because of the temperatures. Looking back, it was a tremendous privilege to be an aide to someone with such a quicksilver mind. Linda was truly a great creator – and dictator!

The six episodes involved double recordings in front of a live audience of radio fans at The Drill Hall in central London. This time, Jon Rolph came on board as producer. 'I left *The News Quiz* when I left radio comedy, but I was tempted back from television to produce the second series of Linda's *A Brief History of Time Wasting*,' he says. 'It was a sitcom of sorts, in that it had recurring characters, but it was much more an illustrated monologue that allowed Linda to go on a brisk half-hour walk round an east London of the mind.'

Jon proved to be a perfect foil for Linda and played a pivotal role in scripting and editing, as did our great pal Jeremy Hardy. If Linda was stuck on an idea or stuck *for* an idea, Jeremy would often come to the rescue. He responded like a kind of email cavalry. Jeremy summed up *ABHOT* when he introduced it on BBC Radio Seven, where it was re-presented as a tribute to Linda some months after she died: 'For those unfamiliar with the programme, it's a sitcom in which Linda plays herself and talks to the listener in the same way she did as a stand-up. The setting is a house in east London, an area where Linda lived for the last 13 years of her life. The characters are over the top, but with quirks Linda found in real people she met and knew.

'The regular characters are: Chris, the camp live-in builder whose work is never done, played by Chris Neill; the determinedly moribund next-door neighbour, Betty, played by Margaret John, who once played Mary Wilson opposite Mike Yarwood's Harold; and Nigerian cabbie Wara, played by Femi Elufowoju Jnr. Other parts are played by versatile stalwart Martin Hyder, and sometimes by me.

'I'd be flattered to think that Linda was seizing an opportunity to celebrate my cruelly underrated talent as a character actor, but I'd be even more flattered to think she just wanted an excuse to have me around. We were very close and loved to talk for ages on the phone. I would find a simple banal comment from me, like the mention on one occasion that I was in Argos when she rang, would inspire a brilliant off-the-cuff remark from her, which would in turn evolve into a routine and find its way into a script.'

Suzanne Phillips thinks she knows how the series originated. 'Linda came up with what I think now was an early version of *ABHOT* in 1992,' she says. 'We got some development money from Radio Sheffield and wrote a proposal for *The Wonderful World of Linda Smith*. I remember it had a range of characters and was told through the main character Linda Smith, a keen gardener. All the characters were based on people in Sheffield who fascinated Linda.

'One of the main ones was the middle-aged transvestite from Darnall who lived with his mother and came to town in a twinset and skirt, non-matching hat and bag. Clearly a bloke in women's clothing who had come shopping. There was a bit of a narrative, but it was very loose. I think it blew Radio Sheffield's mind a bit and they didn't actually commission a script, but I can definitely see how *ABHOT* was a mature constructed version of that idea – always people and their funny ways, never judgemental, always acutely observational. Linda focused on the attributes and details that wouldn't even register with other people. I think the narrative came less easily – intense detail on characters came first. Linda was always happy to sit down and have a go and see what would happen. She wasn't driven.'

Jon Rolph says that the key to understanding the sitcom lies in Linda's personality. 'Chris the builder, Wara the taxi driver, Betty the morbid neighbour, even Sir Cliff the tortoise – Linda's gallery of characters shared a not uncommon flaw – they were all easily distracted from the job at hand. Tea, other road users, impending doom or lettuce would get in the way of whatever they were supposed to be doing, and those distractions were usually the engine of the comedy, which pinged from idea to idea with a speed that belied the characters' indolence. They were all time wasters, and Linda was, I think, keenly aware of that trait in herself. Like many extraordinarily talented people, she would sometimes go to seemingly great lengths not to get down to the job in hand – at least that's how it sometimes seemed.'

Chris Neill earned a cult following for his portrayal of camp builder, Chris. 'Linda was very supportive and encouraging when I became a performer,' he says. 'It was the most generous thing, because she could have got someone a lot better! We talked about who I could be; there was something vague about me being a hotel bellboy as in *Some Like It Hot* – irritating and cheeky. She decided on Jeremy Hardy for lots of voices and was very excited when Maggie (John) came on board.

'The first series was really fun. Linda wrote funny lines for everyone. There wouldn't be feeds for her – she had stand-up style monologues. It was a very pleasant and happy collaborative experience. Jeremy was very good at sharpening up lines on the day.

'Because it was Linda, the audience was hugely warm and very keen to receive it. It was always very jolly; the trip to the pub was always very important. We'd gather and it would be fun. It wouldn't be this awful angst-ridden thing. Linda wanted you to have a good time doing it. She hated the idea that you would be worried about something. She was such a gregarious person and enjoyed other people making her laugh as much as making other people laugh.

'I hadn't realised how much affection there was for the show until Linda died and I read all the message boards with people asking, "When are they going to repeat it?" I think we could have done another series – it would have been great. But I think sitting in a room writing is not so much fun if you are a very sociable person, which Linda was.'

Femi Elufowoju Jnr also remembers rehearsals for *A Brief History of Time Wasting* with fondness. 'I'll never forget her diplomacy in hinting how best she wanted her minicab driver, Wara, to sound over the airwaves. It was a perfect masterclass in how best to inspire an actor to deliver a performance already fully formed in the writer's head,' he says.

'After the warm welcome, initial coffees and just before the first read-through, Linda decided to share with us an anecdote which featured literally half of the characters we were there to play. As she funnelled her way through her hilarious tale, up came Wara, her favourite driver from her local minicab office.

'Up to this point, Linda had in her inimitable and versatile way impersonated each character convincingly, and despite her pinpoint accuracy with the regional accents and ability to convey the heart and soul of a young Ali G aspirant from Streatham, I thought the pomposity and huge world of a Nigerian iconoclast would be beyond her. Before she launched into him, I scurried beneath the coffee table in fear of embarrassment.

'The more I think about what happened next, the more I am convinced that Linda's amazing vocal ability with that instantly recognisable West African dulcet tone was her subtle warning shot to me that anything below that yardstick would spell the end of our professional relationship. It was crafty, but it worked. During her rendition I began to doubt my roots and even questioned whether Linda was indeed a descendant of the Great War tribe from ancient Yoruba land. I had lived in Nigeria for twelve years, yet I began to dread matching Linda's impulsive performance. I love to think she was happy with my Wara thereafter, as she did invite me back to complete the series and a second series too, and in so doing I had the good fortune of working alongside the marvellous Jeremy Hardy, Martin Hyder, Margaret John, Mark Steel and Chris Neill – I feel so privileged to have been a part of it during those fun, unforgettable months.'

Linda wasn't well enough to work in early 2003, but we did manage to have a holiday in Mallorca in late January. We discovered this beautiful island in 2000. At first I needed convincing that it was a place worth visiting, because Mallorca spelt package holidays to me – bucketloads of Brits and Germans sunning themselves to a crisp. And that wasn't us. We enjoyed putting together our own itineraries, sometimes just booking flights and hiring cars and making it up as we went along. But our friend Jane Baker, who was an inveterate holidaymaker on this largest of the Balearic islands, assured Linda that it was a place that would please us. Linda trusted Jane and I trusted Linda. So we gave it a whirl in 2000 and came back for more in 2003 and 2004 – coinciding with Linda's birthday in late January on the last two occasions.

Quite frankly, if you want an active holiday off the beach, avoid the south-east of the island and pack your walking boots to explore the north-west. We flew to Palma, which is a super capital city with a swish centre that's small enough to walk around. Great tapas bars and fish restaurants in the palm-fringed areas of the old town and port. We always sat down at Ca'n Eduardo, beside the fish dock. The waiters are characters and the chargrilled dorado (bream) is second to none. We also enjoyed visiting the modern gallery at the foundation building dedicated to the work of artist Joan Miró, who spent a lot of his life living and working on the island. It was a dreamy experience.

One time we didn't hire a car and took the extraordinary

bumpy old-fashioned train to the north-west of the island. It takes about 75 minutes from Palma to Soller and should be tried at least once. It was originally built a century ago to transport oranges and lemons. It's a grand way to see the countryside and the imposing mountain ridge of the Sierra de Tramuntana. The region is characterised by peaks on one side and plunging cliffs on the other, and everywhere there's just enough hillside land to accommodate olive and citrus groves.

If mountains loom and have a presence, then none more so than over the village of Deià. This became our base for touring the north-west. The area's most famous resident – poet Robert Graves – is buried in the churchyard with the best views out over the coast. We based ourselves here for numerous day trips because it is so atmospheric on a moonlit night and there are plenty of good eating houses. We splashed out and stayed twice at La Residencia, once owned by a business gent called Richard Branson. It has everything, this hotel. The breakfasts were the best we had ever come across. They were like banquets and set you up for a day's hiking in the mountains or walking along the rocky coastline. TV gardener Monty Don and his wife were there on our last stay. It's so relaxed that he was wearing a chunky jumper with holes where the elbows used to be. So Mallorca is fab – I was wrong and Linda was right. No change there.

As Linda recovered from chemo and surgery later in the year, she began to feel much improved physically. In the autumn of 2003 she felt well enough to get back in the saddle and go on tour again and we had a good run of shows. Touring was very uplifting and she went out on the road as much as possible. Work was a huge part of her identity – she hated it when she wasn't well enough to do it. We radically scaled down our outings to the cinema and music gigs. In fact, leisure activities like that gave way almost entirely to Linda's work.

Obviously, the more she toured and appeared on radio and TV, the more press attention she attracted. But it was a source of real puzzlement to us both that the *Daily Mail* – hardly our favourite bearer of news – consistently applauded everything she said and did. Perhaps the management thought they could secretly recruit her to the 'other side', wherever that was. (And wherever it was, she wasn't going near it.)

One morning in November 2003, our friend Dave Cohen rang to ask if we had seen a rave review in that morning's *Mail*. I skipped out to get a copy.

Lynda Lee-Potter had written: 'Recently on *Have I Got News For You*, I saw Linda Smith for the first time. Previously, I'd heard her only on radio, but she's uniquely funny, slightly off-the-wall, fearless and with the hint of danger possessed by the best comedians. She certainly disproves the myth that women don't make great comics.'

Let's just say that Linda was not an avid follower of Lee-Potter, although she didn't loathe her in the way she did Melanie Phillips. Which brings us neatly to Mr Garry Bushell, fellow south-east Londoner and self-appointed arbiter of working-class popular culture. I recall the shock we experienced – the *Daily Mail* piece was more of a surprise than a shock – when we were alerted to a glowing mention Bushell gave Linda in the *Sun*, again in the wake of a winning performance on *Have I Got News For You*. It was astounding.

Sometimes we had to stand back and wonder if Linda

was doing something wrong. The more prominent she became, the more points she seemed to be stacking up with the newspapers and critics of the right. She was never accorded the same level of acclaim by our more natural supporters at the *Guardian* or the *Independent*. On the other hand, she received some tremendous accolades from people who mattered, including the instance in 2002 when she was voted 'Wittiest Living Person' by listeners to Radio Four's *Word of Mouth*.

Along with several appearances on *Have I Got News For You*, Linda was twice a panellist on *Question Time*, where she more than held her own among the politicians. She seemed to be immediately at home and in control. You'd think she'd been doing this sort of programme for years and she didn't betray any nerves whatsoever. She was never one to respect politicians, with the exception of a few individuals to the left side of the Labour benches, such as Alice Mahon and Tony Benn. So she had no qualms about having a go at them when it was justified.

Linda was cautious about not over-stepping the line between being first and foremost a comedian – a professional entertainer – and being seen as a political pundit, and she never saw herself as a rent-a-comment personality. She took a serious dislike to the Andrew Neill show, *This Week*, featuring the ghastly double-act of Michael Portillo and Diane Abbott, and she had no hesitation in rejecting their advances on several occasions. She wasn't going to play court jester to anyone. She had several approaches to write weekly columns in newspapers, but was undecided about the wisdom of taking on this kind of commitment. She never liked to be tied down, unless it was going to be fun. *The News Quiz* was fun, so she mainly stuck to that.

However, she couldn't resist appearing on an edition of the *Great Lives* series on Radio Four in 2003, presented by the late Humphrey Carpenter. Linda chose the subject: Ian Dury, singer-songwriter, painter, teacher, actor, TV presenter and UNICEF ambassador. Ian was a great favourite of Linda's. She admired the man and his music, and identified with his beginnings. She loved his way with words, what she called his 'proletarian poetry . . . the way ordinary people use language in a way that's funny or savage or vicious, in that very creative inventive way.'

She told *Word* magazine, 'I've started this campaign on a Radio Four programme I'm doing called *Great Lives*. I want to get all the Essex towns mentioned in Ian Dury songs to put bits of lyrics on the pavement or wall, in brass. In Burnham-on-Crouch you'd find, "Oh golly, oh gosh, come and lie on the couch with a nice bit of posh from Burnham-on-Crouch." Better than "It's on the River" or whatever their slogan is. Plaistow is probably not so keen on their lyrics – something like, "Arseholes, bastards, fucking cunts and pricks, aerosol the bricks." We'll be contacting the civic heads of these places and see how it goes.'

She enjoyed doing the occasional one-off, but what with hospital appointments to attend and treatments to endure, she tended to stick with her favourite panel shows. Simon Nicholls, producer of *The News Quiz*, was one of the few people she confided in about her illness. 'We used to have these very long chats. I remember a few times we'd natter on for ages about cancer because my mum had died of cancer. Linda would say, "It's this rubbish thing that I've got." She was always quite matter of fact about it.

'I remember the first time Linda came on after being away for quite some time, the first time she was away with the cancer. She came back wearing a wig. I didn't clock it because I'm useless. I just thought she had done her hair differently. I think Andy was the same. I remember that Linda made some comment to Andy about his clothes and his beard being a bit unkempt. 'You want to sort out your personal appearance.' I don't think she told Andy until much later about the cancer.

'He said something like, "Well, at least I don't feel the need to wear outrageous wigs."

'"Oh no!" I thought. But she was totally cool with it and just laughed about it.

'For the first couple of years when I was producing *The News Quiz*, she might have the odd week off, but she was totally on top of it. However, towards the end we were all on alert and Andy would be ready for me to ring him up on a Thursday and tell him that Linda had to pull out, so could he come in? But for the first few years it was business as usual, just a different selection of headgear going on.

'I'd make sure I knew when she was having the chemo and how much it was zapping her. It really knocks it out of you. She usually had it on a Monday and then I'd speak to her on the Tuesday to see how she was doing. By the Wednesday she'd be a bit stronger, but still a bit groggy. Then, come the Thursday, it was like, "Right, let's do it." Sometimes she would tell me that she was quite tired – a bit pooped and low on energy – but she was a right trouper. She would get up on that stage and you would never guess there was anything wrong. Listening back to the recordings, you would have no idea of what she was going through. It was just normal Linda. For that hour and a half of recording she would give it her all. She'd save herself up for that recording, storm it and then go home and presumably flake out.

'No one came up to me afterwards in the green room and asked, "Is Linda all right?" There was none of that. I imagine that *The News Quiz* kept her sane. It certainly kept her busy. She struck me as the kind of person who liked to be busy and doing stuff, but she could just as easily put her feet up and watch *Monk* all day.'

Linda could just as easily spend a whole day reading. Her taste in literature was eclectic, sometimes surprising and always voracious. She loved so many authors: Dickens; Shakespeare; Jonathan Coe; Raymond Carver; Alexei Sayle; Katherine Mansfield; Patricia Highsmith; Thomas Hardy; Beryl Bainbridge; Colin MacInnes; Alan Bennett; and Truman Capote. One of my favourite passages from her stand-up show was tucked away in the second-half autobiographical material about her family and teenage years, where she made a great but subtle point about the social classes. Friends at university would say, 'Well, I was always going to end up doing English because I was brought up surrounded by books.'

Linda would retort, 'Yes, so was I, but they were full of Green Shield stamps. I suppose we could have swapped them for books, but we had our eye on a twin tub.'

Linda once hit the literary note in a magazine Q & A interview:

Q: What book has changed your life?
Linda: I couldn't choose any single one, but I'm a great big fan of public libraries and I used to go to our local one every week when I was a kid. Jean Rhys was one of my favourite writers. I loved *Wide Sargasso Sea*, her prequel to *Jane Eyre*, which explains how Mrs Rochester ended up as the mad woman in the attic. It's extraordinarily powerful.

Q: What happens at the end of *Jane Eyre*?
Linda: It turns out that *she's* Keyser Söze after all.
Q: What's the most trouble you've been in?
Linda: Until the London Borough of Bexley announce
   a library books amnesty, I'm not at liberty to say.

Linda was invited to appear at many literature festivals up
and down the land. She had several approaches from major
publishing houses about writing a book, presumably a
humorous book, but alas time and ill health prevented
anything materialising. So she appeared on the big festival
stages at Hay-on-Wye, Ilkley, Dartington and Keswick in
her usual capacity as mirth maker and bringer of joy to the
book lovers of Britain.

It was at those last two festivals that Linda and I first met
and then got to know the organisers of 'Ways With Words'
– Kay Dunbar and Steve Bristow. 'Linda came to do her
stand-up at "Ways With Words" at Dartington a few times
and also to our literature festival in Cumbria,' says Kay. 'The
audiences loved her gentle, often domestic humour: lost scissors, knitting, woolly hats, town twinning, dark roots from
delayed highlighting sessions at the hairdresser's. She also
researched the area where she was appearing, so that her
stories and jokes had a particular resonance for the local
people.

'Before our Cumbrian festival, she'd noticed all the
outdoor-wear shops in Keswick selling boots, socks, kagouls
and fleeces. So at her show she asked the audience, "Where
do people in Keswick buy their indoor-wear?" Now whenever
we drive through Keswick and see all the outdoor-wear shops
we always say, in homage to Linda, "But where do they buy
their indoor-wear?"'

By now Linda's illness was taking up huge chunks of her life. She became very well informed about it and was keen to experiment with different therapies and treatments. She did plenty of independent research into ovarian cancer, gaining a lot of information from books, pamphlets and the internet, and gradually became a very knowledgeable lay person. She was always swapping experiences with other patients. The doctors and nurses who attended her soon realised they were in the presence of someone who knew more than most about their illness.

Her next referral took us to Tooting, south London and St George's Hospital, where in spring 2004 she attended a clinic run by an eminent research professor who managed to procure a course of the analogue of the formerly controversial drug Thalidomide, which had been proving its anticancer properties in the USA. Linda could remain on this drug, with the co-operation of the American supplier, provided her results were deemed positive. For a while the drug seemed to be having beneficial effects and things were looking good. We were full of hope and very optimistic about the future.

17

Defender of the Faithless

Wanstead, East London to Conway Hall, London WC1

Humanism is a philosophy of life inspired by humanity
and guided by reason. It provides the basis for a fulfilling
and ethical life without religion.

www.humaniststudies.org

Most people join something at some time in their lives.
By that, I mean an organisation whose aims they
support and intend to play a part in, although an initial
enthusiasm can fade quite quickly and result in the non-
renewal of an annual subscription. For instance, a health
club that you join with good intentions in January and then
throw in the towel by February.

But not Linda Smith – she just wasn't the clubbable sort
to start with. Indeed, she often protested in public that she
was not a joiner – that she had never joined anything, never
belonged to an organisation. She was proudly independent
of thought and action. She had for a few years been a card-
carrying member of the Royal Horticultural Society and the
National Trust, but always insisted that 'they don't really
count, do they?' In the early stand-up years she did some
autobiographical material which reiterated her position,
claiming that she had evaded all approaches to join the ranks
of political groups but had once been enrolled by her mum
into the military wing of the Brownies – the Tufty Club!

On a warm summer Saturday in 2004, Linda and I drew up outside Conway Hall in Red Lion Square, central London. On the journey, Linda had been scribbling furiously in a notebook, noting down jokes and anecdotes that she could include in a speech that she was due to deliver in a few hours' time. But this was no run-of-the-mill, 'dash in, do your stuff and dash out with the dosh' corporate gig. Money would not come into the equation. No, this was about personal commitment. Linda had made a big decision around the time of my 50th in April and now she was taking it to its logical conclusion.

Linda headed for the hall whilst I parked at a meter in the square and fed it all my loose change. Then I followed her into the historic home of the South Place Ethical Society, named in honour of Moncure Daniel Conway, the anti-slavery advocate, outspoken supporter of free thought and biographer of Thomas Paine. It's a landmark of London's independent intellectual, political and cultural life, based in the heart of Bloomsbury. We had both been here for various public events over the years, from heated debates and trade union meetings to concerts, and Linda had appeared on its stage at fundraisers for various good causes. I remember one for Nicaragua Solidarity with Mark Thomas in 1993.

Onwards and inwards, we were greeted by a very warm welcoming party led by Hanne Stinson, executive director of the British Humanist Association (BHA). Slogan: *For the one life we have.* We had arrived in good time for the start of the BHA Annual General Meeting in the commodious main hall.

A quick scan of the agenda confirmed that Linda would be on the podium at around 3.30 p.m. – the last item. We chatted with members, browsed the literature on the bookstall and prepared for the next two and a half hours of business. The ensuing debates and discussions helped educate Linda to the ways of the BHA, shining a light on leading personalities and highlighting the range of concerns that drove active members to distraction. One factor was outstanding – the conspicuous lack of attendees under the age of 60/65.

Bear in mind that Linda wasn't the joining kind. She wasn't volunteering for extra-curricular activities. So why was she giving up a whole hot afternoon to benefit this audience? Taking one giant step forward for comedian-kind, she had agreed to become the new president of the BHA, a position recently vacated by the high-profile, highly respected campaigner Claire Rayner. Linda really admired Claire Rayner as 'a good, good woman'. Now she was due to make her presidential acceptance speech in front of an incredibly learned reception committee. The term of office was normally four years, as in the Oval Office in Washington.

In an interview three days later with Professor Laurie Taylor for a piece in *New Humanist* magazine subtitled 'Putting the humour into humanism', Linda explained the circumstances that had led her to break the habit of a life-time. She had recorded a 30-minute programme on Radio Four as part of a series called *Devout Sceptics*, where Bel Mooney interviewed people in the public eye at length about their beliefs. Linda's edition went out at breakfast-time on New Year's Day 2004 and her radical thoughts turned heads in the upper echelons of British humanism. A letter duly arrived from Hanne Stinson on behalf of the BHA. The letter stated that the trustees had reached a unanimous agreement that Linda was the ideal person to head up the BHA. Her recent appearance on *Devout Sceptics* had reinforced their viewpoint.

'The letter took me totally by surprise,' Linda told Laurie Taylor. 'Hanne said she'd the heard the programme and was pleased to hear my humanist views. Until that moment I'd never thought of categorising my views as humanism. But I came and met Hanne and chatted and realised that it was a fair description.

'When I came to the BHA it was exactly as I expected – a little office with a bust of Bertrand Russell. But after we'd talked, I began to realise that I was interested in this little world if I could help to make it part of a bigger world. I didn't want to write off the past. I was pleased that there was a whole history of rational thought. I just wanted to make it more relevant to the modern world. Another reason was all this talk about faith schools. I feel very uneasy about that, as do lots of people. It somehow seemed time for people who don't like these sinister changes to stand up and say so. And finally there was Mark Steel. I had a long chat with him about it all and he said, "Go ahead and do it. It will be a huge laugh." And so I agreed.'

Linda would never have accepted the BHA's offer if she hadn't been optimistic about the future. She was full of hope that somewhere along the line she would find a radical treatment for her illness that would keep it at bay, or perhaps even eradicate it, and would definitely have declined if she thought she wasn't going to be around for the next four years.

'I know that there is only so much that one can do to an organisation, but I want to begin by finding ways of publicising the BHA,' she told Laurie Taylor. 'At the moment people know about it from funerals and possibly from weddings and non-christenings. But it's not so well known for its campaigning work on issues like faith schools and fundamentalism.

'I want to have a go at the Blairs,' Linda warned. 'Him with his God bothering and her with her crystals. That's the trouble; when people stop believing in God, they start believing in anything, in any nonsense. It would be nice if some of the people who stopped believing in God started to believe in humanism. I have the feeling that humanism needs waking up. It needs a much younger profile. It's a bit stuck in history, isn't it? There were people in the audience who looked as though they'd stepped straight out of the past. I noticed one man sitting halfway back who looked exactly like George Bernard Shaw. *Exactly* like him. Very, very strange. And I'd just got used to that when I looked along the row and saw a man sitting almost next to him who looked exactly like Bertrand Russell. It was just extraordinary.'

Linda, the self-confessed 'unconscious humanist', enlivened the proceedings with jokes, which was fitting for a philosophy based on happiness. Shortly after her speech, the AGM wound up and people began to approach her to congratulate her on the tone and content of her address. Among them were the very eminent, now late Sir Hermann Bondi FRS and his wife Christine. Professor Lewis Wolpert FRS and Professor Richard Dawkins FRS are examples of other well-known names attracted to the humanist cause. The crème de la crème of British scientific and philosophical life are among those listed as Distinguished Supporters: Professor Sir Harry Kroto FRS; Professor Stephen Rose; Professor Sir David Weatherall FRS; Sir Anthony Epstein FRS; Professor Simon Blackburn. And down among the plebs are Philip Pullman; Jonathan Meades; Anish Kapoor; and Baroness Blackstone.

Linda's arrival as a new figurehead and ambassador for

the BHA was roundly welcomed by the membership. Her elevation to the role of president may not have been the most obvious move for the BHA but it was hailed as brave and inspired. The media took notice quickly and the *Times Educational Supplement* labelled her 'defender of the faithless' in an article that scrutinised Linda's thoughts about faith schools. As the newly installed 'supreme commander', she made it clear that she was lending her voice to the campaign to halt the expansion of faith schools and to embed humanist beliefs in the RE syllabus.

'I do not think faith schools are a good thing,' she said. 'Generally speaking, faith should not be part of children's education. It should not be presented as a) true, and b) good. You only have to look at Northern Ireland to see how faith schools have failed rather spectacularly to form any kind of social cohesion. My preference would be to have a philosophy syllabus which looks at all the world's beliefs and gives them equal weight, rather than an RE syllabus.'

On the same subject, Linda told Libby Purves, the presenter of Radio Four's *The Learning Curve*: 'Humanists are liberal souls; they're quite happy for people to have their religious faith. They're just not happy for education to be based on that faith . . . because it's divisive. "Faith schools" is quite a cosy name. If you call them sectarian schools, they don't sound quite so nice, do they?

'I don't think it is the business of the state to educate children religiously. Religious faith and culture, that's a job for home. It's not a job for the state. It's not a job for the taxpayer. What children are entitled to from the state is a good general education, where all faiths and beliefs, including humanism and philosophies that don't include God, are equally respected. And that way, I think you have a better chance of achieving the social cohesion that the government claims to be striving for, but in fact is taking measures that are going to bring about exactly the opposite effect.'

Following the AGM, letters of congratulation arrived from members. A doctor wrote, 'Your talk made me almost start believing in the supernatural. Till yesterday, I was Cassandra predicting an unavoidable, "age-related doom" for the BHA. For young people to be attracted towards any idea, there needs to be youth, joy, humour, fun and entertainment. It seems that you can offer it all, and for this, "bless" you.'

One elderly scientist, the self-proclaimed world's longest-serving atheist, who'd criticised fellow humanists for being too po-faced and was positively delighted at the move to make a comedian president of such a formidably intellectual movement, wrote: 'If any group of philosophers can be said to be the progenitors of humanism, it is the Atomists – Democritus, Leucippus and that lot – two and a half thousand years ago. And, when he was not founding the Atomic Theory of Matter, what was Democritus doing? Cracking gags! He was the Laughing Philosopher.'

In her speech, Linda had reiterated what she'd said to Bel Mooney on *Devout Sceptics*. 'I talked about the whole business of the Holocaust and how if God was going to show his face, that might have been quite a good time for him to have done it,' she told Laurie Taylor. 'I mean, was he waiting for something worse to happen before he stepped in? I remember Bel saying that religious people would reply by asking where man had been at the time. But as I said, at least some humans did help.

'God did nothing at all. Missed his big chance. And then I went on to say that I thought of God in much the same way that I think of the royal family. If we didn't live in this toy town with princes and kings and so on, then we might make a better stab at being citizens.'

The *Devout Sceptics* programme was very illuminating. For the first time on air, Linda was provoked into revealing the brushes with religion that had occurred in her early life and the formation of her beliefs in adulthood. There were some terrific exchanges between Linda and Bel Mooney; I fancy Linda may have been one of the trickier customers on that series. Linda never missed an opportunity to remind Bel and the listeners that she could find humour in almost everything. Tune in to Ms Smith in full flow:

Bel: Linda, can you make jokes about God?

Linda: Yes, you can. You can make jokes about anything really, I think. Especially made-up things like God.

Bel: You sure he's made up?

Linda: Pretty sure.

Bel: Well I think we're jumping the gun a little. But there must be no-go areas because you might be afraid of a fatwa?

Linda: Well, you've got to accept that a fatwa might result. Yes, but that doesn't mean you can't make the joke. The consequences are yours to contemplate really, aren't they? But that doesn't mean you can't make a joke. You can make a joke about anything, but it kind of depends who's making the joke, I think. And whether you trust them.

Bel: For instance there is a tradition of Jewish jokes, but they have to be made by Jewish people.

Linda: Exactly. I think mostly they do. I think people in show business sometimes have this kind of progressive Jewish disease, where they think by throwing in a few bits of Yiddish they are in fact Jewish, but they're not. Jewish jokes from non-Jews are strange. But there are plenty of good ones from Jews, I think.

Bel: So we're already establishing no-go areas.

Linda: Well it's not a no-go, you can do it but it's tricky. No, you're right, I've totally contradicted myself in five seconds. That didn't take long, did it?

Bel: Let's unpick where you are coming from here. Let's look at the idea of the devout sceptics, the title of this series. Now, you are a lot more sceptical than devout, that's quite clear.

Linda: Totally.

Bel: But in terms of this idea of, broadly speaking, being devout, would that be expressed to you in terms of the values of Jesus, the liberal values of the sermon on the mount, say?

Linda: I would say many of my own values would coincide. It's not a surprise that a lot of early socialists were Christians and came out of usually non-conformist Christian churches. You can see that line. You can see how a Christian person could look at the broad principles of Christianity and see that socialism was the most compatible ideology with that, I think. It's hard to see how someone could look at Christ's teachings and think that he wanted us to be monetarists and very right wing and to condemn people.

And religion, formal religion, has most often become a means of social control. It's a power base, usually for men, for controlling the community, for controlling elements in it. You look at the medieval church, you look at cathedrals – well, they look wonderful now.

We go to them now and they're National Trust, and you buy fudge in the gift shop. But that's not what they were built for. They were built to dazzle the poor and let people know their place.

The problem over literacy, how opposed the Church was to the idea of people being able to directly read the Bible, for a long time – it's all about social control. And it seems to me that organised religion, over the centuries, has done far more harm than good.

Bel: If you say you're an atheist, you know there's no God. End of discussion.

Linda: Yes, and I do feel that I'm an atheist. When I look inside myself, I find no belief in the existence of God. I ask myself, 'Do I believe in God?' Answer comes back, 'No I don't.' However, I'm loath just to describe myself in that way, because it is so final and it's so [sighs] sensible, very sensible. It's the sensible thing. We weigh up the evidence and there's no evidence on earth to suggest the existence of a God. There's none at all. You can look back at how every religion has developed and you can see all kinds of reasons.

You can trace the history of it; you can look at Christianity as one cult among many in Rome. All that makes total sense and I totally buy that. On the other hand, there is undoubtedly something intangible about people that goes beyond their physical selves, I think. And I think it all comes down to creativity. What is godlike about people is that they create things, they create relationships between them that go beyond death.

You talk about people getting solace from praying in a religion. I think it's the act of doing it, not the idea that's there's anyone there listening to it. People have put that meaning onto it. And you do that yourself. When you lose people that you love, you make up little stories. Perhaps something will happen at a funeral that you'll think is a sign, a bird or an animal, or some coincidence. You'll pick up a record that happens to have a title that's resonant and you build those stories, because that's what people do.

They make their life into stories. People are very creative. I'd call that a godlike thing in people, but it's very much to do with us. I think we underestimate just how brilliant people can be. There is an energy in a group of people together. For example, gospel music. I love gospel music. I'm not a practising Christian, as we have established; however, there is definitely something going on with that music. It's a fantastic feeling and it's just people, people's energy together, vast groups of people.

In this last sequence, I think Bel Mooney unintentionally provided the classic set-up allowing Linda to deploy her full comic powers. They were working as a double act, foil and funny person.

Bel: Is being on the radio a form of immortality?
Linda: No. It's a form of mortality, actually. It's a form of radio, telly, work generally, of just keeping body and soul together. Certainly not a form of immortality. I quite like the idea of getting repeat fees for ever, into eternity; that would be quite nice. That must add up

to about three quid, I would have thought. After 5,000 years. But no, I don't think it is at all. You would be mad if you thought that, wouldn't you? You'd just be a mad person.

Bel: But your energy, your creativity, goes into what you do . . .

Linda: I hope so. And that's why it's such a pleasure. I don't look upon it as a job, really.

Bel: You may have imagined a dark day when there are no jokes. There is nothing funny to be said . . .

Linda: Yeah, probably about next Wednesday. The idea that you would be there at the end of the world going, 'Have you ever noticed . . . ?' There is a slight Battersea Dogs' Home element to being a comedian, an awful 'love me, take me home' thing. Be nice to think that ended one day.

After the programme, Linda wondered how she had come across. 'I thought to myself, "Oh no, I must have been talking complete nonsense." But it turned out that there was a really big postbag following the programme. So many people writing in to say that it was so good to hear a non-religious view on the radio. Of course, there were one or two who said that I was a sinner and that, unless I repented, I would burn in hell. The ones that were signed "Yours in the love of Christ".'

Later in 2005 Linda was invited to become an honorary associate of the Rationalist Association, in recognition of her 'outstanding commitment to the values of humanism and rationalism in your writing and public pronouncements'. Not a bad roll call to join: Noam Chomsky; Eric Hobsbawm; George Melly; Claire Tomalin and Jonathan

Miller, for starters. The same Dr Miller who so impressed us with his BBC TV series *A Brief History of Disbelief* in 2004.

Laurie Taylor reminded Linda that some adherents to humanism, secularism and rationalism were still arguing the toss about the difference between humanism and rationalism. Could one be a humanist without being a rationalist, or a rationalist without being a humanist? I don't think Linda was prepared to hang around to find out. Put in the simplest of terms, she backed the BHA's declaration to support and represent people 'who seek to live ethical and responsible lives without religious or superstitious beliefs'. That's making sense of life using reason and experience. You can find your own way to a definition of rationalism. Enough with the propaganda.

I'll leave the last words to Linda. This is what she told *BHA News* on the announcement of her forthcoming presidency: 'The BHA's work is more important than ever. With fundamentalism of many kinds on the rise, the rational voice of humanism needs to be heard. I see publicising humanism in order that other people might identify themselves not just negatively as atheists, but positively as humanists, as a vital part of my role. I'm looking forward to evangelising – if that's the right word. The future is bright, the future is human!'

Arriving back at the presidential car, we discovered to our disbelief that it was not exempt from the casual cruelty meted out by ever-vigilant parking wardens. Slapped on the windscreen was a £50 fixed penalty notice for 'feeding the meter'. That was not a very humanist gesture on behalf of the London Borough of Camden, was it? I nominate Camden, Hackney and Westminster as London's least motorist-friendly boroughs. Please send me your choices on a postcard.

Postscript: did I mention that we forgot to join the BHA at the time of Linda's installation? Another 18 months would elapse before we realised our embarrassing oversight.

18

In Search of the Perfect Crab Sandwich*

Journeys through England, 1985–2005

For 20 years, I drove Linda around Britain doing shows, mainly on a one-night stand basis. This gave us ample opportunity to savour the attractions and cultural high spots. But there was one aspect that most trading establishments of these places had in common – a propensity to close their collective doors TOO EARLY!

We never found out whether these places, in particular small towns, were subject to a hitherto unannounced European early-closing directive, which relied on public ignorance to make it effective to operate. At least when you go to Spain and other Mediterranean countries, you know there will be a siesta in the afternoon. But here's the difference: the shops reopen and stay that way until quite late in the evening.

Linda observed from her extensive travels around the British Isles that shops, cafés and tearooms had a tendency to close right on the stroke of 5 p.m. Some might stretch to 5.30 p.m. in the summer. As we journeyed from town to town, we envisaged a contest for retailers that involved competing to win the title, 'Earliest closing in Britain'. Half-day closing didn't count. We encountered cafés that proudly hung out a 'We Are Closed' sign at 4.30 p.m. Why, when

* We found it at a seafront kiosk in Deal, Kent, not far from Sandwich.

people go in search of cups of tea and cakes at around 4 p.m. and usually partake of this most sociable of acts past 4.30 p.m.?

In Maldon, Essex, one Saturday afternoon, we had decided to go and admire some of the elegant Thames barges on the River Blackwater, just below the High Street. Spotting a delightful-looking tea shop, homemade cakes, the lot, we made a mental note to finish our walk there. We arrived back at a few minutes past 4 p.m. to find that the bloody place had already begun shutting down. With growing impatience, the staff were applying hot breath on the necks of comfortably seated customers, miming the words of the dreaded expression, 'Don't you know what time it is?' Yes, it was five minutes past four. Helpless in the doorway, we gave up and drowned our sorrows elsewhere. Linda was adamant that teashops had no right to be closing at the onset of teatime.

Before the advent of modern Sheffield, with its myriad coffee houses and all-day bars, it was literally impossible to get a cup of tea in the city centre after 4 p.m. We often ended up walking miles to the cafeteria inside the Midland Railway Station. Madness. I think it might be something to do with old shift working patterns in industrial cities and towns. Workers whose hours were 'eight while four' would be heading home exhaustedly for their tea-time meal. They would not be seeking out tea joints in town, so there was no perceived demand for serving tea then.

'British shops love to be closed,' Linda told *Word* magazine. 'I don't know why we operate a capitalist system in Britain, because we don't like it at all. People don't seem to have got the hang of exchanging money for goods and services. You always get the impression when you go into a shop that they'd much rather you pushed the money under the door, pissed off and left them alone. It drives me nuts.

'I used to have this fantasy about café society: I'll go to Leicester or somewhere, I'll be able to arrive at 4 p.m., walk into a bistro, be able to have a sandwich, maybe a cup of coffee, maybe have a hot dish. But of course, no. Some little rat-faced miserable bastard says, "It's the wrong time. You should have been here earlier." Well, I wasn't fucking hungry earlier!

'And there are some strange rules, like you can't have a glass of wine unless you order hot food. What do they say when you bring your own wine, eh? Or buy something hot and leave it to go cold. Now that could give them a dilemma, wouldn't it? Or buy something cold, and use a blowtorch to heat it up. How would they like that?'

An experience over twenty years ago inspired Linda to re-enact on stage a scene at a Scarborough B&B. This place set a new benchmark for regime ruthlessness. Here she is telling a Sheffield audience all about it in 1986:

'Why is it that British people can't cope with this idea of the paying guest? It's like you pay these people to stay there, but you try and act as inconspicuously as you possibly can. It's like no financial transaction's taken place. It's as though you've just imposed yourself off the street – you've just walked into the house. And they think, "Who the fuck are you? You've not just paid me £25, have you, to stay here?" So you get in and in fact you might as well just rip up that £25 and sleep on a park bench, for all the comfort of the B&B.

'First you try the lounge, the TV lounge. Again, suddenly you are in Poland, martial law, because there's a curfew. You're watching a film – the telly goes off at 11.30 p.m. A bloke stands over you, shouting, "I've got to get up at six o'clock this morning – what time are you going to bed?" "All right, yes, we're going now, we're going now." You go up to bed with a sinking heart that sinks even further when you open the door and find – ughh! – the mauve candlewick bedspread.'

For much of our time on the road we managed to combine our paid work engagements with a zeal for leisure and adventure. We would do research about a town or an area – Linda would normally check out the proximity of a good garden. If we were in a region for a few days, there would be plenty of scope for extra-curricular activity. For instance, if an area of the coast impressed us on a first visit, we would be back, for work if possible, with all expenses paid, or if not, in our own time. And so we developed our list of favourite places.

I have selected five stretches of the English coast – no offence to Wales, Scotland or Ireland, because we had wonderful times in those countries, but the list could go on for ever. Linda loved being near to the sea and often expressed a desire to live on the coast. We did explore the possibilities in different locations, but never took the plunge.

Linda loved the great outdoors and nature in the form of trees and wild flowers and was a keen amateur bird-spotter. So any walk that turned up trumps in those departments earned bonus points. If there was a good beer and food pub on the trail – add another one. If there was a tea room – add one more. And so on.

In order to construct days out that were the motoring equivalent of circular walks, these criteria for selection should be applied:

a) The ability to reach the destination for a day out with an early start and a late finish
b) Motorways to be avoided, preference for A and B roads, scenic routes when available
c) Spending most of the day on the coast, beside the sea
d) Good for walking and people watching
e) Reliable teashops and fish restaurants in the vicinity
f) A good garden or National Trust public property

I've tried to encapsulate our whistle-stop visits in a series of mini-commentaries. And I have reserved special praise for the following four coastal tours, which became popular in our household when we resettled in east London.

North Kent coast:
A12 / A2 / A28 / A259 / A28 / A299 / A2 / A12
First stop off the old A2 London road was on the edge of Faversham for a quick browse around Brogdale 'World of Fruit' – the home of the National Fruit Collections. It boasts the largest collection of fruit trees and plants in the world. I could bore you with the stats – for example, there are over 2,300 different varieties of apple tree. Visit the 150 acres of orchards in blossom time or take a guided tour in late summer and autumn, when the ripe fruit is ready for picking. We often popped to the plant centre there and did buy a couple of espalier apple trees for our new garden.

The next town visit always seemed like a pilgrimage for Linda, with her Kentish roots and intense interest in literature. To Broadstairs on the Isle of Thanet, a delightful and sedate seaside town that has a distinctly 1950s/1960s feel about it. There are old-fashioned shops and Italian ice-cream parlours with remnants of their original decor. I would rate this as one of Linda's favourite places, partly because it is synonymous with Charles Dickens. Linda was intrigued by towns that had literary antecedence and she was a *big* fan of Dickens.

The fort-like Bleak House, now a maritime museum containing domestic furniture from Dickens' time, stands overlooking the sandy beach of Viking Bay and the compact old town and its twisting streets. The celebrated novelist spent many a summer here, and most importantly, this is where he wrote *David Copperfield* and planned *Bleak House*. Linda was big on detail, so I'm obliged to mention that a house on the seafront was once the home of Miss Mary Strong, the model for the character Betsey Trotwood in *David Copperfield*. It is now the Dickens House Museum. I suppose readers should also know that Broadstairs goes crazy for a week in June each year with a Dickens Festival, when people dress up in Dickensian costume. Unfortunately, some of the locals went mad at a general election and were crazy enough to vote in the disgraced Jonathan Aitken as their MP for South Thanet. I wonder what Dickens would have made of him.

On the north side of the Isle of Thanet – an island now only in name – is Margate, where thousands of London urchins of our generation lost a mountain of pennies in the slot machine arcades at the giant Dreamland amusement park.

We visited Whitstable many times with different sets of friends. It always felt very low-rise, unassuming and relatively unchanged. That was until changes became apparent, activated by entrepreneurs who decided to accommodate the London middle classes and take more than a few pennies off willing Islingtonians who flocked here for weekend breaks in the converted fishermen's huts off the beach. We thoroughly enjoyed Whitstable, although neither of us sailed or liked oysters. Its prime asset is its location. Once the port for Canterbury, it still has a fishing fleet and a thriving fresh fish market. The boardwalk at the beach stretches almost to Seasalter and provided a most satisfying stroll for nosy people like us, because it's easy to peer into residents' gardens and front rooms. In the other direction is Tankerton, with grassy slopes and a fine shingle beach for shell collecting – another of Linda's pastimes. On arriving at or departing from the beachfront car park at Whitstable, Linda would always delight in showing friends 'The Peter Cushing View' – or a bench inscribed and dedicated to the great Hammer Horror film actor, who was the town's most notable resident. It would be a cue for her to sing a chorus from a punk anthem that celebrated Cushing's importance to the town – by local band Jellybotties. It goes something like this: 'Peter Cushing lives in Whitstable / I have seen him on his bicycle / I have seen him buying vegetables.'

South Kent coast:
A12 / A2 / A21 / A262 / B2067 / A259 / A268 / A21 / A2 / A12
And so to the English Channel and Kent's garden coast, an area that Linda got to know well on childhood holidays, but began to appreciate many years later, when she took me on day trips there. We would kick off our visit to Britain's sunniest corner, west of Folkestone at Sandgate, the one-time home of H. G. Wells. It's an improving fishing village that boasts a parade of antique shops, a few good pubs and the excellent Sandgate boutique hotel and restaurant.

Along the sea road is Hythe, one of the Cinque Ports, a pleasant town where the older part is separated from the largely Victorian resort by the Royal Military Canal, dug during the early 19th century as part of the defensive system against Napoleon. These days Hythe has Nepalese restaurants in the High Street and the area itself has the largest Nepalese settlement in the UK, due to Gurkha troops being stationed in Kentish barracks. Hythe has a grand promenade above a shingle and sand beach and a Martello tower – a circular early-19th-century fortress tower – a familiar feature of this coastline from the Napoleonic era. Once people feared the French invasion. Now they look forward to the regular invasion of French market traders and their goodies.

Hythe is the northern terminus of the Romney, Hythe and Dymchurch Railway, a miniature steam railway that runs parallel to the coastline for nearly fourteen miles through Dymchurch and New Romney to Dungeness. Known to enthusiasts as 'The Line that Jack Built' (that's Captain J. E. P. Howey, its founder) the world's smallest public railway celebrates 80 years of service in 2007. Miniature engines and carriages are one-third full size. It's a joy – particularly if you've got long legs. The area's literary connection is with Edith Nesbit, author of *The Railway Children*, who once lived in a cottage alongside the current station at St Mary's Bay. The book and film were firm favourites of Ms Smith, whose family holidayed in the area in the 1960s. To do the whole railway experience takes just over one hour each way, but the five-mile trip (then return) from New Romney to Dungeness is a tip-top twenty-seven minutes, and that should fill your boots. During the changeover at the Dungeness end, nip in for a quick cuppa at the Light Railway Café.

I'll leave Linda to set the scene for those early-life holidays in Romney Marsh. She based a wonderful episode of her radio sitcom on a trip to this part of Kent and she always managed to work up a full head of steam in her stage act: 'If we didn't go to the Isle of Wight, we'd take a little trip to Romney Marsh . . . in Kent – now, might have mentioned we lived in Kent – don't know what was going through their heads. "Mmm, we need a break. I know, let's go deeper into Kent. But I know, as we haven't got a car, let's go to the bit of Kent untouched by public transport; that'll be an adventure." Michael Palin could have done a whole series on our trip to the coast, basically.

'We'd leave our house in Erith. We could get a normal sort of train from there to Ashford, and from Ashford you could get a Green Line bus to Romney – then from Romney you had to get a spacehopper or something to New Romney, and from New Romney, the only way of getting to the coast was the Romney, Hythe and Dymchurch light railway. A lovely little model steam train, lovely it was, but we were going for a fortnight. We had deckchairs, suitcases, lilos, inflatable whales, water wings, rubber rings . . . cats, donkeys . . . my Dad's six foot two – we're sat on there with our knees around our ears . . . by the time we get to Dymchurch we've all got deep vein thrombosis.'

Time to explore the flatlands of Romney Marsh, which are very remote and mysterious but retain a beauty in their bleakness. The marsh is anything but a boggy swamp. It has vast dry shingle wastes, golden sand dunes and rich pasture-land that is home to numerous sheep. The wool trade was its making. Nowadays, Romney Marsh lamb is a popular item on local pub menus. Famous for having thirteen medieval churches, much of it was once owned by the wealthy monks of Canterbury. Linda showed me the best known, St Mary the Virgin at St Mary-in-the-Marsh, where E. Nesbit is buried. Noël Coward was another Marsh luminary who once lived at Goldenhurst in Aldington.

We invariably ended up at Dungeness, an intriguing and dramatic place to take a long walk on the shingle promontory and watch the hopeful anglers at the water's edge. Wild, beautiful and windswept. There's the occasional chuffing and puffing of the steam trains, two lighthouses, a pub, and various clapboard and tarred timber temporary-looking houses and shacks concentrated on the far side of the road that separates the residents from the beach.

Looming in the background, never out of sight, is the nuclear power station. This is also a potential site to build one of the new generation of nuclear generators, if the government gives the go-ahead. But what with the RSPB reserve acting as a wintering ground for thousands of migratory birds, and a dazzling array of wild flowers and plant life surviving the conditions on the beach, nature is still winning. These combined features in a surreal setting made Dungeness one of Linda's favourite places in Britain.

Linda and I found a picture-perfect place for late-afternoon cream tea – the Romney Bay House Hotel on Coast Road, Littlestone. It's yards from the beach below New Romney. We would sit on the terrace and be transported back to a bygone era when people played tennis and croquet in stripy jackets. We stayed there a couple of times and I can vouch for the spectacular views of the English Channel from the front-facing bedroom windows. This historic white building was built in the 1920s for the American actress and gossip columnist Hedda Hopper, and was designed for her by Sir Clough Williams-Ellis, the architect of Portmeirion in Wales.

Thence over the border into East Sussex, where we often made time for a quick flurry on the huge dunes at Camber Sands. This is where the sea goes out for half a mile at low tide, but beware the dangers of the fast incoming tides. From there on to Rye Harbour with superb walks out into the nature reserve and its shingle ridges, salt and grazing marshes, gravel pits and lagoons at the mouth of the River Rother. Prime 'birding' terrain – we spotted various terns and plovers before twilight. Then it was supper in Rye and home.

Suffolk coast
A12 / B1078 / B1084 / B1069 / A1094 / B1122 / B1125 / B1387 / A12
To get to the Suffolk Heritage Coast, you have to rely on the A12. Coming from the south, once you turn right for the sea, it's country B roads – a pleasure to negotiate. First turn off to Orford – an attractive village with a fine square. We were patrons of the Crown and Castle Hotel run by David and Ruth Watson – food writer and Channel Five TV's 'Hotel Inspector'. Superb breakfasts. We always made a point of sampling the produce of two particular smoke-houses. Richardson's profess to use only pure salt as an additive to food that undergoes long, slow, oak-wood smoking. Try the salmon, trout, mackerel and cheeses. The Butley–Orford Oysterage has similar foods, but also offers a simple but delicious range of very freshly prepared fish and seafood to consume on the premises.

Then walk this little lot off along the quayside, which was the first place we ever saw an avocet, a striking black and white long-legged wader with the upward curved beak. It's a beautiful creature that's become symbolic of the returning bird life in both Suffolk and Norfolk.

On through Snape and past the magnificent Maltings buildings, which house a lovely concert hall where Linda recorded *Just A Minute*. Onwards to Aldeburgh and its splendid shingle beach and elegant Georgian main street. This place has become seriously upmarket over the past decade – it was always posh and conservative, but has gone through a commercial uplift. Best avoided during peak times of the year, especially the height of summer. It's hard to resist the local fish and chips, but hold on for Southwold, if you can, and try the modest riverside shack of Mrs T's – so that's what she's up to now! The winner of the 'we're proud to close at four-thirty' contest goes to Cragg Sisters in the High Street. The best local restaurant in Aldeburgh and our regular evening haunt was The Lighthouse.

No time to dawdle, so we're off to Minsmere RSPB reserve via Westleton – a village with several greens and a bookshop run from a former chapel, where we once encountered the proprietor serving customers in mid-afternoon wearing his pyjamas and a dressing gown. Minsmere offers many walks between the bird-spotting hides. One of the best is near the entrance in a clearing, where we scrambled up a ladder to a raised feeding station and were rewarded by the sight of black and red Spotted Woodpeckers snacking. Minsmere is very good for spotting wading birds and all paths eventually lead down to the beach, where a mugshot of Sizewell B nuclear reactor greets you. It's not pretty.

Along the beach and a short climb up to the coastguard cottages at Dunwich Heath. This area is a stunning lookout point, rich in wildlife. It is what remains of the once extensive Sandlings heaths, with open tracts of heather and gorse, ablaze with colour in late summer and early autumn.

Once we sped through the lanes to get to a last cup of

tea of the day. Fingers tightly crossed, we pulled into the National Trust tea rooms car park at Dunwich Heath on the stroke of five o'clock. We raced out of the car to find the staff cleaning up and checking the takings. We must have put on our, 'But we're Trust members and we're desperately thirsty and sorry, but if you could just see your way to . . .' act. And they did. A win. But we had ten minutes to drink the tea and get out, as they mopped around us. When we arrived back at the car, Linda overheard a couple of people whispering.

'I'm sure it's that Linda Smith off the TV.'

'It can't be her – she wouldn't be getting into a Renault Clio.'

If there's time, do visit Blythburgh on the way to Walberswick. This little village on the edge of the marshes was an active port at one time, before falling victim to the silting up of the River Blyth. The Church of the Holy Trinity is a visible landmark for miles around. Both its exterior and interior are worth a look, especially the carvings that depict the Seven Deadly Sins.

Walberswick is a special place with a good beach and a network of paths and boardwalks through the reed beds. But it's also become too cute for its own good. Hordes of casual day visitors pour in to upset the delicate balance achieved by residents and family groups who come year on year to savour its combination of sands, marshes, river and sea. It's also attractive because of its proximity to the amenities of Southwold, which can be reached by crossing an iron footbridge further down the banks of the River Blyth. In summer, the lazy can zip across by ferry rowboat.

If Walberswick is outgrowing its physique, then Southwold is far too hip. It's Sunday broadsheet travel supplement land par excellence, but somehow the locals have hung in and made a determined attempt at blending the past with consumer pressures of the present. Linda and I first came here in the late 1980s on a speculative trip, foolhardily expecting to escape the freezing cold of Sheffield, only to be met by the biting cold winds of an East Anglian mid-winter. We ventured out to the reed beds in the marshes, but surrendered within a short while to the elements and went back to the Swan Hotel to pamper ourselves. In Sheffield we would have been labelled 'nesh' for our abrupt about-turn. The Crown Hotel, like the Swan, is part of the dominating Adnams family business and an excellent place for bar food. If we didn't finish the day here, it would be in Aldeburgh. We always stuck to what we knew.

Southwold has several green spaces above its unpretentious seafront, with about 250 brightly coloured beach huts – reckoned to be among the most expensive to buy in the UK. The pier is a must-see, particularly because of a madcap and marvellous collection of homemade slot machines housed in the weird amusement arcade. Go see the 'Under the Pier Show' by artist, cartoonist and engineer Tim Hunkin, and keep good time by his sublime Water Clock.

In the summer of 2003, Linda recorded two editions of *Just A Minute* at St Edmund's Hall during the traditional summer repertory theatre season. It was a memorable night for two reasons. Firstly, the chairman Nicholas Parsons and panel – Sir Clement Freud, Paul Merton, Graham Norton and Linda – were on sparkling form. Secondly, on a very hot and close evening, the conditions were made bearable only by opening the fire doors, thereby exposing all on stage and those in the audience to the gaze and ridicule of a gang of local juveniles who knew that the spotlight was on them.

There were some interesting and hilarious exchanges when the lads realised they were in the presence of BBC national radio.

North Norfolk coast
A12 / A130 / A131 / A134 / A1065 / A148 / A149 / A10 / A406

One thing to remember before you set off on a trip along this coast is that it's a strictly outdoor experience in cagoule and fleece country. There are no indoor distractions to speak of, other than sitting in pubs and cafés waiting for it to stop raining. A lot of hardened visitors come for sailing, or walking and bird spotting on the vast salt marshes under the huge Norfolk skies. We were smitten with it on our first visit during a crowded August bank holiday weekend, never ideal circumstances to make judgements about a new place. One aspect we did like was the sparseness – plenty of villages but few towns between Sheringham in the east and King's Lynn in the west.

The best place to start a tour is at Holt, a small town just a few miles in from the coast. It's distinguishable by an assortment of period colour-washed buildings with signs proclaiming it as a Georgian town. On the surface it seems quiet, peaceable and respectable, but there is plenty of activity to keep you occupied. As well as having ample eating and drinking places, it is tops for browsing, with lots of shops peddling antique and high-class curios and bric-à-brac. This had instant appeal for Linda.

Perhaps our finest discovery was Old Town in Bull Street, a singular, independent, small-scale manufacturer and retailer of work-wear-style clothing, run by Marie Willey and her partner. A major influence on their output is the period either side of and during the Second World War. They use British cottons, woollens and linens and their garments are individually cut, sewn and finished. They work in classic fabrics such as Harris tweed, corduroy, moleskin, cavalry drill, Irish linen, superfine cotton, Aertex, brushed cotton and Sudbury silk, sourced from the best suppliers. Their clothes are designed for simplicity of line, consistency of detail and durability of construction. Over the years Linda and I bought a steady supply of shirts, trousers, dresses, jackets and bags – in fact we used to joke that we were 'dressed by Old Town'. Recommended.

What I don't recommend is the rather unpleasant surprise we had one evening in Holt, when we managed to get a late booking at Yetmans restaurant, a charming place with 30 covers and very good food. The ambience and our concentration was firmly knocked for six when we realised that two of the four diners at the next table were none other than former prime minister and hot lover John Major and his long-suffering wife Norma. One of their other two companions was a significant Tory who was sporting an MCC 'bacon and egg' tie. Forgive me for going on about this, but Linda and I could never come to terms with leading Thatcherites like Major and Kenneth Clarke being the public standard bearers for cricket and modern jazz respectively. Two of *our* passions!

Down the shaded lanes to the coast and Salthouse for a handsome seafood and smoked fish salad at the inimitable Cookies Crab Shop, where you can sit out on any day of the year and enjoy a meal and gaze across the salty marshes. Salthouse, in common with neighbouring Cley and Blakeney, is a former port cut off by the receding sea. We whiled away

many an hour here in contemplation, glowing with satis-
faction. Linda was quite a connoisseur of cooked crab in
all its forms and she proclaimed Cookies as 'very hard to
beat' – fair praise from someone who had sampled crab all
the way around the Kent coast, and for that matter just
about every other coast in Britain.

Minutes along the coast road is the intriguing Cley next
the Sea (pronounced 'Cly'). For us, the Cley marshes were
bird-spotting central and Linda would stride along to get
to a series of hides, binoculars around her neck, concen-
trating hard on the breathtaking sight of marsh harriers in
flight. We chit-chatted in hushed tones with real birders who
spend most of their waking leisure hours tracking these birds
of prey. The pay-off came when the birders relented and
offered Linda the amateur a better view of the action through
a powerful scope, which brought us almost face to face with
this impressive predator. But still no reclusive bittern to be
heard or seen – maybe we were just plain unlucky, although
we did see an outline of one in a reed bed at Lee Valley
Park in Essex.

Blakeney is a flint-walled village with a neat harbour and
a good line in crab sandwiches. But the rush is on to get
to next-door Morston Quay and squeeze on board for a
very rewarding boat trip to the common and grey seal
colonies at Blakeney Point. A bonus here is to witness the
summer nesting and feeding grounds for migrant birds,
especially terns – little, common, Sandwich and the quite
rare Arctic ones. And turns they certainly are – we marvelled
at their aerial acrobatics, diving headlong into the water
and emerging with fish or sand eels.

The best walking in north Norfolk is probably found on
the vast stretches of Holkham beach, where you can stroll

for miles when the tide goes out. Linda was always recommending it to whoever was mildly interested in a trip to this coast. You can see and hear skylarks, wheatear and meadow pipits on the sands and in the dunes. Then, with binoculars at the ready, make for the George Washington bird hide and see the grandeur of spoonbills, little egrets, sparrowhawks and more marsh harriers. Beach and birds together – what an indulgence!

Retire to the soothing surrounds of Titchwell Manor Hotel for tea and cakes – Linda and I tasted our best ever slice of homemade ginger cake here. Last stop in this very hectic day would be Brancaster Staithe – a staithe is a bank, or landing stage in Old English. Here we would fantasise about living a contented existence, feasting on top quality crab and locally-caught fish – until the phone would ring and it would be a producer at the BBC asking if Linda had written that script yet. More strolling, or in Linda's case striding, before wrapping up proceedings with a mighty good fish dinner at the White Horse Hotel.

North Yorkshire coast
A630 / A19 / A64 / A169 / B1416 / A171 / B1447 / A171 / A169 / A64 / A19 / A630
Heading out of South Yorkshire, skirting West Yorkshire and making for York. No trip to the northern part of the county would be complete without a visit to a branch of Betty's Café Tea Rooms in St Helen's Square. This is the flagship of the chain, with other fine eateries at Harrogate, Ilkley and Northallerton. It would be a challenge to any gastronome to fit in a meal at all four branches in one day. We settle for a light brunch in the art deco elegance of a dining room based on one of the staterooms of the luxury

cruise liner *Queen Mary*. Betty's founder, Frederick Belmont, was a man of great style in all respects. His family has kept up the highest standards of bakery ever since 1936, when a dilapidated furniture store made way for a centre of sophistication.

Next stop is the market town of Pickering at the southern end of the wonderful North Yorkshire Moors Railway. Time for a nostalgic ride on a complete steam train, with thrilling views of the national park on the way through to Grosmont. We travelled just a few stops up the line to Levisham, before returning to Pickering. Then on to the breathtaking car ride along the top of the heather-covered moors with panoramic views, eventually dipping down to the picturesque village and former fishing and smuggling centre of Robin Hood's Bay. When we were on foot with backpacks we would stop off here for refreshments on our section of the Cleveland Way from Scarborough to Whitby. The full walk is an impressive 110 miles of path in a horseshoe-shape. It starts at Filey, takes the coast to Saltburn-by-the-Sea and turns inland, ending up at Helmsley.

The walk from Robin Hood's Bay to Whitby and back is guaranteed to gee up your appetite, if you haven't ruined it with an overdose of the walker's friend – Eccles cakes. Move on to the fishing port of Whitby, and if the tide allows, take the short stroll along the wide beach to the next-door resort of Sandsend. Make haste on the return leg because, as supper-time approaches, big queues start to form outside our all-time favourite fish and chips establishment, the Magpie Café on Pier Road. Expect fabuloso battered fish and splendid seafood salads. It's hard to top their sticky toffee pudding.

Take the gentle winding road into the tranquil evening air of the Esk Valley – fine trekking country – to the moortop village of Goathland, where moorland sheep rule. They are everywhere, so don't mess with them. This village is perhaps better known as Aidensfield in the TV drama *Heartbeat*. There's a super walk from here along the ridge of Wade's Causeway, one of the best-preserved sections of Roman road. One more hop to the last stop of the day, the enchanting Beck Hole, where a tiny bridge crosses the Ellerbeck. This has been a popular travellers' rest for centuries. For us it meant the superb combined bar room and shop of the Birch Hall Inn, with regionally sourced nourishment in the form of a pint of Theakston's bitter and a packet of Seabrook's ready-salted crinkly crisps.

Together, we saw so much of Britain that it seems rough justice to reduce a lot of other places to an honourable mention, but space on the page dictates it. So here goes:

Derbyshire – the White Peak, singling out the Tissington Trail / Dove Dale and the village of Hartington.

Round Sheffield Walk – a circular walk that we could pick up a short distance from our front door.

Essex – Mersea Island westside and the seafood haven of The Company Shed.

Dorset – Isle of Purbeck / Studland / Brownsea Island.

Northumberland – the deserted coast and beaches and a tea of Craster kippers.

Devon – for Dartmoor and Exmoor.

Cornwall – St Mawes and the Roseland Peninsula.

Lancashire – the Forest of Bowland walks.

West Wales – Mumbles and the Gower Peninsula.

North Wales – Portmeirion / Snowdonia and the Lleyn Peninsula.

Cotswolds / Sussex – Arts and Crafts houses, in particular Standen.

19
Tests, Trials, Tests, Trials

East London to Sutton, Surrey

Between spring and autumn 2005, there were some weeks when it felt like we were spending more time in traffic on the southern section of the M25 motorway than we were at home. During the periods of intensive treatment Linda was receiving at the Royal Marsden Hospital in Surrey, we were making the return journey every other weekday. Depending on the appointment time, the trip might take an hour or so, but twice as long if we hit the Blackwall Tunnel and Dartford intersections during the morning or evening rush hours.

Occasionally, Linda had an overnight stay and I headed back home, accompanied by the pumping sounds of the Virgin Radio evening request show. Virgin Radio was designed for 'Orbital Rock' and I needed its help as I sped along. There were days when I felt out of my mind on a combination of anxiety and weariness. Virgin on top-notch volume was the drug of choice to keep my adrenalin topped up under my personal bonnet.

In the early morning we would take alternative routes to beat the southbound traffic to the tunnel. Linda would be in control of the airwaves and we would have Radio Four's *Today* programme on for sheer enlightenment. After a while Radio Four would give way to the up-tempo Radio Five Live phone-in topic of the day show. Bored with speech, Linda would then decide to chivvy us up. She would try everything on the dial before settling down to Virgin, where one in three tunes would be to our mutual liking. That's not a bad ratio for a commercial station.

Virgin Radio helps the small motorist in their Renault Clio; it ratchets up their confidence to compete for road space with continental juggernaut lorries and, more importantly, the men in white vans who believe *they* are the kings of the tarmac. We were behaving ourselves, trying to mind our speed, but jockeying with the kind of drivers who are desperate to maintain pole position. This is where 'Orbital Rock' meets 'Combat Rock'. There is no margin of doubt available to driver or passenger, no time to relax into finger-tapping on the steering wheel while cruising along. This wasn't toe- or foot-tapping country while doing a steady 60 mph in the slow lane. We had to get there on time, so it was life in the fast lane, as the Eagles would have it.

Virgin plays perfectly palatable middle-of-the-road rock, has reasonably unobtrusive DJs (less irritating than other stations) and shortish ad breaks. I imagine it's the station of choice for the Clarkson Tribe – Music Radio Bloke terrain. It tends to reinforce prejudice, evoking one of two reactions: *still like it* or *still loathe it*.

Linda took the role of Roman Emperor, giving the thumbs up or thumbs down to the various tunes on the Virgin playlist – mainly singles taken from albums in the upper reaches of the charts or the odd all-time fave rave like David Bowie ('The Jean Genie'), The Clash ('Rock the Casbah'), The Specials ('Ghost Town') and Van Morrison ('Brown Eyed Girl').

The songs she liked stayed on; those she didn't, didn't. The thumbs-up category would include the Scissor Sisters, Magic Numbers, The Killers, Paul Weller, Kaiser Chiefs,

Franz Ferdinand, Black Eyed Peas and Goldie Lookin' Chain. Thumbs-down certs were James Blunt ('You're Beautiful'), any Coldplay track, any Keane song or David Gray number. If Linda was snoozing, then I could get away with Oasis, Red Hot Chilli Peppers, Stereophonics or even Green Day. If she woke up during one of those I would get 'the look' and be punished by a return to Melvyn Bragg on Radio Four talking about some obscure saint who did good works in the north-east of England.

During periods of inactivity or frustration with the NHS system, Linda attended the Harley Street consulting room of a socialist-inclined medical practitioner, Dr Etienne Callebout. She was inspired and uplifted by his beliefs and practice. He became her pathway to sourcing other therapies as we sought a breakthrough, at a time when conventional medicine seemed to be distinctly unpromising. Obtaining non-toxic beneficial substances unavailable to NHS patients came at a financial cost. And the regime that accompanied them was very rigorous, sometimes too rigorous for Linda to endure.

Linda accommodated chemotherapy in tandem with other therapies. She never tried *the* radical alternative – the abandonment of chemotherapy in favour of a reliance on other methods and treatments. This course of action was followed by Michael Gearin-Tosh, as outlined in his acclaimed book *Living Proof*. Gearin-Tosh prolonged his life for years by keeping to a strict regime of zero chemotherapy. Linda admired him and was very sympathetic to his approach.

During the course of her illness and as an NHS patient, Linda had reason to visit nine hospitals in the London area for emergency treatment, blood tests, scans, drug trials, surgery and chemotherapy. These were: Newham General; Bart's; St George's; St Thomas's; the Royal Marsden,

Sutton; St Anthony's; Charing Cross; Marsden, Fulham; and Whipps Cross.

We moved on to the Royal Marsden from St George's, Tooting, because the positive effects of Thalidomide had hit a plateau and begun a reversal, meaning that Linda had to succumb to the inevitable and stop the drug. The Royal Marsden Hospital and the Institute of Cancer Research form the largest comprehensive cancer centre in Europe. Linda was receiving experimental treatment at the brand-new Oak Centre, which had just been opened by Gary Lineker. She'd been referred there from Bart's Hospital and had signed up for clinical drug trials. The first of these had been in the previous spring, for a completely untried drug supplied by the US manufacturers Chiron Corporation, which was one of several pharmaceutical giants trialling new anti-cancer drugs in tandem with public hospitals and patients in research programmes around the world.

Patients on these first-phase trials are going into pioneer territory by taking a drug, or a particular combination of drugs, which has never been given to people before. Linda was in a batch of only 30 to 50 patients testing out this particular therapy. It was to be taken in 7- and 14-day cycles with appropriate gaps. Constant tests had to be made for possible side effects and in order to assess any measurable changes in a patient's condition – so blood tests at regular intervals were a big feature, along with checking the levels of the protein CA125.

Unfortunately, the results from the first completed cycles did not signify any noticeable improvement in Linda's overall disposition and she was taken off this drug. This was yet another knock-back, but we waited in line for the chance to be eligible for other drugs that were deemed suitable for a trial run. There weren't any new ones in the pipeline for a while, so Linda opted to try Caelyx, a standard chemotherapy treatment.

During the hiatus period in June between the two drug programmes, Linda went back to work and appeared on a couple of episodes of the new BBC TV topical comedy panel game, *Mock the Week*. It was at the end of her second appearance, the fourth episode, that life took another turn for the worse. After a long and exhausting recording, she came into the hospitality room at BBC White City studios looking very troubled and worn out. She led me out to her dressing room and showed me an alarmingly swollen left leg. It so happened that I had been chatting to the partner of show host Dara O'Briain, who was a medical doctor. She came to look at Linda's leg and advised us to get down to nearby Charing Cross Hospital as soon as possible. It turned out that Linda had a case of deep vein thrombosis (DVT), not uncommon in cancer patients. From that night onwards she had to take anti-coagulants and found walking more than a short distance quite problematic.

Linda's outpatient appointments at the Marsden fell on certain Mondays – and at the Oak Centre on Thursdays. They usually lasted at least a half-day and sometimes went through to the evening. Now this was the summer of England's astounding cricketing success against our old enemies, Australia, and Linda and I were completely swept up in the hysteria surrounding the proceedings. We both loved cricket. Unfortunately, the appointments for the Caelyx drug programme coincided with the Thursday opening days of three of the Test matches. By the time we got round to the morning appointment on Thursday 8 September, the fifth and final Test at the Oval was starting. The tension had become unbearable for both hardened cricket lovers and the millions of new converts to the national cause. England were two to one up and only needed to draw this match to win back the Ashes. Linda's various tests and her treatment were set to go on for hours and would mean that she was attached to tubes and generally quite drowsy. She was exasperated at not being able to watch or listen to the match.

This is where I came into my own again as her tried and trusted informant, Linda's eyes and ears. It was my job to go periodically to the canteen on the ground floor and watch a few overs, then I would report back to Linda and her fellow patients upstairs, giving them the latest score and a summary of play. England batted well that day and went on to secure the draw that brought home the Ashes, ending 18 years of drought and Aussie dominance and creating much merriment for the long-suffering English cricket public. Commentators considered it one of the greatest series of all time. It certainly helped to distract Linda and me during a long hard summer.

I must point out here that Linda knew her Graham Dilley from her Peter Willey. She was Kent to my Essex when we decided to get fierce and competitive about cricketing loyalties – although Linda was always cautioning people not to get too wound up and territorial on behalf of pieces of land that were most probably owned by the government, Church, monarchy or the Oxbridge colleges. In her youth, she had worked in the local parks one summer and assisted the groundsman at Dartford, which used to host a festival of Kent county cricket matches. That's where she came across Graham Dilley in his debut season, a powerful, locally born, golden-haired youth, raised to bowl fast for his county, going on to bowl fast for his country.

Our sporting rivalries would bare themselves in the football season, too. Linda supported West Ham United because when she was growing up, they were the nearest first-class team – albeit directly across the Thames. Charlton were still a fallen giant, yet to undergo their modern-day trans-formation, and the thought of supporting Millwall was beyond the pale. Far too rough.

For me, I had always been Arsenal, following in my dad's footsteps and rejecting overtures from most of my other male relatives, who were staunch Tottenham Hotspurs – 'the Yids' as we Jews say. We made a few trips to see West Ham and Arsenal engage in sporting battle. I recall a game at Arsenal's old Highbury stadium where we had seats in the very partisan North Bank grandstand. I became almost apologetic when Arsenal were leading 4–0 at half-time.

Then there was the occasion we went to a hectic and exciting clash between West Ham and Newcastle United with comedy mates Phill Jupitus, a big Hammer, and Richard Morton, a discreet but proud north countryman from Hexham. It was a terrific game and memorable for Linda because of the chants and counter-chants from the respective sets of fans. As usual, Newcastle were very vocal, but West Ham refused to be trumped and tightened the south–north economic screw with a wicked rendition of 'In Your North-ern Slums'. It didn't help their cause on the playing field – Newcastle won by quite a margin, aided by Alan Shearer.

Linda had always been fascinated by sporting chants. Here she is live on stage at the Lescar Hotel, Sheffield, in 1993: 'It's nonsense now, of course, but we still think we should win at everything. And so, like I say, we are playing cricket with Pakistan and the Pakistanis are winning by the expe-dient of being quite good at cricket . . . and so the English fans – I was there at the time – started taunting the Pakistani fans, shouting, "One Salman Rushdie – there's only one Salman Rushdie . . . you can't beat the boy from Penguin, the boy from Penguin, he's our boy!"

'And I thought, well, I can see what you're getting at there, lads, really. They're trying to find an upside to everything – they're trying to see a little good in everyone. And I think . . . well, at least it's an educated heckle – at least it's a literary heckle – I quite like that. You know, the Pakistanis should have responded in kind. They should have started chanting, "William Shakespeare – William Shakespeare, you're not writing any more, you only write when you're alive – write when you're ali-ive, you sonnet-writing slap-head." That would get the lads.'

When Linda was in the Marsden for the day and there were suitable breaks between medical tests, I would spring her from her chair or bed and we would go off on little local jaunts. We went to several places neither of us had visited before. We lunched, shopped and browsed for collectibles in Banstead, Dorking and Reigate and took in the spectacular views of the North Downs from Box Hill. We escaped occasionally to the quaint world of the nearest National Trust house and garden at Polesden Lacey for tea, and even found time between blood tests to race to Wakehurst Place Gardens beyond Gatwick Airport. It was sometimes a hairy drive back to the Marsden. But if we had a short hospital stay, Linda would always want to visit her spiritual home at the RHS gardens and HQ at Wisley. This has a superior garden centre and she would always emerge with a few trophies to take home, in the expectation that she would be fit and well enough to plant new varieties in the ground or in one of the large pots she had acquired.

Sadly, she was never physically able to realise her third

large-scale garden project, at our new home. She had been waiting a long time to be the mistress of such a domain, but it was not to be. She managed some light planting and instructed me in various clearance duties, which were intended to make space for her plans. It was so frustrating for her. Likewise, her lack of stamina meant she only fulfilled one day of hard graft at a nearby allotment at Empress Avenue, which she and our friends, Sue, Jen and Karen, had spent ages wresting from slothful Redbridge Council. Linda took on a new role as adviser to the willing and able first-time volunteers.

In summer 2005, between hospital appointments and periods of treatment, we also managed to squeeze in trips to our absolute favourite coastlines of Suffolk, north Norfolk, north and south Kent, as well as visiting the amazing art deco interiors of Eltham Palace, and the great gardens at Sissinghurst and Great Dixter.

Linda's last working day fell on 24 November, when she gave her most candid ever interview to Dawn French for a new BBC2 TV series that she was fronting called *Girls Who Do Comedy*. Surprisingly, for two near-veterans of the modern comedy business, it was Linda and Dawn's first meeting.

They settled down to chat and I retreated to the back of the room, but within earshot. As the make-up ladies made their applications, I overheard Linda and Dawn comparing notes about their favourite contestants in the hottest series on cable TV, *America's Next Top Model*, one of Linda's regular distractions during her many enforced days at home. It was a wonderful interview. Linda talked to Dawn very openly about her childhood and family life and how it had inspired her comedy.

*　　*　　*

The interview was in the afternoon and afterwards we returned home to east London at tea-time with barely an hour to turn around, have a bite to eat, and for Linda to collect her thoughts and take some painkillers. She was already physically exhausted as she got into the car and we drove off again.

But Linda was so determined that nothing was going to stand between her and that night's episode of *The News Quiz*, especially since she had missed out on every episode of the autumn series, despite producer Katie Tyrrell's best efforts to keep a spot open for her every week. It was now or never. There were only two editions to go before Christmas and she was in no mood to let down the rest of the panel, the producer or the audience. She would have to draw on all her reserves and canniness to get through.

We drew up at the Drill Hall about twenty minutes before the warm-ups for the recording. Linda slipped through the side entrance to join her colleagues and prepare herself. When they and she were introduced onto the stage, no one in the auditorium, other than me, knew the true state of affairs.

She was in good company for what turned out to be her last ever appearance on the BBC flagship show. She was among some of her favourite co-panellists and mates – Andy Hamilton, Alan Coren and Armando Iannucci. Buoyed up by an amalgam of Doctor Theatre and pure adrenalin, she was on great form as usual, indulging in plenty of sparkling repartee. Laughing away. It was business as usual. But by the time we said our goodbyes and left the venue, she was completely wiped out. It took her a couple of days to get over this twin-burst of activity.

The last Christmas dinner that Linda and I shared together

was at her sister Barbara's home in Bexleyheath a few weeks later. It was touch and go whether we would make it over there until just a few hours before we set off from east London. Linda had been feeling consistently unwell for months and had only been able to work a couple of times during that period. She had been on a ruthless regime of medication, which left her fatigued and generally unable to walk more than a very short distance. She was also troubled with pain and numbness in her right arm and hand. The routines of daily life we take for granted were getting increasingly difficult for her to negotiate. I had become her full-time carer months earlier – it was a pathetically seamless graduation from being our part-time domestic.

A few weeks before Christmas we had attended the Royal Marsden Hospital in Fulham and Linda had been detained overnight for various tests and scans. The outcome of these was dreadful. Linda was told that her cancer had spread and that she probably only had a few months to live. All that could be offered was short-term treatment to alleviate the symptoms. Linda was so brave and strong. I felt weak and just wanted the earth to swallow me up. Linda's ever-positive attitude made her a tower of strength when I was feeling low, although I would never let it show.

Linda did Christmas pagan-style. There was enough symbolism for her in having a tree for the season. We always went down to Columbia Road Flower Market in Bethnal Green, east London, to get the right size tree, which Linda would decorate. She carefully unwrapped the family heirlooms inherited from her mum, a range of eye-catching glass figures and glittering baubles. Everything about this act was perfect, from the design concept to the lighting rig. Linda was an artist and she was in her element dressing the Christmas tree. Everyone that visited, and for that matter passed by the house, complimented her on her creation.

But as we approached this Christmas we knew that we would have to rely on family and friends to carry out all the physical duties. And so it was one evening that Linda sat in her reclining chair giving minimal instructions to her sister, brother-in-law Terry, close friends Debra and Hattie, and to me, the self-appointed tea and coffee maker. The job was done by midnight and Linda must have felt a real glow transcending her tiredness. We had not let her down.

Linda died at home on 27 February 2006 with close family members around her. I was so glad that we'd been able to make sure that she didn't die in hospital. Lots of people came to see her in her final week and on that last day an amazing number assembled at our home. All her closest friends and family were there, including many friends from the comedy world. It was an extraordinary day. After Linda died, we all gathered in the front room and raised a glass of malt whisky to her. I made a little speech – actually, it was one of my 'Castro' speeches. I'm known for my overlong speeches.

Linda's humanist funeral was very private, just for family. Two versions of 'I'm Forever Blowing Bubbles', the West Ham United anthem, were played during the service, one by Vera Lynn and the other by the West Ham supporters. The next day there was a big commemoration and celebration of her life, attended by hundreds of her friends.

I will close with Linda's own words, from the interview she gave to Bel Mooney for *Devout Sceptics* broadcast on BBC Radio Four on 1 January 2004.

Bel Mooney: People always think of those who make their living from being funny as perhaps having a melancholy side. You've obviously got a very serious side. Do you find it easy to be optimistic, to see the funny side of things?

Linda: Oh yeah, definitely. I don't want to paint a picture of me as this terrible maudlin clown. Like one of those paintings on velvet, with a 3-D tear just trickling down my face. That would be awful. Oh no. No, I'm very optimistic. I just think like lots of people – mood swings. Doesn't take much to cheer me up. I could be feeling really, really miserable but a small thing can really cheer me up.

Bel Mooney: What kind of thing?

Linda: Hello, three hours of *Columbo* on Granada Plus. Brilliant, that'll cheer me up, or a brilliant old film, black and white. If you see the words Alastair Sim in the credits, you immediately perk up, don't you? You think, We're in for a treat here. Again, nice bright sunny day, look out of the window, sun shining, that's a result, isn't it? You're already points ahead.

Bel Mooney: They are all solitary pleasures so far.

Linda: Oh really, are they? Also friends. Having a laugh would be the top of them all, which for most people is the case, isn't it? Cos everyone's funny. I'll qualify that. There's a small group of people who are never funny and they are people you would go a long way to avoid. Most people, if you think about it, friends you have, they are always going to make you laugh at some point, because that's what groups of people do for each other, isn't it? I mean, in really terrible situations, people still manage to laugh, don't they?

Find funny things, because it gets people through.

Bel Mooney: Is that what makes us human?

Linda: I think it may well be. I've never seen a fish laugh! Never seen it. They maybe have a little bit of a smirk, maybe they like that more sideways look. There might be a little troupe of octopus doing a sideways look at undersea worlds somewhere. Animals, they're lovely but they are not big on the jokes generally, are they? You'd wait a long time before a cat came out with a really good one-liner. That's as fair a definition of what makes us human: the ability to have a laugh.

Bel Mooney: Linda Smith, thank you very much.

Linda: Thank you, Bel.

THE END

Epilogue

I began writing this book during two bouts of hospitalisation in early 2007. The whole scenario in my ward was reminiscent of *The Singing Detective (SD)* – one of Linda's all-time favourite TV series. Linda had endured longish stints in hospital herself. I often wondered when I departed for the night and left her to her thoughts whether she was having one of those *SD* moments – she must have had.

Ordinarily, she could easily slip into her own parallel world. We are all capable of that. While I may have fancied myself as an amateur Philip Marlow, I never managed to conjure up any of those riotous vaudevillian song and dance routines involving consultants, their medical teams and nurses. No 'Dry Bones' by Fred Waring's Pennsylvanians for me, although a hard-working cleaner who mopped and hoovered in rhythm to his own singing had enormous potential and would have been a sure starter in my contemporary hospital combo.

For the past seventeen months, I have striven to honour Linda's memory in public and in private by trying to preserve and represent all she stood for. Linda had died on the eve of Ovarian cancer awareness month. I must confess that I was unaware of the campaign's existence until a journalist from the *Mail on Sunday* rang me to talk about Linda and alerted me to its imminent launch. Therein lies the problem – lack of awareness. There was a flurry of newspaper articles highlighting ovarian cancer in the days immediately after Linda's death. I've tried to distil some of the essential facts below to demonstrate why there is such a crying need for greater dissemination of this information and why I am determined to do what I can to assist in this cause, not least by donating a share of royalties from this book to Ovarian cancer action.

Key facts at the time of writing:

- Every day, 12 women in the UK die from ovarian cancer.
- 7,000 women in the UK are diagnosed with ovarian cancer each year.
- It's the fourth most common form of cancer in women in the UK.
- The UK has the second lowest survival rate in the western world.
- About 75 per cent of cases are not detected until its latest stages.
- Survival rates remain depressingly low, with only 30 per cent of women living longer than five years, compared with 80 per cent of those with breast cancer.
- Earlier diagnoses and quicker treatment could increase survival rates to 95 per cent.
- One in 48 British women, mostly over 50 years, will develop the disease at some point during their life.
- 85 per cent of the women diagnosed with ovarian cancer are over 50 years old.

Linda educated herself in order to understand what she was taking on and the prospects she was facing. The statistics are very scary and upsetting, but she was never daunted by them. She continued to lead her life to the full and didn't complain. I pay tribute to her and to the many thousands of women who have died from this terrible disease and, of course, to the increasing number of women who have overcome these odds and survived.

At the time of Linda's death, I knew I had to be strong and clear about what was to happen next: a very small humanist-run family funeral one day – no friends, no fuss; the next day a public commemoration and celebration of Linda's life, orchestrated by her social friends and close colleagues in comedy and broadcasting. It was an extraordinary event staged at the Theatre Royal, Stratford, east London, where 450 people, including many of comedy and broadcasting's finest, stood, sat, laughed, cried and applauded in honour of their recently departed friend.

Since that unforgettable day in March 2006, there have been fundraising tribute concerts organised in Linda's name at the Lyceum Theatre, Sheffield; the Victoria Palace Theatre, London and the Assembly Rooms, Edinburgh Festival. There have been tribute programmes devoted to Linda and her humour on BBC Radio Four (three), BBC Radio Seven and BBC Two TV. October 2006 saw the publication of an anthology of Linda's best material, entitled *I Think the Nurses are Stealing My Clothes: The Very Best of Linda Smith*, edited by myself and our friend Ian Parsons and marked by not one, but three separate launch events in London and Sheffield, that raised funds for Ovarian cancer action. Shortly after came Linda's posthumous induction into the Radio Four Hall of Fame, along with her comedy heroines Hattie Jacques and Betty Marsden. And in March 2007 Linda received a posthumous accolade from the Chortle Comedy Awards in recognition of her Outstanding Contribution to Comedy.

While I have acted as guardian of the Linda Smith legacy in public, my true desire has been to mark Linda's life in a more sedate and unseen way – more in keeping with the person herself. With a wonderfully active and supportive group of friends, we organised a truly memorable day in the Kent countryside and seaside en route to a communal scattering of Linda's ashes in her home county. A coach full of 65 hit the trail for an old-fashioned charabanc ride to a series of stopping-off places that had very special meaning for Linda and me.

Continuing on the outdoor theme, I pledged myself to persevere with Linda's beloved back garden project, which she was physically unable to complete. This was planted last summer and is in spectacular full bloom as I write, thanks to the imagination and skill of my sympathetic garden designer and Weedfinder General, Anna Wardrop. Anna drew inspiration from the English cottage garden plants that Linda had so loved and planted in her previous gardens, as well as from the gardens that Linda most loved, the White Garden at Sissinghurst and the spectacularly mixed borders at Great Dixter. The result is a beautiful thing, with a meandering path leading to a seating area under a chestnut tree – a path that, as Anna puts it, 'takes you on a journey through all the things Linda loved about gardening'.

Over the last few years, in particular since Linda's passing, I have drawn strength from a core of close friends and family members who have supported me all the way. Without them, little of what has been achieved in Linda's name could have materialised. They have worked with me at all times; given me breathing space; been there to prop me up just as I was falling. No names; they know who they are. This informal grouping has found an official role in the last year as an organisation known as The Friends of Linda Smith.

The Friends of Linda Smith exists to undertake programmes of work, in the UK and abroad, which reflect Linda's likes, interests and passions. We initiate projects that she would have approved of. In so doing, not only do we undertake some exciting projects and activities but we also help to keep her name a living memory.

Linda was committed to assisting several causes she came across in her private and public life. Her friends are trying to raise money in order to support a range of projects that reflect Linda's interests across the spectrum of popular culture, education, young people and international relations. These projects are constantly updated on www.lindasmithcomedy.co.uk.

The success of the concerts in Sheffield and London relied on the goodwill and co-operation of a chain of comedians, musicians, speakers, technicians and theatre managers. But without two particular individuals working with me on a day-to-day basis, these shows could not have happened. My thanks forever to Mike McCarthy, who masterminded the Sheffield 'reunion' and to Carol Benjamin, who orchestrated the London extravaganza and then went on to steer us through the Edinburgh Festival.

None of the events that have taken place recently in Linda's memory would have been possible without the talent and generous participation of literally hundreds of people. Here's the roll call of all those people who appeared at the various events. I salute you.

10 March 2006
Theatre Royal, Stratford, east London
'A Celebration of the Life of Linda Smith'

String Quartet of BBC Symphony Orchestra; Bill Bailey; Jane Baker; Caroline Black; Jo Brand; Barry Cryer; Stephen Daldry; Mark Damazer; Graham Downes; Kevin Eldon; Ronnie Golden; Steve Gribbin; Andy Hamilton; Jeremy Hardy; Hattie Hayridge; John Hegley; Phill Jupitus; Ann Lavelle; Mike McCarthy; Chris Meade; Karen Merkel; Paul Merton; Richard Morton; Chris Neill; Henry Normal; Debra Reay; Sandi Russell; Brian Shade; Arthur Smith; Mark Steel; Hanne Stinson; Laurie Taylor; Mark Thomas.

14 May 2006
The Lyceum Theatre, Sheffield
'In Praise of an English Radical – A Celebration of Linda Smith'

Margaret Barraclough; The Chuffinelles; Deborah Egan; Denise Fitzpatrick; Steve Gribbin; Jeremy Hardy; John Hegley; Sylvia Jones; Ann Lavelle; Jane McCauley; Roger Monkhouse; Brian Mulligan; The Mysterons; Chris Percival; Rony Robinson; Sandi Russell Trio; Kate Rutter; Joy Skelton; Betty Spital; Don Valley and The Rotherhides; Rachel Van Riel.

4 June 2006
The Victoria Palace Theatre, London
'Tippy Top – An Evening of Linda Smith's Favourite Things'

The Blockheads; Jo Brand; Tim Brooke-Taylor; Corrie Corfield; Barry Cryer; Peter Donaldson; Graeme Garden; Charlotte Green; Steve Gribbin; Andy Hamilton; Jeremy Hardy; Hattie Hayridge; Simon Hoggart; Phill Jupitus; Humphrey Lyttelton; Paul Merton; Richard Morton; Brian Mulligan; Chris Neill; Nicholas Parsons; Brian Perkins;

Sandi Russell Quartet; Arthur Smith; Mark Steel; Liza Tarbuck; Mark Thomas; Sandi Toksvig.

22 August 2006
The Music Hall, Assembly Rooms, Edinburgh (Festival)
'A Tribute to Linda Smith'

Tim Clark; Ronnie Golden; Jeff Green; Hattie Hayridge; John Hegley; Adam Hills; Fred Macaulay; Chris Neill; Mrs Barbara Nice; Lucy Porter; Liz Stephens; Count Arthur Strong.

30 October 2006
The Drill Hall, Chenies Street, London
I Think the Nurses are Stealing My Clothes: The Very Best of Linda Smith
Book launch

The Bettertones; Gurpreet Bhatti; Bob Boyton; Jo Brand; Stephanie Calman; Dave Cohen; Corrie Corfield; Barry Cryer; Ivor Dembina; Peter Donaldson; Femi Elufowoju Jr.; Ronnie Golden; Charlotte Green; Steve Gribbin; Andy Hamilton; Barb Jungr; Phill Jupitus; Jenny Lecoat; Sean Lock; Brian Mulligan; Chris Neill; Nicholas Parsons; Brian Perkins; Eve Polycarpou; Ian Saville; John Sergeant; Ian Shaw; Arthur Smith; Mark Steel; Liz Stephens; Sandi Toksvig.

ACKNOWLEDGEMENTS

My personal thanks to all those people listed below, and apologies to anyone whom I have accidentally omitted from this roll call. Without their combined efforts, friendship, kindness and support, this book could not have been written and produced.

For their initial encouragement and for making me believe I could do these books – Pat Hehir and Carol Benjamin.

The Lakin production team: the ever dependable research and transcription partnership of Ian 'Mr Find-o' Parsons and Gail 'The Judge' Elliman, readers and advisers Sarah Broughton and Debra Reay, and my superb editor Rebecca Cripps.

The Friends of Linda Smith projects manager: Graham Downes.

Special thanks to staff at Whipps Cross Hospital, Leytonstone, east London for twice making me better during the early stages of writing this book.

At publishers Hodder & Stoughton – Nick Davies, Nicola Doherty, Hugo Wilkinson, and Karen Geary.

At literary agents Curtis Brown – Jonny Geller and his assistant Doug Kean.

To author Graham McCann for his valuable advice.

For contributions to the Erith years:
Pauline Daniels (Pauline/Lucy Trask), Alison Dark (Travers), Barbara, Terry, Scott and Austin Giles; Sean

Acknowledgements

Hayden, John Hogan, Peter Howard, Michael Howard, Justin Lorentzen, Sharon Noonan-Gunning, Philip Sanderson, Brian Shade, Sharyn Smith, Stewart Wentworth, Ian Williams.

For contributions to the Sheffield years:
Jane Baker (Betty Spital), Margaret Barraclough, Margaret Bennett, Janet Bray, Carolyn Carmichael, Jean Clarke, Kate Collier, May Corfield, Nicky Cowan, Stephen Daldry, Denise and Barry Fitzpatrick, Annie Goodchild, Frances Gray, Elb Hall, Richard Haswell, Amy Horton, Dave Humphreys, Mark Hurst (Miwurdz), Sylvia Jones, Karen Koren (The Gilded Balloon), Tony Lakin, Ann Lavelle, David 'Little Brother', Ben Lowe, Alex Manning, Valerie Marks, John (Agraman) Marshall, Mike McCarthy, Pat McCarthy, Chris Meade, Tony Mercer, Henry Normal, Joy Palmer, Simon Parrish, Julie Pearn, Chris Percival, Suzanne Phillips, Araya Reddah, Dave Rees, Rony Robinson (BBC Radio Sheffield), Kate Rutter, Jane Salt (Sheffield Newspapers), Ian Saville, Maria de Souza, Rachel Van Riel, Chris Ward-Brown, Mea Webb, Celia Woolfrey.

For contributions to the London years:
Julie Balloo, Helen Boaden, Tina and Leigh Borrett, Jo Brand, Arnold Brown, Stephanie Calman, Jo Caulfield, Dave Cohen, Keith Collins, Kay Dunbar and Steve Bristow (Ways With Words festivals), Simon Elmes, Femi Elufowoju Jnr, Stephen Fry, Lol Gellor (sound radio), Charlotte Green, Steve Gribbin, Andy Hamilton, Jeremy Hardy, Sue Harper, Hattie Hayridge, Sally Heaven, Simon Hoggart, Claire Jones. Barb Jungr, Liz Kneen, Ken Loach, Jenny Lecoat, Maureen Lipman, Cathie Mahoney, Karen Merkel, Will Merkel-Downes,

Brian Mulligan, Chris Neill, Simon Nicholls, Joe Norris (Off The Kerb Productions), Karl Phillips, Susie, Jennifer and Tony Reay, Jon Rolph, Kate Rowland, Sandi Russell, Mavis Seaman and all at The Drill Hall, London, Katherine Seddon (Chester Literature Festival), John Sergeant, Andy and Angela Smith, Janet Staplehurst, Mark Steel, Prof. Laurie Taylor, Dr Kerrie Thomas, Don Ward and Barbara Herbin (The Comedy Store, London), Anna Wardrop, Richard Wolfenden-Brown (The Plough Arts Centre, Great Torrington), Hanne Stinson and Caroline Black (British Humanist Association), and Allyson Kaye, Annwen Jones, Jill Davis, Deborah Granville (Ovarian cancer action).

SOURCES

The author gratefully acknowledges the following source material:

Epigraphs:
Extract from 'The Passing Show', lyrics by Ian Dury from the album *Mr Love Pants* by Ian Dury and The Blockheads (Ronnie Harris Records, 1998)
Extract from *Devout Sceptics*, BBC Radio 4 on 1 January 2004. Linda Smith in conversation with Bel Mooney.

Print:
Stephen McClarence, *Sheffield Star*, 7 May 1985
Stephen McClarence, *Sheffield Star*, 1988
Dr Oliver Double, University of Kent, September 1989
Alison Hurndall, *Sheffield Star*, 26 July 1990
The Stage, 8 November 1990
Jane Tadman, *Sheffield Telegraph*, 16 November 1990
Helen Fox, *Northern Star* magazine, 31 October 1991
Stephen McClarence, *Sheffield Star,* 21 November 1991
Ian Soutar, *Sheffield Telegraph*, 31 January 1992
John Highfield, *Sheffield Star*, 11 May 1992
Alfred Hickling, *Yorkshire Post*, 10 June 1992
The Scotsman, September 1992
David Belcher, *Glasgow Herald*, 22 August 1994

Dave Douglass, 'All power to the imagination!', The Class War Federation, 1999

Venue magazine, Bristol, 13 April 2001

Wayne Burrows, *The Big Issue In The North*, 4 June 2001

Radio Times, 7 July 2001

Susan Jefferys, *Daily Mail*, 7 July 2001

Independent on Sunday, 2 June 2002

Malcolm Hay, *Time Out* magazine, London, 19 June 2002

Bruce Dessau, London *Evening Standard*, 24 June 2002

David Sexton, *Sunday Telegraph*, 8 September 2002

Mickey Noonan, *Manchester Metro*, 27 June 2003

Mike Barnett, *Manchester Evening News*, 27 June 2003

Craig Manning, *Wirral Globe*, 16 July 2003

Janet Marsh, *Eastern Daily Press*, 27 September 2003

'An Education in the Life of Linda Smith' by Jonathan Sale, *Independent*, January 2004

Sian Pattenden, *Word* magazine, February 2004

South Wales Echo, 15 May 2004

Sally Whitman, *Eastern Daily Press*, 7 June 2004

Times Education Supplement, 9 July 2004

New Humanist magazine, Laurie Taylor, September 2004

'College Days', Katie Shimmon, *Guardian*, 21 June 2005

Time Out magazine, London, 22 June 2005

Broadcast:

All BBC-owned material reproduced by arrangement with the BBC.

Arthur Smith, *Aspects of the Fringe*, BBC Radio 4, August 1989

Susan Hill and Henry Normal, *A Good Read*, BBC Radio 4, July 1995

Sources

Late Edition, BBC Radio 4, 22 November 1995

'My Life in CD' (non-broadcast pilot), Andrew Collins, 11 September 2001

Humphrey Carpenter (late), *Great Lives* (Ian Dury), BBC Radio 4, 28 November 2003

Michael Rosen, *Word of Mouth*, BBC Radio 4, 2002/03

Devout Sceptics, BBC Radio 4, 1 January 2004

Libby Purves, *The Learning Curve* BBC Radio 4, 13 July 2004

Emma Wallace and Liz Jaynes, *Hold On Tight, Please!*, BBC Radio 4, August 2004

Simon Fanshawe, *Pick of the Week*, BBC Radio 4, 5 March 2006

Girls Who Do: Comedy, Dawn French, BBC TV, 13 August 2006

Material from *Question Time* editions, 26 June 2002 and 25 November 2004 for BBC TV, reproduced courtesy of Mentorn TV

Material from *The World According to The Simpsons*, for Channel 4 TV, reproduced courtesy of Nobles Gate Film & TV, November 2004

Material from *Clive Anderson's Chat Room*, for BBC Radio 2, reproduced courtesy of Above The Title Productions 25 November 2004

Picture acknowledgements:

Many of the photographs are from the author's own collection, with kind contributions from Barbara Giles and Mea Webb. Additional sources: Ken Clay 9 above; David Corio 10 below; Robin Hammond 16; Caroline Laidler /IRIS 9 below; Martin Jenkinson 14.

Two audio CDs of Linda Smith's live performances are available from Hodder & Stoughton Audiobooks:

I THINK THE NURSES ARE
STEALING MY CLOTHES

is available as a two hour audio CD – a collection of previously unheard recordings of Linda's performances from throughout her career, introduced by Hattie Hayridge.

LINDA SMITH LIVE

is a classic recording of Linda's live stage show on two CDs

A collection of Linda Smith's best material is published by Hodder & Stoughton:

I THINK THE NURSES ARE
STEALING MY CLOTHES
The Very Best of Linda Smith

Available from all good bookshops.

INDEX

Index

BRITISH HUMANIST ASSOCIATION
for the one life we have

'The British Humanist Association's work is more important than ever – with fundamentalism of many kinds on the rise, the rational voice of Humanism needs to be heard.'

Linda Smith
President of the British Humanist Association (2004–6)

The British Humanist Association (BHA) gives a voice to the many non-religious people in the UK who seek to live good lives without religious or superstitious beliefs. We:

- Campaign for human rights and a secular state, with an end to state-funded faith schools, and religious privilege and discrimination, wherever it is found
- Work in education, promoting humanism to the public, lobbying for the inclusion of humanism in school syllabuses, and providing educational resources
- Promote a rational humanist approach to public ethical issues, from sex education to assisted dying for the terminally ill
- Provide humanist funerals, weddings, civil partnership celebrations and baby-namings, meeting a real and growing need in the community

Our work depends on the support of our members and donors. Please join or donate today.

You can join the BHA through our website or request a membership pack by telephoning the number below. You can also make a donation online or send a cheque payable to 'British Humanist Association'.

British Humanist Association
1 Gower Street, London, WC1E 6HD
020 7079 3580
www.humanism.org.uk

Taking action now to save women's lives

Amongst those of us involved with **Ovarian cancer action**, we have lost too many women we have known and loved to ovarian cancer. Whilst we sadly can't help these women any more and nor can Warren help Linda, we feel we must change the future for those unknown women, friends, lovers, mothers, sisters who get the disease. The breast cancer charities have shown us that improvement in survival can come about in leaps, but ovarian cancer survival is at 30%, unchanged in decades.

We urgently need to raise funds for the newly established **Ovarian Cancer Action Research Centre** at Imperial College, London), the UK's first ever research facility entirely dedicated to ovarian cancer. We are creating an international research hub with a crack team of researchers to address the problem of ovarian cancer. Prevention, early detection and better treatments are the key to saving lives.

To donate, or for further information about ovarian cancer and our work, please visit us at www.ovarian.org.uk

Thank you for your support.

Allyson J Kaye
Chair, Board of Directors

Annwen Jones
Chief Executive

Ovarian cancer action
raising awareness | funding research | giving a voice

Bush House
The Waterfront
Elstree Road
Elstree
Hertfordshire
WD6 3BS

Registered charity no. 1109743